Cruel Banquet

MONICA STRAUSS

Cruel Banquet

THE LIFE AND LOVES OF

FRIDA STRINDBERG

HARCOURT, INC.
New York San Diego London

Library of Congress Cataloging-in-Publication Data
Strauss, Monica J.
Cruel banquet: the life and loves of Frida Strindberg/Monica Strauss.
p. cm.
Includes index.
ISBN 0-15-100290-8
1. Uhl, Frida, 1872–1943. 2. Strindberg, August, 1849–1912—Marriage. I. Title.
PT9815.S68 2000
839.72′6—dc21 99-046228
[B]

Designed by Trina Stahl
Text set in Fournier
Printed in the United States of America
First edition
A C E G I J H F D B

To Sylvia, Jane, and Bo

CONTENTS

ACKNOWLEDGMENTS

PIECING TOGETHER FRIDA UHL Strindberg's life in several countries and four languages would not have been possible without the generous assistance of many individuals and institutions.

I owe the biggest debt of gratitude to two friends. The consummate editor and fine printer Jane Timken was the first to encourage my interest in Frida Strindberg and urge me to write this book. Her support was constant. At all hours of the day and night, at home, in restaurants and coffee shops, on one occasion on a park bench in Union Square, she good-naturedly offered her keen comments on the several drafts. Bo Persson, Swedish filmmaker and cosmopolitan intellectual, was instrumental for my work in his country. He introduced me to archives, libraries, and scholars, assisted with the language and, most important, kept me on my toes with his perceptive queries and suggestions through every phase of writing.

I am particularly grateful for the help of Dr. Friedrich Buchmayr, librarian at the Stiftsbibliothek St. Florian in Austria. His pioneering work on Strindberg's Austrian sojourn, as well as his discovery of the hitherto unknown Weyr family archive, gave me a foundation on which to build. In sharing sources, checking rare references, taking the time for a personal tour of the Strindberg sites along the Danube, he was an exceptionally generous colleague.

This book could not have been written without access to Frida's personal archive, donated to Stockholm's Kungliga Biblioteket, by her grandson, Kristof Sulzbach. In making the material available for research, he has been a crucial figure in advancing the cause of Strindberg studies. I am grateful for his friendship and that of his wife, Gudrun Sulzbach.

Strindberg scholars the world over have benefited from the devotion and knowledge of Margareta Brundin, curator of the Strindberg manuscripts at Kungliga Biblioteket. She not only was responsive to all my requests but also went out of her way to suggest materials that might be useful to me. Her interest in the project never wavered even though the library was undergoing restoration and her department seemed to be constantly on the move throughout the years of my research.

I am grateful to the Strindbergssällskapet for giving me a six-week stay at the Strindberg Museum, located in the Blue Tower—Strindberg's last residence—in the heart of Stockholm. Agneta Lalander, director of the museum, and her assistant Marie-Louise Jaenssen made me welcome.

Also in Stockholm, I wish to thank Barbro Ek, the archivist of Bonniers publishing house, for her invariable goodwill in assisting me and making me comfortable in her domain. Thanks are due also to Dr. Magnus Ljunggren, for his suggestions regarding Frida's connections to Russian writers, and to Professor Brigitte Steene for pointing out the comments of Asta Nielsen. During my summer stay, Siv and Leif Björk and Karen and Axel Strindberg were hospitable and gracious in relating their memories of Frida.

In Austria, the late Maria von Weyr, granddaughter of Frida's sister, Mitzi, opened her home to me on two different occasions to enable me to study the papers of the family archive. I am sorry she could not live to see the book completed. I owe thanks to her family—Mr. and Mrs. Haas and their daughter, Petra—for making my first stay in Villach such a pleasant one. In Vienna, Dr. Barbara Lesák, curator of the Österreichisches Theater Museum, eased my way both professionally and personally. I am thankful also for the help of Dr. Weissenbock, curator of manuscripts at the same museum, and the good advice offered me by the Viennese antiquarian Georg Fritsch. Christof Lettner, director of the new Strindberg Museum in Saxen, was kind enough to give me a private tour and much-appreciated attention.

The *Editions und Forschungsstelle Frank Wedekind* in Darmstadt, Germany, assisted me at the very beginning of my research, and Elke Austermühl, Hartmut Vincon, and Eleanor Waldmann continued to answer my queries in the years that followed. I would also like to thank the librarians at the Deutsches Literaturarchiv in Marbach and the Handschrift Abteilung of the Stadtbibliothek in Munich, which houses the Wedekind archive. Carola Regnier, Wedekind's granddaughter, generously offered hospitality at her home in Munich and much useful information about her family.

It was through the auspices of Jasia Reichardt and Nicholas Wadley in London that I was able to meet Frederick Gore, the son of Spencer Gore, one of the decorators of Frida's cabaret. He kindly showed me his father's papers. Michael Holroyd, author of the compelling biography of Augustus John, was generous with time and assistance and helped resolve the mystery of the whereabouts of *The Way Down to the Sea*. Strindberg's English biographer, Michael Meyer, not only spoke to me at length but also invited me to the 1995 Edinburgh Fringe Festival to see a performance of his play *A Meeting in Rome*, depicting a fictitious encounter between Strindberg and Ibsen.

In New York, I was able to draw on the holdings at the New York Public Library for the Performing Arts at Lincoln Center, and the Elmer Holmes Bobst Library at New York University. The New York Society Library, with its excellent collection and generous lending policies, was essential for my research. Friederike Zeitelhofer, the librarian at the Austrian Cultural Institute, assisted me on many occasions, as did members of the staff of Goethe House. The cooperation of the Edward Kroch Library, Cornell University, Ithaca, New York; the Harry Ransom Humanities Center, Austin, Texas; and the Syracuse University Library, Syracuse, New York, was much appreciated.

Thanks are also due to Susan Gibbs in Oslo, Marina Vidas and Bengt Boeo in Copenhagen, Dr. Marianne Eaton-Kraus in Berlin, Dr. Janusz Spyra in Cieszyn, Despina and Bernhardt Leitner and Frantisek Lesák in Vienna. In New York I benefited from the assistance and support of Caryl Avery, Dr. Eszter Salczer, Mr. Helmut von Moltke, Oren Jarinkes, Armin Baier, Dr. Herbert and Lottie Strauss, and Linda Florio.

Throughout this long but rewarding endeavor, the patience and faith of my family—Sylvia Spitzer, Jacqueline Strauss, and Mark Roblee—made all the difference.

INTRODUCTION

FRIDA UHL STRINDBERG was born to the cultural purple. Her father, Friedrich Uhl, was one of Vienna's most important drama critics in a city of passionate theatergoers. It was a world the young Frida was hungry to enter. Only twenty and just one year out of convent school when she first met August Strindberg in 1893, she believed marriage to the forty-three-year-old Swedish dramatist, one of the most controversial on the European scene, would open the door.

As an ambitious young woman, Frida was not unlike Strindberg's first wife, who married him, in part, to launch an acting career. The playwright was clearly attracted to women with independent minds but, once tied to them, he could not tolerate the freedom their work demanded. In the exuberance of courtship, he offered Frida a free hand in the management of his affairs. Once married, he was unnerved by her independent spirit and, above all, her erotic appeal; he accused her of sexual betrayal. The marriage was short, but its effect lifelong. Three generations of women—Frida, her daughter, and her mother—remained obsessed with the troubled genius.

These two strands of Frida Uhl Strindberg's existence—her stubborn pursuit of a cultural role and her continuing struggle with the aftermath of her youthful marriage—are the focus of this first biography of her life. It was her fate to have been born in a period of transition for women. At the time of her birth, in 1872, few questioned the right of a father or a husband to determine a woman's destiny. When her formal schooling ended, twenty years later, the women's emancipation movement had begun to threaten such assumptions, and the reaction among men ranged from intransigence to uncertainty. Although some doors were grudgingly opened to women, others were irrationally kept shut. The writers and artists of Frida's generation were particularly sensitive to the radical shift in human relationships implied by the growing independence of women. Many of them masked their anxiety by an increasing obsession with the subject of sex. From the time she married Strindberg, Frida was caught in the crossfire of that fixation.

Her father's contemporaries—the revolutionaries of 1848—had fought for social emancipation, but over time became rigid and conformist in protecting their hard-won status. For their sons, individual freedom was the rallying cry, and defiance of bourgeois morality their symbolic weapon. They invited women to share in their sexual liberation, while denying these same women the social emancipation they craved. Strindberg might have feared Frida's sensuality, but her subsequent lovers encouraged it. And yet when she followed their prompting and declared herself a "*grande amoureuse*," it served her no better than her innocence had with her husband. Even men flaunting liberal sexual attitudes were uncomfortable with a sexually assertive woman. Thus, when Frida served as a model for characters in the works of Strindberg, Frank Wedekind, and Arthur Schnitzler, and a compelling reality in the autobiographies of Wyndham Lewis and Augustus John, she was often depicted as that fin-de-siècle specter—the insatiable femme fatale. It took the iconoclastic Ezra Pound to admit, many years after meeting her in 1912, that he had not been advanced enough to "appreciate Frida."

Frida never married again but sought further alliances with creative men. Like her fellow Austrian Alma Mahler, she clasped her cultural heroes to her bosom, but once she made a conquest, she assumed her lover's ambitions as her own. In the process, she became a talented and persuasive cultural impresario among the bohemian enclaves springing up throughout Europe at the century's close. These loose associations of temporarily impoverished young artists and writers were not merely hotbeds of sexual experimentation, but also sources of adventurous cultural enterprises: provocative publications, private theater societies, cabarets. It was among these rebellious individualists that Frida refined the cultural instincts that ensured her survival. In the atmosphere of bohemia, she could ignore traditional expectations of women's behavior, consider men as colleagues, and, like them, speculate in art, literary properties, and theatrical ventures. From the 1890s to the 1920s, in Berlin, Munich, Vienna, London, and New York, she improvised the career that made her a "carrier" of culture, across the continent to the new world.

FRIDA'S WAS A peripatetic life. In the course of her seventy-one years, she lived in five countries. Between the time of her childhood and middle age, she had no permanent home. What this meant for her biographer was that some periods of her private life were richly documented, while others offered scant primary material. The same was true of her cultural contributions. Her major accomplishments—including the founding of London's first cabaret and the well-received memoir of her marriage to Strindberg—were given much attention. Her quieter achievements, behind the scenes, were recorded in the small print of an article, or remembered as a passing reference in a lover's letter or a colleague's diary. Thus the chapters in this book vary in their emphasis: in some, her public life takes precedence, in others, it is the personal dramas with which her life was punctuated. If these variations reflect the exigencies of the sources, they also speak truly of Frida's existence.

As Friedrich Uhl's daughter, she had a public persona from the start of her life, and her vision of her roles—wife, mistress, lover, even mother—made little distinction between the private and the public. Frida never hesitated to draw on the feminine emotional arsenal—sexual reproach and maternal concern–to hold or launch a protégé; nor did she spare her lovers, or her children, the calculations of a businesswoman. Her associations with the creative spirits of her time and her forceful engagements with them were at the core of every aspect of her story.

Cruel Banquet

· I ·

The Editor's Daughter

Otherwise there is not much happening in dear Berlin. But I had an unforgettable evening.... August Strindberg was among the guests and since he doesn't speak German especially well and is rather reserved as far as the ladies are concerned, I had him entirely for myself for almost three hours in a neighboring room.... His nerves are badly strained—but it is an inspired madness. Curiously, it did not take very long for him to be open with me, indeed it happened so soon that I believe he was no longer aware of what he was saying.... His manner of relating the most intimate details of his life and character as if he were dreaming gave me a very strange feeling. Strindberg would be someone you could talk to.[1]

WRITING TO HER FATHER, the fledgling Austrian journalist Frida Uhl could not hide her fascination with August Strindberg after the bewildering intimacy of their first encounter on January 7, 1893. Only twenty, she was well aware that the man she had met was twice her age and had a considerable career behind him. By then he had written twenty-six plays, several novels, a series of veiled autobiographies, and collections of stories, poems, and essays. His dramas of the last decade exploring the conflict between the sexes with a new and disturbing candor had established his reputation as a major writer in Europe. What the young Fräulein Uhl could not know was how much these explosive pieces drew upon the courtship of his first wife, the Baroness Siri von Essen, their troubled marriage, and the bitter crises that brought it to a close.[2]

Flattered by Strindberg's attention, intrigued by his lack of reserve, Frida looked forward to meeting him again. At the end of January, however, she received a curt and disquieting note from her married sister, Mitzi Weyr. Conveying a message from their father, Mitzi wrote Frida that she would have to leave the "morally poisonous" atmosphere of Berlin immediately and return to a supervised existence in Munich or, worse yet, join their mother in the remote little hamlet of Dornach in Upper Austria.

Friedrich Uhl, editor in chief of the *Wiener Zeitung*, Austria's official government newspaper, had agreed to his younger daughter's living alone in a foreign city while reviewing books and theater for his paper, but he had forbidden her to go out without a chaperone. Frida had other ideas and had written freely to her sister about her unorthodox life in Berlin—her solitary walks in the city's poorer districts and Jewish quarters and her easy relationships with her father's male colleagues, whom she received in her rooms or accompanied to exhibitions and the theater.

Mitzi, as her father's confidante, could not turn a blind eye to her younger sister's blithe rejection of his strictures. No matter how innocent Frida's enthusiasms, a young unmarried woman of her class could not go about in the independent manner she described in her letters without reflecting badly on herself and, more seriously in Mitzi's eyes, her eminent father. In the Uhl family, the editor's reputation was sacrosanct. For the sake of his standing in Viennese society, sacrifices had already been demanded of his wife and his older daughter. Frida was not to be left off the hook.

In 1893, when Frida first met Strindberg, Friedrich Uhl was at the peak of his profession. Though his position was precarious—as editor of the mouthpiece of the Habsburg court, his life was under constant scrutiny—he had managed to hold on to his job for more than twenty years. This success had come at a price, however—both personal and ideological. Like many of Vienna's influential figures in the last quarter of the century, Uhl was part Jewish and a *zuagraster* (outsider), a label still applied by the Viennese to denote the lesser status of those not born within its precincts. His father had been a manager of one of the estates of the Habsburg archduke in Cieszyn, Upper Silesia (now southwestern Poland), and his mother, though baptized a Catholic on marriage, came from a prominent Jewish family in the region. In 1842, age seventeen, Uhl had gone to study philosophy at the University of Vienna and to dedicate himself to his two passions—writing and theater, the latter nurtured by the lively theatrical life for which Cieszyn had been known since the early eighteenth century. Soon he was penning short pieces for the Sunday newspapers, and in 1846 published his first book, *Tales from the Land of the Vistula*, stories from the landscape of his childhood.[3]

In later life, Uhl's status as an outsider fueled his ambition to belong, but in the exuberance of youth he was a rebel writing incendiary verse in support of the 1848 uprising. He joined the university students taking to the streets in revolt against the paralyzing censorship imposed by Metternich, the chancellor who had held the reins of power since the defeat of Napoleon in 1815. Soon after the student protest began in March, the rebels achieved one of their objectives when Metternich fled. The Habsburgs, however, consumed with the fear of regicide that pervaded Europe, chose to interpret the insurrection as an attempt to topple the monarchy. Seven months later, after a brutal military assault, Vienna was placed under martial law and a new emperor, the eighteen-year-old Franz Josef, was crowned in the name of reaction.

The young ruler's faith that he was divinely appointed to restore the glory of the Habsburg dynasty held up social and political reform for more than a decade, but the 1848 uprising had brought about a more effective vehicle of change in Vienna: social mobility. The feudal aristocracy, having fled the city in fear of revolution, ceased to be a dominating presence. Bankers, financiers, entrepreneurs of the infant Industrial Revolution took their place. As new opportunities arose, class barriers began crumbling and enterprising young men saw their chance. For many members of the generation of 1848—and Uhl was not the least of these—the lure of advancement began to take precedence over liberal principles.

Having participated in the birth of the modern Austrian press, when dozens of newspapers emerged from the euphoria of revolution, Uhl lived through the neo-absolutism of the early years of Franz Josef's rule by working for *Die Presse,* a paper dependent on the wily political machinations of its editor. Expediency had replaced revolutionary fervor, and staying alive in the world of print meant learning to be devious. In Uhl's memoirs he recalled that "at the time you learned the detours of writing, how to lay a veil over speech. And the public learned to read between the lines, to understand the language of a phrase broken off midway, to interpret the irony of the title of an article."[4] Journalists became adept at expressing political views within the literary essay known as the feuilleton. In fact, becoming a brilliant feuilletonist was one of the highest aspirations for Austrian newspapermen, and the most successful practitioners, Uhl included, had learned their trade in the censors' school.

In 1861, change was in the air as the emperor, weakened by a series of military defeats abroad, appointed the liberal Anton Ritter von Schmerling as premier. By then Uhl was one of three editors responsible for getting out the daily morning and afternoon editions of *Die Presse,* which had become the most successful of the Austrian newspapers. He also had charge of the contents of the "Vienna Chronicle," an influential gossip column. When he was extended a personal invitation to attend one of the premier's receptions, he had no illusions about the purpose of the gesture. Nevertheless, the event was Uhl's first experience of the privileges of power. He never forgot the festive glow of the grand rooms where ministers, generals, and high-ranking civil servants mingled below the great chandeliers.[5]

Uhl's subsequent praise of the evening in his column did not go unnoticed, and two years later the editor was invited to work on *Der Botschafter* (*The Diplomat*), a new paper published under the premier's auspices to reflect the views of his regime. Although the paper survived only for the four years Schmerling held power, Uhl was able to experiment with ideas that would later emerge in the *Wiener Zeitung.* He placed an emphasis on culture, published long critiques of books and plays, serialized novels, and wrote extensive feuilletons. His greatest coup resulted from his unflagging support of Richard Wagner. When the composer completed *Die Meistersinger,* he gave Uhl the privilege of printing the first act on the front page of *Der Botschafter.*

From the start of his career, Uhl had tried to hide his Jewish ancestry, but as he advanced in society this became more difficult. In mid-nineteenth-century Vienna, the offspring of a mixed marriage, even after the conversion of the Jewish partner (demanded by law), was still socially categorized Jewish. This was true even after the Patent of Toleration issued by Emperor Joseph II in 1781 had given Jews a new mobility by permitting them to attend secular schools and universities, set up businesses, and participate in German culture. By the time Uhl arrived in Vienna in the 1840s, Jews were an increasingly dynamic presence, gradually changing the character of the city. Officially, however, they were "outsiders" until 1867, when they were finally declared citizens equal before the law. Although Jews predominated in the world of Austrian journalism, Uhl chose to distance himself from his heritage as clearly as possible. Had he not done so, certain political positions such as his subsequent appointment to the *Wiener Zeitung* would have been closed to him.

Under Schmerling's patronage, Uhl had access to a higher class than the one he usually occupied as a bachelor journalist taking his meals in a local café, but he lacked the social standing to take full advantage of his new opportunities. Such standing could come only through family connections or wealth. By birth Uhl could not claim the former, nor had journalism provided the latter. Only marriage could remove these obstacles. The match he made a year after he received his appointment from Schmerling appeared to serve the purpose well.

In 1863, Uhl, thirty-eight, married the eighteen-year-old daughter of a wealthy and very Catholic family. On the surface the alliance seemed appropriate. Her parents lived like members of the landed gentry in the hamlet of Dornach, Upper Austria. Actually, the fortune of Uhl's father-in-law, Cornelius Reischl, had only recently been acquired through questionable real-estate speculation in Vienna's mid-century building boom. With this money, Reischl had set himself up in elegant style in the hinterland, expanding a simple one-story house on his vast property into an imposing, if architecturally unembellished, structure with three stories and two wings. Assisted by a large staff, he and his family lived the country life: his wife managed a dairy farm, while he indulged in the aristocratic sport of hunting with a pack of thirty-two dogs.

The seclusion of this country seat appealed to both Uhl and his father-in-law. Reischl's wife, the former Maria Watzl, a great Viennese beauty in her youth, had given birth to twin girls at the age of eighteen without the benefit of marriage. According to family legend, their father was a Jew. Later Maria Watzl married Reischl, but her daughters retained her family name. Such irregularities occurred in many families, but for those with social ambitions they had to be hidden. The chances of the Watzl twins finding appropriate suitors in Vienna were small: their origins were less obvious in the country.[6]

Uhl and his father-in-law made the kind of coldhearted arrangement typical of many middle-class families in the nineteenth century. Women were pawns for the men's aspirations. When the younger Maria Watzl became Maria Uhl, the two families' questionable ancestries—illegitimate on one side, Jewish on the other—cancelled each other. A culture of concealment paved the way for social mobility, but it also brought inflexibility into private lives threatened by exposure.

After Schmerling lost power in 1865 and *Der Botschafter* folded, Uhl was invited by two former colleagues to join the newly created *Neue Freie Presse,* a paper that was to become the largest and most important in Austria. Thus by 1872, when the emperor appointed him editor of the *Wiener Zeitung,* Uhl could be considered part of the establishment. As a writer, he was the author of several "backstage" novels describing the lives of artists, actresses, and opera singers. As a journalist with the *Neue Freie Presse,* he not only sent back skillful dispatches from arenas as diverse as battlefields and industrial expositions, but also was considered a first-rate stylist. "The briefest piece by Friedrich Uhl," a fellow journalist noted, "is precise—it outlines the subject, says what is required and, nevertheless, nearly always reveals a personal outlook. He is a born polemicist."[7] Uhl's skills as an editor had become legendary. It was said that he was capable of reducing a novel to a novella, a novella to a feature article, and a feature article to an aphorism. But he lacked autonomy, and this is what the *Wiener Zeitung* had to offer, even though he would now be a civil servant running the paper characterized by an Austrian humorist as "the most irresistible contemporary... sleeping pill."[8]

Uhl was not completely comfortable within the emperor's inner circle—the most conservative in Vienna. By background and inclination he remained a liberal and negotiated the political vise of his position by reserving for himself the role of drama critic for the *Wiener Abendpost*, the paper's evening supplement. Under the protective mantle of culture, he could support a new revolution, the one begun by Ibsen in the theater.

Ibsen's plays made bourgeois life—the discontents of middle-class domesticity, the corruption of small-town politics, the unthinking adherence to convention—the stuff of drama and tragedy. Since the characters were not idealized types but troubled complex human beings, the plays forced audiences to think about themselves. Until works by the Norwegian playwright appeared on Vienna's stages in the early 1880s, Viennese audiences expected to be diverted by a well-made farce or to have their cultural standing confirmed by performances of classical tragedies by Shakespeare, Schiller, and Goethe. Theater was a cultivated pleasure in Vienna, not an arena for confronting the perils of existence. Ibsen presented them with an entirely new view of theater, a view that first appeared threatening in a society where predictability made culture comfortable.

With their stress on the importance of the individual's needs over the demands of society, Ibsen's plays were harbingers of modernism. To Uhl's credit, he knew exactly what he was seeing when he wrote, "Just because Friedrich Schiller once lived doesn't immediately imply that Ibsen is a fool or a criminal.... Yes, some of these pieces give us pain, but from our wounds come thoughts and perceptions; one learns to look into people as into clockwork and learns to understand them better one way or another. That is also something, that is a great deal."[9]

The division between Uhl's cultural liberalism and the political loyalty demanded of him as a civil servant could sometimes be awkward. In the evening edition he might assert that Ibsen had taught his contemporaries to study their conscience, but in the official Habsburg bulletins he had no choice but to varnish the continual crises of the monarch's personal life. On one occasion, he was forced to print a false headline to cover up the dual suicide of the crown prince and his mistress in the famous tragedy at Mayerling in 1889. In bold type on the front page, Uhl reported that His Royal Highness Crown Prince Rudolf had died suddenly of a heart attack while sleeping alone at his hunting lodge. Even after admitting to the suicide a few days later, the *Wiener Zeitung* never mentioned the name of the eighteen-year-old Baroness Vetsera, who had been shot by her lover and whose body had been spirited away by her uncles, permitting the Habsburg scion a Christian burial.[10]

Uhl's public position placed demands on his private life too. Initially, the union of Friedrich Uhl and Maria Watzl, the *mariage de convenance*, had the intended effect. Maria had found a respectable and influential husband, and Uhl had gained socially and financially. Their first child, Mitzi, or Marie, was born in 1864, the year after they married. Marie Friederike Cornelia, known as Frida, followed eight years later. But the cultural divide between man and wife became increasingly difficult to ignore. Maria Watzl Uhl was an intelligent but provincial and pious woman, while her husband was a cosmopolitan and agnostic. Her passions lay in the religious studies she conducted with her twin sister, Melanie. She could not share Uhl's love of theater, his dedication to literature, and his taste for worldly companions. Nor could she conduct a household that attracted theater directors, diplomats, and other members of Vienna's upper echelons, with whom Uhl liked to socialize. Although still fond of each other, they decided to live apart after fifteen years of marriage—a problematic decision for Uhl's career. As a civil servant of a Catholic monarchy, he could not officially separate or divorce.

By the late 1870s, Uhl occupied a unique position in Vienna. As the editor of the newspaper representing the imperial court, he had direct access to the emperor, a privilege granted only the highest members of the government and the so-called first circle of the feudal nobility. He was one of the most important theater critics in a city where theater was the favorite pastime of a large segment of the population. And Uhl enjoyed the privileges—the first-class travel arrangements, the best seats in theaters, the wine and delicacies that arrived from the court every New Year's Day. He had to devise another balancing act—a semblance of marriage that would somehow allow him and his wife to separate.

Uhl's generation of self-made men shrouded their arriviste status by building grand family homes and filling them with antiquities suggesting ancient lineage. When, in the 1860s, Vienna's medieval city walls were torn down and land became available, it was primarily this class of wealthy entrepreneurs and professionals that occupied the historicizing palaces lining the newly created boulevards of the Ringstrasse. Uhl resorted to a similar tactic, but in a more secluded spot. Soon after being appointed editor, he built a sumptuous villa in Mondsee, a resort in the Salzburg region, close to the emperor's summer quarters. It was completed shortly after Frida's birth in 1872.

To give the lakeside residence a pseudo-historic pedigree, a Roman foundation stone discovered nearby was incorporated into the structure. On the façade, Renaissance masonry formed an uneasy alliance with indigenous carved wooden eaves and balconies; inside, rooms in different styles housed Uhl's growing collection of Gothic, Renaissance, and Baroque artifacts. When the tip of one of the towers of Vienna's cathedral was removed for safety reasons, the fragment, taller than a man, became the centerpiece of Uhl's Gothic chamber.

In front of the villa, with its view of the Schafberg, the mountain dominating the Mondsee range, a long, sloping lawn descended to the lake. On the shore a small bathing hut housed gear and equipment for the trout fishing that was Uhl's favorite Mondsee pastime. Ostensibly the magnificent Mondsee complex was the family home, but the family as a whole resided there for brief periods only. The villa was kept for required joint appearances six weeks every summer. The rest of the year, to hide the reality of the broken marriage, parents and children led separate lives. Maria Uhl returned to her father's house in Dornach alone. Had the children accompanied her, the separation would have been too obvious. Mitzi, at fifteen, was sent away to a convent school. Frida, seven, was left alone in the care of a nanny at the Mondsee villa. Uhl made a home of his editorial headquarters in the capital.

A young reporter, invited for an interview, left a vivid description of the crusty newsman in his lair. Uhl inhabited two small rooms, one for working, the other for living and sleeping, but in both of them the walls were covered with blotting paper for the editor's instant use. He often wrote seated on his bed, which was covered by a reindeer skin, the gift of a North Pole explorer and now hard as a board. Observing him working there by the light of two candles, the young visitor was amazed that Uhl "did not go up in flames [because] his dry comments provided combustion enough."[11]

Husband and wife remained on cordial terms and wrote each other often. On the surface, Maria Uhl appeared to accept her situation, but when writing to Mitzi's prospective husband, she gave herself away. Aside from Uhl's stinginess and slovenly ways, she wrote, "and that he absolutely does not love me, I cannot blame him for anything. He is a dreamer, an idealist, a visionary, but at the same time cold, calculating, particularly self-indulgent—no ordinary person."[12] These equivocal protestations hinted at the emotional cost of the circumstances foisted on her by Uhl's ambition. The absence of a husband and the loss of intimacy with her children left her yearning for some new attachment.

Like many lonely children, Frida, left behind in Mondsee, sought solace in books and spent hours in her father's library absorbing what she could without interference. Untrammeled, she became an imaginative child, formed her own opinions, and bridled at restraint. But no matter how comfortable her surroundings, how attentive her caretakers, how unrestricted her freedom, nothing could make up for the absence of her parents. In the mind of a child, so radical a desertion could mean only one thing: she had been found wanting. Why else expel her from the paradise of the family? When her efforts to please did not effect her return, obstinacy supplanted docility, and she learned to fend for herself.

At nine, she too was sent away to a convent school—a radical change, since she had little experience of other children. In St. Zeno, Reichenhall, the first of several schools she attended, she felt miserable and uprooted among the one hundred twenty girls who boarded there. From the run of the house in Mondsee, she was now subject to discipline, a strict routine, and little physical comfort. Since her isolation had bred the inimical qualities of self-reliance and a desperate need for affection, her teachers found her an odd child, difficult to direct. It took a while for Frida to realize that her long hours in the library at Mondsee could stand her in good stead. By the time she was a teenager, at the Jesuit convent of *Les Oiseaux* run by the Society of the Sacred Heart in Paris, her mind had taken fire. She became an outstanding student despite the quality of the education she described years later.

The nuns all came from aristocratic families and the hatred of revolution was in their blood. They avoided, on principle, anything that smacked of the new and the free. The upbringing inside the sacred walls was conducted just as it had been the century before. We learned nothing of life or for life, despite the fact that an incredible amount of information was fed to us in miserable fashion. The nuns were our teachers and since they had as much belief in authority as they lacked in knowledge, they read aloud to us the textbooks recommended by the Bishop and we had to regurgitate the information precisely—if possible down to the exact word.[13]

How could the liberal editor send his daughter to be educated in so reactionary an institution? There was little choice. Secular secondary schools for women were a new phenomenon, and it was only in 1892 that the first girls' school to offer a classical education opened in Vienna. The cloistered precincts represented a long tradition of girls' education, even if the emphasis remained on feminine pursuits of needlework, music, and languages. Social ambition also came into play. Middle-class girls were sent to boarding schools, but the daughters of the Austrian aristocracy were still immured in convents for the duration of their adolescence. And Uhl was certainly not averse to the convent school's pedagogical philosophy that an emphasis on chastity accompany a girl's exposure to knowledge.

Once Frida completed her studies at *Les Oiseaux* in 1889, with the prize in history, however, Uhl was forced to recognize that his daughter's gifts demanded more solid fare. Although most girls left school at seventeen, he gave her three final years at the Dominican Convent of the English Ladies in Haverstock Hill, London. There she could prepare for the Oxford Senior Exam, a privilege only recently extended to women. Frida's mentor, Sister Theresa, wrote Uhl that his daughter had a "superior intelligence."[14] But Uhl's benevolence could go no further. Although university education was available to women at a few faculties in Europe, it was too new and radical a development for a man in Uhl's position to consider.

From the letters Frida addressed to her father during these last years of her schooling—written, on paternal demand, in French—it is clear that she knew the life of the mind would interest him. On her arrival in England in 1889 she wrote him of her ambition: "I work all day—English, French, music, needlework. Time seems to be too short for the big things I want to accomplish. The more I advance in my studies, the more I have a taste for them." She offered assessments of her reading: Wilkie Collins did not meet with her favor but Byron inspired her. Taking a playful and humorous tone, she felt free to tease her father with provocative opinions: "I'm always convinced that Sacher-Masoch was a German Jew . . ." she wrote him. "His simple French has a certain German profundity. . . . None of his compatriots succeed as well in giving a sense of tears. Heine, Mosenthal, Masoch. Really the Jews don't do so badly in our day. They persuade us that the muse lives in the ghetto—*un beau prospect*."[15] In this little gibe, Frida revealed an acceptance of her mixed inheritance far different from that of her father's generation. By the 1890s, Jews, converted or not, were becoming the dominant cultural figures in Vienna and a bright student such as Frida wanted her father to know she had noticed.

As a result of the family's complicated arrangements, Frida's adolescence unfolded in competing environments as she was shuttled between Mondsee, Dornach, Paris, Vienna, and London. Although a sense of humor and capacity for irony enabled her to cope with her peripatetic existence, she had no real sense of where she belonged. She was too bright for her outdated schooling, too educated for the simple pieties of Dornach, too much the *jeune fille* to share her father's world. What kept her going was Uhl's faith in her intelligence and his encouragement of her intellectual ambition. Unable to take her father's true measure, Frida believed she was being groomed to be an active participant in cultural life.

Unfortunately for Uhl, Frida's long, archaic incubation could not last. When she left the cloistered precincts in the summer of 1892, she was a spirited young woman of twenty, fluent in English and French and with a long-suppressed appetite for life. Petite, buxom, with thick brown hair and dark eyes set above a delicately curved nose and a full mouth, she was attractive, overeducated, and, without a suitable admirer in sight, a threat to her father's tranquillity. No moment was more nerve-racking for a nineteenth-century Viennese patriarch than a daughter's coming-of-age. A sexual lapse—a love affair, a pregnancy—could erase years of hard-earned respectability for a family and eliminate possibilities for social advancement.

Nine years earlier, Uhl had managed to marry off his older daughter by a ruse. When Rudolf Weyr, a successful forty-year-old sculptor who had been given some of the most lucrative public commissions in Vienna, expressed his interest in seventeen-year-old Mitzi, the editor made sure there would be no opposition. He arranged for the two to get to know each other, and when Mitzi was reluctant to accept a proposal from the much older Weyr, who she felt was temperamentally unsuited to her, Uhl accused her of compromising herself and so forced the marriage.[16] Once assured that all threat of scandal had passed, however, Uhl invited his newly married daughter to exercise her literary talent as a contributor to the *Wiener Zeitung*.

Just as Uhl had attempted to navigate the hazardous terrain between his loyalty to the emperor and his appreciation of Ibsen, so he tried to straddle two worlds when it came to his daughters' upbringing. As a bourgeois patriarch, he did not hesitate to exercise authoritarian control, but as a liberal journalist and intellectual, his outlook was more advanced. Frida could not help but see that her father applauded attitudes on the stage he would not countenance in life. His forte as a critic was his capacity to judge plays as works of art, while other critics wrangled over controversial subject matter. In 1890 he was able to praise Ibsen's *Ghosts* when others were caught up in the shock of the drama's direct confrontation of hereditary syphilis. A central motif of the play was the sad effect of forced marriages, and there before Frida's eyes was Mitzi's unhappy union. The gap between her father's social conformity and his intellectual risk-taking made Frida a skeptic regarding traditional social expectations. Marrying *her* off would not be easy.

When Frida completed her schooling, Uhl was in a quandary. He had no permanent household from which to present a marriageable daughter. Although appropriate suitors had not yet appeared, an inappropriate gentleman was already on the horizon. No sooner did Frida come home from England to summer in Mondsee than she embarked on a serious flirtation with Herman Sudermann, a married German writer fifteen years her senior who had come to see her father. Sudermann had written short stories and novels and in 1889 made his debut as a dramatist in Berlin with his play *Die Ehre* (*Honor*) touching on the fragility of concepts of honor when it came to conflicts between social classes. The critics, including Friedrich Uhl, greeted this first effort with enthusiasm and thereafter Sudermann was considered a playwright to watch. His reputation reached its apogee with his third drama, *Heimat* (*Hometown*), the unfinished version of which he wished to discuss with Uhl when he came to visit in the summer of 1892.

In going to Uhl for advice on this play, Sudermann was following the example of many promising dramatists who sought out the highly respected Viennese critic for assistance with works in progress. But on receiving the playwright in Mondsee, Uhl unwittingly provided him with a more passionate interlocutor in the form of Frida, emerging from the chrysalis of the cloister. *Heimat* seemed written for her.

Sudermann's heroine, Magda, is a successful professional singer returning to her hometown for the first time after a long absence. Twelve years before, her father had ordered her out of the house in disgrace after she had refused the husband he had chosen for her. With her triumphant return, a reconciliation is attempted, but, once again, her father cannot resist trying to force his daughter to bend to his rigid code of honor. In the character of Magda, Sudermann created a young woman whose success as an artist released her from accountability to the man—father or lover—attempting to control her. The most affecting parts of the play are her speeches in defense of her hard-won survival and achievements.

Things would have been different if I had remained a daughter of the house like Maria, who is nothing and can do nothing without the protective roof of some kind of home, who goes directly from her father's to her husband's house—who gets everything from the family: bread, ideas, character. Look at me. I was a free bird—I am the kind of creature that stumbles around the world unprotected like a man, with only her hands to rely on for work.

I will not be a pendant to the Prodigal Son. If I returned as a daughter, as the lost daughter, then I could not stand here with my head high, then I would have to sink into the dust before you in full awareness of all my sins. I don't want that—I can't do that—because I am who I am and it is myself I cannot afford to lose.[17]

As Frida and Sudermann strolled among Uhl's carefully tended rose gardens or enjoyed the summer breezes on the lake, they discussed and debated the radical and stirring lines in which Magda defended her right to her profession, her illegitimate child, and, most daring of all, her sexual life, which she had refused to repress in the vain hope of finding a husband. "Why shouldn't we give to men what our own being cries out for?" Sudermann had his heroine ask. "Gag us, make us stupid, lock us in harems and in cloisters—maybe that is best. But if you give us freedom, don't be surprised if we make use of it."[18]

For Frida, these were heady sentiments, far removed from any she had heard from her parents and teachers, and more inspiring. It did not take long for the shining light of *Heimat*'s message to shed its glow on the bearer. Sudermann appeared to take her seriously, solicited her opinions, made her feel she had something to contribute. But she could not have been unaware that her youth and beauty held as much appeal for him as her eager intelligence.

The plot of *Heimat* had its relevance to Uhl's predicament as well. Unlike Magda, Frida had not yet disobeyed her father, but she was to be driven out nonetheless. The manner in which Uhl achieved this was audacious for a paterfamilias of the 1890s. He would give his bright daughter a career—but a career he could supervise. As Frida recalled, the course he had decided upon appeared to begin with a spontaneous gesture. One day, glancing at her sharply through his pince-nez, he handed her a book, saying, "Here, read it, write about it, give it six paragraphs." Then he added a touch of his own philosophy of journalism. "But don't tear off all the flesh; we are friends and you might need him." Frida did not hesitate.

The assignment was flattering and surprising, and to review a friend of father's did not faze me. I was, namely, just six weeks out of school and until then at least twice a week in my literature classes, I had criticized greater names. Whoever gets used to fearlessly expressing opinions of classic writers . . . a Viennese feuilletonist is clearly not going to be threatening. And even if the book did not fascinate or attract me, I was, nevertheless, obedient in refraining from ripping it apart, and even gave him credit for the not completely empty charm and grace of his gossip. . . .[19]

Frida had the article ready by sundown. Uhl looked it over, glanced at its nervous creator, and with "a satisfied growl" told her to send it to the deputy editor to be printed for the Sunday edition. The piece appeared two days later, and Frida experienced great satisfaction, even though neither she nor Mitzi ever received a byline. "This would have had to happen sooner or later . . ." she wrote afterward. "I came into the world with ink in my veins. My profession had found me."[20]

Uhl had Frida write a few more book reviews for the *Wiener Zeitung*, baptized her a journalist, and, in the autumn, sent her off to Munich as his cultural informant. It was a token freedom. By making Frida his employee and thus dependent upon him for both personal and professional largesse, Uhl could easily rein her in from a distance. He also made sure she would be chaperoned by arranging for her to live with family friends. Initially, Frida thrived in the Porges household, which, although solidly bourgeois, had a lively cultural atmosphere. Heinrich Porges, an old ally of Uhl's in the defense of Richard Wagner, was still involved with Bayreuth and the Wagner family, and in Munich he directed and conducted a large choir.[21]

Many years later, Else, one of the daughters of the house, remembered the impression Frida made when she arrived fresh out of the convent. Shy and needy, she was so grateful for the warmth extended to her that in no time her affectionate nature had broken down all formalities. She hugged and kissed members of the family and began calling the parents Mother and Father. She was a beauty, Else recalled, with her delicately rounded cheeks, the dark glimmer of her eyes, the yearning hinted at in her smile. "She had 'sex appeal,'" she wrote. "The word did not yet exist—but it could have been created for Frida."[22]

The men in the Porges circle made much of the newcomer, and Franz von Lenbach, one of Munich's leading artists, wanted her to model. But these conquests seem to have been of less interest to Frida than her eagerness to work, to test her critical responses to theater and literature, and to get to know actors, singers, and bohemians. Sometimes her haste to see and do all she had missed while behind convent walls startled her hosts. "We were concerned but never angry," Else remembered, "because Frida was good—good-hearted."[23]

Initially Frida was enchanted by her new surroundings. She had a new home, new friends, even new clothes to replace the drab convent uniforms. But being in the bosom of a family, even an enlightened one, was restricting. Nothing that happened in Munich could compete with the exciting encounter with Sudermann the summer before. When Frida discovered that he would be in Berlin preparing for the January premiere of *Heimat,* she took her fate in her own hands. Leaving Munich without her father's permission, she was settled in a pension on Berlin's Lützowplatz by early December.

It was an impulsive and daring move. In order to declare her life her own, Frida braved the displeasure of the man on whom she was wholly dependent. Sudermann, through the instrument of his play, had suggested there might be other and freer choices for women, and Frida, in her youth and inexperience, took art for life. Hadn't Magda, after all, poured scorn on bourgeois values and urged her sister to shake off responsibility and honor and go away with the man she loved?

Years later Frida wrote of her joy on being at liberty in Berlin, the "gold-rush town . . . where the gold miners saw art as a sleeping beauty they wanted to wake with hammer, spade, and shovel rather than kisses."[24] The city in the 1890s was a brash, prosperous capital where the puritanical censorship of the resident Prussian monarchy was at odds with the interest of the young in the provocative work of Ibsen, Strindberg, and other modern writers. Their books and plays broke long-established taboos—particularly about sex—and raised controversial social and psychological issues. To circumvent official constraints, the youthful enthusiasts founded their own journals, publishing houses, and private theater societies. It was their rebellious enterprises that gave Berlin's cultural life its robust vitality.

One of the most important of these ventures was the *Freie Bühne*, or Free Stage, a private theater club and publication. Established in 1889 by Ibsen enthusiasts Otto Brahm and Paul Schlenther, it was intended to circumvent the double trap of censorship and commerce. As a result of their efforts, Berlin had begun to surpass Vienna in the excitement of its theatrical life.

Brahm's inspiration had been the small independent *Théâtre Libre* founded in Paris in 1887 by André Antoine. A passionate fan of contemporary theater, Antoine had funded his venture by subscription. Brahm decided to follow the model in Berlin. With a committee including the young publisher Samuel Fischer and the playwright Ludwig Fulda, nine hundred subscribers were recruited before the *Freie Bühne's* first performance, a production of *Ghosts,* in the fall of 1889. The young directors compensated for the lack of a resident theater and acting company with their bold vision. At the end of their third season, they had staged several plays by Ibsen, launched the career of Gerhart Hauptmann, Germany's most important new playwright, and given Strindberg his German debut with productions of his sexually charged dramas of the 1880s. Their choices were criticized, as a contemporary cartoon revealed, but it was the *Freie Bühne's* enthusiastic support of the literary avant-garde that brought the city international attention.

Uhl was dismayed by Frida's independent move but held back from asserting his authority until he could think of a better plan: he could no longer ask the Porges family to police his daughter. To gain time, he told Frida which theatrical premieres she should report on for him and begged his German colleagues in the Prussian capital to keep an eye on his impetuous child. Maria Uhl took a darker view of Frida's impulsive move. "The child has a downright hostile feeling toward anything associated with suitability or order and, like the salamander, does not feel right unless she lives close to the fire," she wrote her husband.[25]

Frida, living independently in her small boardinghouse, but with her father's literary friends looking after her, embarked enthusiastically, but not without self-irony, on her own literary efforts. Soon after her arrival she wrote to her sister.

At the moment I am writing a play in the naturalist style—"Maiden's Honor"—I'm afraid you'll turn somersaults with laughter. Two scenes are finished and now I am waiting and can't go further. If

Fulda comes—he's such a lamb, I don't have to be ashamed in front of him. I am too afraid of the others—they always laugh when I begin to be a free-thinker.[26]

She relied on her father's reputation to gain her entrance to the salons of Berlin's cultural elite; once inside, her intelligence and wit enabled her to hold her own. Full of youthful energy, eager and curious after years of seclusion, she settled with delight into the role of cultural reporter for the *Wiener Abendpost*. In a light conversational style, but with decided opinions, she reviewed the German and French writers her father assigned, including Alphonse Daudet and Gerhart Hauptmann. The latter she declared "equal to Zola when it comes to truth and clarity, but through and through German in the depths of thought and violence of his brushstroke."[27]

Her sudden arrival must have been disconcerting to Sudermann. A married man's gentle flirtation under the eye of a young girl's father was one thing, making up to the daughter of a leading critic in his absence quite another. But before Sudermann could protest, Frida had taken on the role she would play in all her subsequent relationships. She made it her business to foster his ambitions. Soon after she arrived in Berlin, she arranged a private luncheon for him with Max Burckhard, the director of Vienna's *Burgtheater*, and her father's close friend. It was a valuable contact for the playwright, since Burckhard was intent on bringing some of Berlin's theatrical excitement to the Austrian capital.

Shortly after this profitable encounter, Sudermann must have made clear that friendship was all he had in mind, because in a letter on New Year's Eve, Frida broke her connection with him in no uncertain terms. "From now on . . . I ask you to deal with me as a total stranger . . ." she wrote him. "Friendship cannot exist between us, nor can I maintain a friendly disposition toward you because your manner of thinking and feeling has grown alien to me." She closed with an admonition: "Don't kiss any more girls you don't love."[28]

What had Frida expected of her married admirer? Had she hoped Sudermann would divorce? If the pattern of this first flirtation was anything like those that followed, Sudermann had probably encouraged Frida to believe she could be of use to him. The degree of Frida's response to her suitors would always be tied to their creative achievements, but it was not the glitter of their fame that attracted her. The seduction lay in the extent to which they invited her dedication to their gifts. By being of use, she earned their love, in the same way she had come to believe she had to earn her father's.

Even though Friedrich Uhl had given her an opportunity to work, Frida knew she must marry eventually. Lacking a parental home, she had less choice in this matter than other young women of her class. Her father had set her up in a masculine profession with none of the male prerogatives. She might write for his paper, but she was still a "daughter," subject to his goodwill. She knew he would not permit her to live in her present unorthodox manner—alone in a boardinghouse—for long. The only possible hope for a meaningful future lay in an alliance with a creative man who would understand her need to use her mind to some worthwhile end.

After *Heimat*'s premiere on January 7, 1893, Frida attended a festive soirée at the home of Julius Elias, a wealthy literary patron, close friend of Ibsen's, and one of the founders of the *Freie Bühne*. Dutiful correspondent if not dutiful daughter, she had gone to the performance at her father's behest and arrived at the party with mixed feelings—moved by the play, saddened by her recent break with the author. Burdened by the emotional upheaval over Sudermann, she was unable to share in the general merriment. She withdrew into a quiet room where another man of letters ripe for adoration and assistance had also taken refuge.

AUGUST STRINDBERG'S LIFE had been at low ebb when he set his sights on Berlin in the fall of 1892. His fifteen-year marriage had ended, he had little contact with his three young children, much of his new work had been rejected, and his financial prospects were grim. To help him escape his misery, his friend the Swedish writer Ola Hansson urged him to come to Berlin and take advantage of his growing renown in Germany. In his desperate reply from the cold summer cottage he was still inhabiting at the onset of autumn, Strindberg told Hansson he could not leave Sweden without paying his debts. On the other hand, he continued slyly, "If I had the 200 marks needed for the journey, I would run."[29]

Hansson managed to raise the money by calling attention to Strindberg's plight in the *Freie Bühne* and in the first issue of a new and provocative journal, *Die Zukunft* (*The Future*). He even published the sad epistle Strindberg had sent him, embarrassing the playwright. In his preface to the letter, Hansson wrote that in urging Strindberg to come to Germany he was motivated by his high regard for him, which was shared by the "freest and most critical among German progressives." He also wished to "tear him free from the soul-destroying narrow atmosphere of Sweden."[30]

Strindberg's popularity in Germany was not exaggerated by Hansson. The intelligentsia went out of its way to welcome him on October 1, and an article in the popular literary periodical *Magazin für Literatur* expressed the hope that Germany would provide the support Sweden had denied. This effusive greeting had been penned by the magazine's editor, Otto Neumann-Hofer.

Although he would be one of those designated by Friedrich Uhl to look after his daughter, Neumann-Hofer was to be instrumental in fostering Strindberg's courtship of Frida.

Hansson and his German wife, Laura Marholm, took Strindberg home with them to Friedrichshagen, a haven for Scandinavian and other expatriate artists equally disaffected with their homeland. Strindberg had begun to correspond with Hansson in the late 1880s when the younger writer published a collection of stories that paralleled Strindberg's interest in the unconscious. Hansson had enlarged on the theme in a series of literary essays published in Germany and he was now the central figure of a coterie of writers and physicians eager to explore new discoveries in psychology. To them, Strindberg was the most eminent spokesman for the drama of the inner man, and he did not disappoint his supporters at the welcoming party in Friedrichshagen. He enthralled them with his scientific theories and views of literature, embarrassed them by the candor with which he discussed his private life, and in the early hours of the morning entertained them by taking his guitar and singing Swedish songs.

But Strindberg soon began to chafe under the Hanssons' patronage. Laura Marholm, who wrote about women's issues and was as active as her husband in promoting Strindberg's work, was certain to rouse his suspicions of managerial women. She soon recognized that beneath the brilliant and charming exterior of their protégé was "an unmitigated distrust, a mistrust without boundaries, a mistrust for the sake of mistrust, a mistrust on principle, as a prerogative of a superior spirit."[31]

After two months, Strindberg had had enough and, accusing the Hanssons of hiding or reading his mail, he left Friedrichshagen and settled in a small residential hotel in Berlin. On the nearby Friedrichstrasse he discovered a hospitable tavern ironically named *Das Kloster* (The Cloister), but which he dubbed *Zum*

Schwarzen Ferkel (The Black Piglet), after the porcine wineskin above the door. Adding insult to injury, he lured other members of Hansson's circle from "*Friedrichshölle*" ("Friedrich's Hell"), as he had begun to refer to his former residence. In the small room at the back of the *Ferkel*, and under the influence of hundreds of intoxicants, from Swedish punch to Japanese rice wine, boasted of by the proprietor, it was Strindberg who now presided over the raucous company.

At about the same time that Strindberg shifted the center of gravity of Hansson's circle from the suburbs to the city, another Scandinavian, the Norwegian painter Edvard Munch, was shaking up Berlin's cultural establishment. For reasons no one later was able to understand, the conservative Artists' Club had agreed, sight unseen but on the recommendation of a Norwegian member, to give Munch his German debut with a one-man show in their renovated galleries. Munch, then twenty-nine, arrived in Berlin at the end of October with fifty-five pieces he himself proceeded to hang. Uproar and outrage followed the opening on November 5. Among the paintings were some of Munch's now-classic depictions of sexual and social malaise, including *Puberty*, *Despair*, and *Evening on Karl Johan Street*. A meeting of the Artists' Club was called immediately and, despite the threat of a riot by a small minority of members, an unprecedented decision was taken to close the exhibition in the name of "respect for art and honorable artistic ambition."

To the habitués of the *Ferkel*, however, Munch's psychologically fraught images seemed the very embodiment of their ideas. He was soon a part of the tavern's inner circle, and brought with him some member of the so-called Kristiania Bohème, a group of artists and writers from Norway's capital who had been notorious in the 1880s for their credo of sexual freedom. Among these were the painter Christian Krohg, his wife, Oda, and the playwright

Gunnar Heiberg, who were living in Berlin as a ménage à trois. Regulars at the *Ferkel* included the writers Adolf Paul from Finland, Holger Drachmann from Denmark, the young German poet Richard Dehmel, and two local physicians and patrons of the arts, Carl Schleich and Max Asch. Strindberg made a particularly strong impression on Schleich, who was struck by the writer's resemblance to Beethoven.

His high brow had something in it of Prometheus; the same spirit spoke from his curiously sharp yet at the same time sorrowful grey-blue eyes, seemed to ruffle his unruly hair like flames and even expressed itself in his short, energetic mustache, which lent a defiant and ironic touch to his very soft and beautiful mouth, femininely small and finely pursed.[32]

After Strindberg, the most dynamic presence was the twenty-three-year-old Polish medical student Stanislaw Przybyszewski, whose appearance someone described as that of a Slavic Christ with something maniacal in his features. Shortly before Strindberg's arrival, he had published *The Psychology of the Individual,* a small book of essays in which he suggested that the uninhibited impulses of the unconscious, however demonic, were the prime sources of artistic inspiration. *Rausch* (intoxication), whether induced by alcohol, music, dance, or sex—particularly the last—obsessed Przybyszewski and some of the others at the *Ferkel*.[33]

This motley crew reveled nightly, combining heated discussions of art, psychology, and the opposite sex with music and carousing. Strindberg amused the company by singing student songs accompanied by his untuned guitar; Przybyszewski's wild renderings of Chopin and Schumann on the tavern piano left his inebriated companions feeling unhinged. The doctors fed the writers' interest in the working of the mind; the artists took the more flamboyant figures as models. Munch depicted Przybyszewski as a brooding sensualist, Strindberg as a man filled with tension under a surface of forced calm. The same wary quality made itself felt in Christian Krohg's likeness of Strindberg, even though he presented him as a Nietzschean *Übermensch* larger than life in his imposing overcoat. Dehmel saluted Strindberg in verse. At the end of one memorable evening, he leaped upon a table, smashed a few bottles with his walking stick, and recited a poem comparing Strindberg to a giant prehistoric badger who every once in a while "grabs a human brain to feed on."[34]

Issues of sex and emancipation that absorbed the habitués of the *Ferkel* were also on view in Berlin's theaters. In January, Frida attended premieres of three plays in succession in which an independent woman causes a man to die—Sudermann's *Heimat,* Ibsen's *The Master Builder,* and Strindberg's *Creditors.* Sudermann's Magda, although the most pliable of the three heroines, nevertheless causes her father's death when she denies him the moral victory he craves. Ibsen's young Hilde Wangel is a more threatening phenomenon: the sexual recklessness of her youth proves fatal for the much older master builder Solness. Strindberg's creation, the twice-married Tekla, is the most fully rounded of the three women. When Adolf, her second husband, suspects her of infidelity, her responses are playful and sensible. Strindberg gave her the key line when he had her tell Adolf to control his imagination. "That is what makes men beasts," she warns him. And, indeed, the fears that lead to Adolf's death are not actually caused by Tekla, but by the vengeful doubts about her placed in Adolf's mind by her first husband. In demonstrating the tragic potential of the power of suggestion, Strindberg was drawing on his own destructive personal obsessions.

Strindberg found his way as an artist when he realized that his own life provided the best fuel for his work. As a man who cultivated, rather than suppressed, opposing aspects of his nature, he discovered that the conflicts within himself, or in battling with society at large, could be a constant source of inspiration. Early in his career, identification with his mother's lower-class origins clashed with his intellectual ambitions. As he matured, he rejected the Puritan pietism of his youth, but this left a patina of guilt over every assent to life's pleasures. He was attracted to strong, independent women who invariably ended up threatening his zealously guarded ego. In his public life he refused circumspection, and the controversies provoked by his work and pronouncements caused further difficulties. Sometimes he even fanned the dying embers of a dispute with the very work of art it had originally inspired.

As a newly arrived celebrity in Berlin, Strindberg was also courted by the middle-class members of the intelligentsia—the directors and patrons of the *Freie Bühne* and the editors of the liberal journals. At their soirées and receptions—sedate affairs conducted with traditional bourgeois decorum in elegantly furnished drawing rooms—Strindberg was a more discreet presence than at the *Ferkel*. It was on such an occasion, taking refuge in a quieter room from some of his more intrusive admirers at a reception following the premiere of *Heimat*, that he first encountered Frida.

2

The Misogynist and the Maiden

FRIDA HAD COME CLOSE to the truth when she wrote her father that Strindberg had spoken to her as if in a dream. When they passed each other on the street a few days after their first meeting, he failed to recognize her. Many years later, in the opening sequence of *Klostret* (*The Cloister*), an autobiographical novel, Strindberg rechoreographed their first encounter to explain why he had overlooked Frida.[1]

Axel, as Strindberg called his narrator, wakes on a winter morning in Berlin and replays in reverse order the occurrences of the night before. Midnight had found him in a questionable nightspot earnestly explaining his philosophy of life to some ladies of ill repute. When his companions had chided him for discussing serious matters in such company, his response, in recollection, pleases him: "Because all women are the same to me," he had replied.

Before this late-night rendezvous, Axel had attended a so-called Vienna Ball, a costume ball at which both homosexuals and lesbians consort openly with their same-sex lovers under the eyes of the police. Axel, somewhat ashamed of being an onlooker, felt pity for them, understood the power of their obsession, and was amazed that even under the double disguise of costume and sex, the same virtues, the same proprieties were observed as in polite society.

Earlier in the evening, he had been the honored guest at an elegant party. There he had engaged in a long conversation about literature with a young woman, a correspondent for a newspaper. When she expressed some views on women's emancipation, he had chosen to leave. Since the young woman had not been flirtatious nor had drawn attention to her looks, he took no notice of her appearance.

Reversing the narrator's description of that fateful night, the point of the sequence becomes clear. As the evening begins, Axel meets a woman who attempts to impress him with her mind, rather than her appearance. He cannot see her as a woman, and it makes him uncomfortable. Here we have his first view of Frida, a woman whose essence he cannot grasp because the feminine is overlaid with other qualities. At the Vienna Ball, the sexes are even more confused, nothing is as it seems and even so-called vice turns out to have its virtuous side. By the time he reaches the late-night café, he is too tired to deal with his awareness of shifting identities. By discussing philosophy with whores, he puts the world back in order and reassures himself momentarily that roles are fixed; all women are the same.

A month after the meeting with Strindberg, which had left so strong an impression on her, Frida was still in Berlin despite her father's order to leave. She had managed to convince the ever-thrifty Friedrich Uhl that an instant departure would require the payment of a penalty at her pension, and thus it would be less costly if she stayed on for a few more weeks. But she knew that compliance with his wishes could not be avoided much longer.

It was during this reprieve, at a dinner party given by the

Neumann-Hofers, that Frida encountered Strindberg a second time. When the hostess pointed Frida out to him as one of Vienna's young beauties, Strindberg was encouraged to look more closely at the woman he had confided in so intimately at the *Heimat* soirée. When he described this meeting later in *The Cloister*, it was not Frida's appearance he recalled, but her conversation.

> *During that evening she had been treated like a child, they had made fun of her writing and influence and she had only smiled in response. He—the stranger, the woman-hater, which they justifiably but not justifiably called him—was the only one to take her seriously. And he had seen that this was no child but a woman, a woman with whom he could discuss everything that interested him—about people and books without for a single moment having to explain what he was talking about.*[2]

It was a remarkable impression for a woman as young as Frida to have made on a worldly playwright. Strindberg must have seen that beyond her cosmopolitan education and quick mind, there was a precocious grasp of culture and its politics. Having observed her father function as both a severe critic and a sympathetic mentor in the theater world, Frida could draw on experiences that spoke directly to Strindberg's own predicament as a controversial writer.

Free from family surveillance, Frida followed her instinct that there was much to be learned from a friendship with the magnetic playwright. When Strindberg escorted her home that night, she took the first of many initiatives: she invited him to dine with her and a friend the next day. If she was not aware of the unorthodoxy of her invitation, Strindberg certainly was. Despite his bohemian reputation, he respected the conventions which did not permit a respectable middle-class woman to entertain a man in her rooms. But when Frida went on to explain that it would be only a simple occasion, since her rooms were small and her landlady strict, her naïveté aroused his curiosity and he accepted.

And what did Frida expect from Strindberg? She had met the most lionized playwright in Berlin on two separate occasions, and each time he had conversed with her at length in a manner neither paternal nor patronizing. How could the daughter of Vienna's leading drama critic, a newly baptized cultural journalist, and a young woman who venerated literature, not pursue so flattering and stimulating a connection? When Strindberg arrived at her lodgings for their dinner engagement, the promised friend was nowhere in evidence.

Strindberg was disconcerted at first on finding Frida alone, but he was soon disarmed by the easy and open manner with which she welcomed him into her pleasant room, well furnished with comfortable chairs and a large oak desk. Covering the divan was a leopard-skin coat—courtesy of a hunter friend of Friedrich Uhl's—and on the wall hung a reproduction of Rembrandt's *Man with a Golden Helmet*, a favorite of Frida's.

The variety of impressions Frida made on Strindberg that evening confirmed his sense that his new acquaintance offered dramatic possibilities. The evening began pleasantly enough as the two foreigners shared experiences of life in Berlin. However, as Frida, elegant in an Empire-style black silk dress, confidently served the food and poured the wine, Strindberg began to suspect she might be a divorcée. When she gestured toward a large bouquet of roses left by a "friend," he was convinced she was engaged. But when she knelt before the flowers to cut a blossom and, still on her knees, placed it in his buttonhole and then saluted him with a glass of wine, he was amazed and charmed by her audacity.[3] After their meal, Frida insisted he stay longer, but his sense of decorum suggested otherwise. This did not prevent him from writing her immediately.

> *. . . I must thank you for an unforgettable evening. I must tell you that I didn't forget the rose, but left it behind so as to have the excuse to come and get it the following day although my courage failed me at the decisive moment. In short, I have so many things to tell you even with the risk of losing your respect, which I value less than your sympathy. In awaiting a friendly word, I beg of you to have faith in me.*[4]

When he was told of Frida's imminent departure, Strindberg insisted on seeing her daily before the inevitable separation. "Your friendship has already so thoroughly displaced that of my drinking companions," he wrote her, "that I don't want to miss one of the remaining five days in the fear that after your planned departure, I will be even unhappier to be left behind."[5]

Through two acts of defiance—moving to Berlin without Uhl's permission and now leaving it slowly and reluctantly—Frida had stood up to her father. And yet, as a letter to him during this dramatic time reveals, it had not been easy to disobey him. While admitting that their conflict was inevitable, Frida confessed to the anguish she felt over his alienation from her. "I have thrown away your love," she wrote him. "In my yearning for you I feel what I have done thereby."[6]

All did not go smoothly for Strindberg either, as he tried to overcome his resistance to Frida's startling initiatives. Their first evening out together set the tone. Frida suggested the restaurant, a small wine bar near the Zoo, and although Strindberg agreed, he was uneasy about her familiarity with the place. She had, indeed, been there with Sudermann.

As Strindberg recalled several years later in *The Cloister,* the most terrifying moment occurred when Frida removed her leopard-skin coat: he was struck by his strong sexual attraction to her.

> *A clinging moss-green dress revealed the figure of an eighteen-year-old and her hair which she had brushed smoothly made her appear like a grown-up schoolgirl. He couldn't, confronted with such enchantment, hide his state of mind, and instead, looked her up and down as if he could discover a hidden enemy with a searchlight.*
>
> *(Eros! Now I am lost, he thought, and from that moment on he was.)*[7]

But there were more complications before the evening ended. When Strindberg briefly left the table, Frida took it upon herself to pay the bill. Her protests that he was her guest were in vain as Strindberg threw his money down and ushered her out in a fury. Later he wrote that two interpretations of her spontaneous misconceived gesture crossed his mind. Perhaps she was unaware of social codes, unaware in the same way she had been when she invited him to her room. Or she really felt emancipated and believed herself to be an independent woman who could treat a man as her equal.[8] In fact, both were true. Her gesture reflected her artless assumption that theirs was a collegial relationship and therefore free of sexual conventions.

Frida was confronted with a suitor who was both attracted and repelled by her virtues; her intellect stimulated him but her unorthodox attitudes threatened his manhood, her youthful beauty drew him to her, but her erotic appeal made him vulnerable. Still, Strindberg persisted. Before meeting Frida, he had already embarked on some short-lived entanglements with students and freethinking wives, but he was essentially a bourgeois at heart. Frida fulfilled one requirement the members of bohemia lacked: her bold gestures and unconventional behavior were cloaked in the appearance of middle-class respectability. Strindberg soon perceived that they stemmed from neither rebellion nor self-display, but reflected the innocence of "the grown-up schoolgirl" sent out into the world alone.

And so a courtship began, and, through evasive maneuvers, Frida extended the time for her departure from five days to four weeks. The two met often, took walks in the Tiergarten, dined in discreet restaurants, and encountered one another at dinners and soirées. As had become her practice, Frida also tried to introduce Strindberg to the people in publishing and theater who might be of use to him.

Aware of her father's rattling his saber, Frida took the next step a day or two before her departure for Munich. When Strindberg brought her home after an evening out, she pulled the veil on her hat down over her face, kissed him on the lips, and, before he could embrace her, hastily disappeared behind the door. Shaken, yet delighted, Strindberg did what was expected of him and the next day sent a letter asking for her hand in marriage—but not without an ironic warning. "Now the woman-hater lays his head in your lap as a sign that your goodness has had the power to overcome my evil: but don't misuse your power, because the inevitable fate of all tyrants awaits you."[9]

Strindberg never forgot the captivating kiss. When he wrote his play *To Damascus*, long after his second marriage had ended, that kiss became the decisive seductive gesture at the end of Act One. And when the play was in rehearsal prior to its Stockholm premiere in 1900, Strindberg fell in love with the actress Harriet Bosse as he instructed her how to move "when the kiss has to be given with the veil down."[10]

Once again Frida seemed to have acted on impulse. Perhaps the kiss was intended as a gesture she felt free to make before going away. Perhaps she did not want Strindberg to forget her. Perhaps she understood that Strindberg would never make the first move. But now that she had captured her prey, her first reaction was hesitant, even fearful, and she rejected his proposal.

"I love you honestly as a friend," she wrote, "and am ready to do anything to serve you or give you pleasure. But I am unable to feel anything that even remotely resembles a real passion and I think that is a good thing." She ended the letter with a perceptive insight into the self-regarding nature of Strindberg's emotional life. She was convinced, she wrote him, that he did not love her. Rather, he was enamored of the idea of love, of the dream of himself in love. He sought to make a reality of that dream, and so deceived himself.[11]

But now Strindberg would not let her go. He would borrow two thousand marks, he wrote her, and they could leave Berlin as an engaged couple to meet her parents in Vienna. From there, he fantasized further, they could go to Italy. "An answer," he demanded.[12]

Calming her suitor down and heading off the threat of a meeting with her family, Frida agreed to a secret engagement. Still very much her father's child, she would go to Munich to pay off the debts she owed him from her move to Berlin, attempt to regain his good opinion of her, and try to finish her novel. Suddenly businesslike, she insisted that Strindberg organize his finances. He could follow her to Munich, but they would have to work at their respective tasks if they were to marry. Only then could they announce their engagement to the world. This seemed a reprieve for each of them. Frida, assured she would not be forgotten, could try to regain her father's affection. Strindberg, momentarily released from the demands of propriety, could return to his world at the *Ferkel.*

THE MONTH OF March was a comedy of errors for the secretly engaged couple. Strindberg was alone again and unsure how to proceed. Should he follow Frida to Munich, as she urged in her first letter, or should he await her return to Berlin? Confused about his new liaison, he confided in the Neumann-Hofers. They responded that scandal was to be avoided and Strindberg should stay put. "If I leave Berlin," he wrote Frida, "everything is lost—my future and yours. Neumann-Hofer has simply forbidden it, because he is responsible for you. As long as rumors circulate about an engagement, it is fine and honest, but if talk is of an affair . . . Pfui."[13]

Lonely and at loose ends, Strindberg returned to the *Ferkel*, where a friend of Munch's, a young woman with an enigmatic and seductive manner, now held court. Dagny Juel was a twenty-five-year-old piano student from Norway studying at the conservatory in Berlin. Tall, slim, graceful, she dressed to display her figure. Reddish-blond curls fell over her forehead, and her heavy-lidded eyes gave her a languid, mysterious air. She had arrived in Berlin as an independent agent—no family nipped at her heels—and quickly became the erotic focus of the company at the tavern. She pounced first on the newly engaged Strindberg, who cried for help in a letter to Frida before succumbing to the more knowing temptress.

> *What are you doing? Come here and protect me so that I can work—otherwise everything will go wrong. Bad conscience, poor reviews from Stockholm, uneasiness, drives me to the* Schwarze Ferkel. *Don't stay away any longer. I won't eat you. You must become a writer and stay independent if that is what you want. There is a kernel of manliness in you, a droplet of the feminine in me. That makes for a beautiful, wonderful couple. Isn't that true?*[14]

He continued to bombard her with letters and telegrams begging her to return to save him. He was so weak without her, he wrote. And, more broadly, in another letter: "I have so many sins on my conscience the last few days since you left that I want to die. . . . How do you believe I can stay at home the entire hypochondriacal evening when you are no longer at my side guarding me with your sweet benevolent eyes?"[15]

Frida, however, content in Munich and determined to appease her father, did not care to read between the lines. She had found a sun-filled room with a view of the Isar River and wrote Strindberg that she loved the city although it did not offer the excitement of Berlin. She was busily summing up that excitement in an article for the *Wiener Zeitung*. By describing the bohemian life of the artists and writers in Berlin, "who for the most part are denied entry into bourgeois circles but create their own sunny world full of the pleasures of life and spirit," she had the subversive pleasure of promoting her secret fiancé in her father's paper.

> *Berlin has now become the hometown of the great Scandinavians. In a cul-de-sac off the "Linden" empty oyster shells, red wine bottles and the figure of a wild pig can be discerned in front of a little wine bar cheerfully paneled in brown wood.* Zum Schwarzen Ferkel *is the name of the artists' hangout where the foreign artists gather every evening. August Strindberg, Holger Drachmann, Gunnar Heiberg, Adolf Paul—the painters Munch and Krohg—all meet together here. The small colony of great men is not a small part of the pride of literary Berlin.*[16]

Frida went on to cite the theatrical triumphs of Strindberg and Sudermann and concluded with a poetic image of the heated debates their dramas provoked until "the stars come up over the heads of the antagonists and the water rustles softly at their feet under the Potsdam Bridge."

The immediate reality at *Zum Schwarzen Ferkel* was far from the idyllic picture painted by Frida as Strindberg confronted another woman who defied his expectations. Like Frida, Dagny was the daughter of a prominent family, her father a doctor and local politician, her uncle Norway's prime minister. In that crucial period for young women between the end of adolescence and marriage, Dagny's life followed the usual pattern: a stint as a governess, enthusiastic piano study but no great ambition, and traditional mating games at the balls and parties given by her relatives in Kristiania.[17]

More tempting was the social life conducted by the Kristiania Bohème. Its founding members had been to Paris in the early 1880s and had returned to their native city determined to create a bohemia in which the same freedom could flourish. But amid the predictable and inflexible social life of a small and pious provincial capital, a group of men and women enjoying each other's company in the neutral social spaces of cafés and studios appeared new and shocking. Whereas in Paris the artist's bohemian existence, the ease with which he moved among all sectors of society and mingled casually with the opposite sex represented an organic development in a society in flux, in Kristiania, the assertion of such freedom was an artificial construct demanding justification.

Hans Jaeger, the writer and political activist who was one of the instigators of the group, cleverly provided one by declaring that the bohemians had a special mission. They would offer an alternative to the social hypocrisy and sexual repression of Norwegian society and point the way to a more tolerant society. The behavior of his coterie would demonstrate the advantages of sexual equality, the freedom to be had by shaking off the shackles of family, church, and state, and the opportunities available to those willing to take their fate in their own hands. Write your own life, he advised his followers, urging them to voice their personal desires.

Jaeger applied his ideas to women as well as men. Both sexes, he argued, should be allowed to initiate relationships, separate when tired of each other, and feel free to express themselves with the same degree of sexual candor. Predictably, the men in Jaeger's coterie were students, artists, and writers who could socialize in studios and cafés with impunity. Since the women who joined them were not the *grisettes* or poor working girls traditionally associated with Parisian bohemia, but members of the middle class like themselves, theirs was the greater risk. Some were the men's wives or sisters, but others were young women attempting, if only for a brief period, to escape marriage by studying music or art and experimenting with social freedom.

As Munch recalled, in the small, isolated, provincial world of Norway's capital, the effect and influence of the little group around Jaeger was far greater than it might have been in Paris or Berlin. Indulging in the drink and tobacco symbolizing their emancipation, Jaeger's followers were determined to meet as equals and embark on a variety of sexual alliances, including ménages à trois. Jaeger himself was involved with the painters Oda Lasson and Christian Krohg, and Munch fell in love with the married sister-in-law of a fellow artist. Lasson and Krohg, who were married but continued to indulge in affairs, had the inner strength to survive the emotional upheavals of this radical freedom, but Munch's suffering in this uncharted terrain was more typical. The anguish and existential doubt arising from the inevitable guilt and jealousies of these love affairs became the subject of his art for many years. Even his later descriptions of that time read like verbal renderings of the overheated atmosphere in his paintings. "The time of Bohemia came with its free love—God, and everything, was overthrown and all joined in a wild mad dance—a blood-red sun stood in the heavens—the Cross no longer atoned. But I could not free myself from a fear of life and thoughts of eternity."[18]

In 1885, Jaeger incorporated the ideas of his radical coterie in a novel titled *From the Kristiania Bohème.* Embedded in a tale recounting the nihilistic lethargy of two antiheros were Jaeger's frank descriptions of the pain of thwarted adolescent sexuality (for both sexes), and cogent arguments for the advantages of free love over the hypocrisy of prostitution. "The day will come," he prophesied, "when women will tear down the prison of marriage."[19] The book was banned on the day it appeared, and Jaeger was imprisoned a year later. His case became a cause célèbre as enlightened writers and critics in the Scandinavian countries decried the injustice of the sentence and praised Jaeger's courage.

Responding to these so-called immoralists of the 1880s, the Scandinavian "moralists" took action. Tracts appeared in Norway and Denmark accusing Jaeger, Krohg, even Zola, of causing a moral decline. By the 1890s not only Strindberg but also most of the members of the Kristiania Bohème were living abroad. Jaeger was in Paris, Munch, Krohg and Lasson in Berlin. In early 1893, Dagny Juel, whose emancipated attitude and original way of dressing had already led to comments in Kristiania society, followed.[20]

In Berlin, Dagny chose lovers freely and disposed of them easily. She drank, smoked, and accompanied gentlemen to cafés. While the freewheeling atmosphere of *Zum Schwarzen Ferkel* may have reminded Dagny of Kristiania, most of the Berlin bohemians were far more conservative than Jaeger regarding women. His vision had included a generous concern for the equality and well-being of both sexes. At the *Ferkel* the attitude toward sex had a Nietzschean cast: it was accepted as a means of self-intoxication, but involved no larger agenda of emancipating women. In fact, it was at the *Ferkel* that the Greek term *hetairai* was first used to describe the educated women of bohemia, relating them to their forebears in antiquity as women capable of sharing men's intellectual interests but sexual objects first and foremost. Munch, remaining faithful to Jaeger's ideas, never criticized Dagny for her various liaisons. But no such inhibition muzzled Strindberg or, in the long run, Przybyszewski, who eventually married Dagny, but was later to turn on her for what he considered the promiscuity of her past.[21]

In the initial euphoria of having been pursued by the beautiful newcomer, Strindberg spoke in her honor and baptized her "Aspasia," after Pericles' mistress. To him it seemed an apt appellation for a modern *hetaira* who was, as he saw initially, "more of a spiritual than a physical seductress. A vampire of the soul with a yearning for higher things."[22] Happy to be speaking to a woman in his own tongue, he found himself responding to her delicate probing of his engagement to Frida and began confiding in her. In *The Cloister,* he recalled the irony that talking about the absent Frida brought him closer to Dagny. Even as he continued writing amorous letters to Munich, he allowed Dagny to reinforce his doubts about the engagement until, in his words, "he had given the lamb to the wolf and was watching as it fell upon its prey."[23]

Dagny's emancipation was more calculated and programmatic than Frida's. In taking on a bohemian persona, the seductive Norwegian flaunted her freedom. Frida, driven to rebel by the desire to participate rather than display, was not tempted by notoriety. Although she knew she had fallen from grace in her father's eyes, she took no pride in his disapproval. The provocative behavior of the bohemians held so little appeal for her that during the first weeks of her acquaintance with Strindberg, she often begged him to give up his visits to the *Ferkel.*

An enigmatic telegram from Annie Neumann-Hofer urging Frida to return to Berlin left her unmoved. "Impossible and useless," she cabled back.[24] The ardor of Strindberg's letters made her feel secure and, at the same time, she had gained precious freedom to work and satisfy her vigilant father. She made it clear to Strindberg that her obligations to Friedrich Uhl required a six-month stay.

> *My father is the dearest, best and gentlest person in the world and will welcome you with the greatest pleasure—will also be a real friend to you—if we can first succeed in resolving the one point that will cause him to look mistrustfully or even turn against our union. Naturally, that is once again the* fatal *question of money. He, himself, has nothing to give me. So first I have to prove that I am capable of surviving on my own.*[25]

To accomplish this, Frida had given up her allowance and was seeking other newspapers to write for, as well as attempting to finish her novel. Strindberg, too, was to help: he had to pay off his debts, she instructed. For her part, she had bought a Swedish dictionary so they could get rid of his translators.

Less cool was Frida's letter to her mother, to whom she could not resist divulging the secret of her engagement and her excitement at being chosen by a "poet-prince." At the same time, she revealed her confidence in being able to manage her eminent fiancé, whom she defined as "the most important writer, whom everyone in Berlin virtually worships." And, in turn, she boasted playfully, this man worshiped her as if she were "Miss Innocence just descended from God's throne."

But, as both she and her mother knew, it was not the Almighty but Papa Uhl who would be judging Frida. She reassured her mother that she would not marry until her father was satisfied that she had reimbursed him for her impulsive move to Berlin. "I don't want to take my dirty maiden's laundry into my new house," she bravely asserted.[26]

In Berlin, meanwhile, distracted by Dagny, Strindberg acceded to the wait, but not without hinting that there might be consequences for Frida's "all too earthly husband." He added that if they were to be separated for so long, he must be allowed his independence.[27] Was he hinting at his entanglement with Dagny, or did he want to discourage Frida from reprimanding him for his visits to the *Ferkel* and his failure to socialize with her more respectable friends?

Frida took it to mean the former, but with the equanimity of the innocent, surprised her suitor yet again by granting him permission to be untrue to her.

> *As far as your independence is concerned, naturally, my dear friend, you can have that as* you will always have it, *without limits. I want to be your friend, not your master, you understand. You are free to do what you wish. Above all don't feel obligated to be true to me. I give you permission for any escapade your heart desires. I know that means nothing as far as love is concerned. Also, in any other way, do what you wish. I ask only one thing:* think it over *before you act. Think, for example, that you would make our wedding impossible (even after 6 months' spiritual marriage as you call it), if you throw money out the window, instead of striving to pay off your debts.*[28]

Strindberg had once confided lightheartedly to Adolf Paul that Frida was a new type for him—"gentle, buxom, dark, and an utter rogue"—but this letter, with its combination of sexual laissez-faire and economic vigilance, brought out an old litany of fear and anger. Strindberg answered that she had misused her power and made him her "laughable slave." Despite his dalliance with Dagny, he felt free to write that her "dispensation" to be unfaithful had hurt him and could only be read as a sign that she did not love him. As for his financial affairs, she was to have nothing to say from now on.

Frida had not known Strindberg long enough to grasp that she was the object of anxieties from an earlier life. In his play *The Father,* Strindberg had given naked expression to men's fear of controlling women. At the drama's close, when the virile Captain has been tricked into a straitjacket by the women of his household, he calls his wife "Omphale," comparing her to the Lydian queen who had unmanned Hercules by taking his club and lion skin and forcing him to spin wool for her, dressed as a woman. Now Strindberg warned Frida that she was playing the same role. "You have cast your silken net over my head," he wrote to her. "I am already wiggling in it and if things continue as they have up to now, my Omphale, I can foresee the moment when your Hercules will take hold of your spindle."[29]

Frida crumbled before this document, resorting for the first time to the intimate *Du* form, and begging forgiveness for her impersonal tone. But what she refused to accept or could not understand was Strindberg's fear that she wished to usurp him. "You are right about my tone," she wrote, "but not in the idea that I want to take over your powers. I can only love a man who is my superior."[30]

Unable to lure Frida back to Berlin, Strindberg took up another, more threatening tactic, without consulting her. He decided to accept an invitation to Vienna to attend the premiere of *Creditors* and urged Frida to join him there. "First love, then business," he wrote her, delighted with his cleverness at breaking their stalemate.[31]

So much for Frida's carefully laid plans. To forestall disaster, she cabled her mother to join forces with her in the inevitable confrontation with her father. Maria Uhl replied that she was delighted at the prospect of becoming the mother-in-law of the "poet-prince," and added judiciously that Frida should bring *Hemsöborna* (*The People of Hemsö*), a novel by Strindberg, for her father.[32]

With her mother as an ally, Frida asked Annie Neumann-Hofer to notify Strindberg that an arrangement to meet had been made. But by the time her telegram arrived, Strindberg had changed his mind. He claimed that an argument with the director of the *Burgtheater* caused him to cancel his visit to the Austrian capital. But the real reason was probably a last-minute realization that he did not, indeed, have the financial wherewithal to confront Friedrich Uhl. After this failure to live up to his own daredevil gesture, Strindberg's letters were noticeably cooler and more circumspect. In fact, other "creditors" had begun to threaten him—rumors of his engagement to a thus-far-unknown woman had reached Scandinavia and people there to whom he still owed money had begun to press for payment.

At this juncture fate overtook the courtship. In the early hours of March 29, Friedrich Uhl, reviewing his competitors' morning editions as usual, came upon an announcement pertaining to himself in the *Deutsche Zeitung.*

> *We have heard from Berlin that Strindberg is coming to Vienna for the production of his play* Creditors. *It should be of interest to the Viennese that in the past weeks, Strindberg became engaged to Frida Uhl, the daughter of the Councillor Friedrich Uhl.*[33]

Within moments, Uhl had summoned Mitzi to his office. She found her father smoking his sixth "Virginia" cigar—the chewed and bitten tips of its predecessors were strewn about. He handed her the offending article to read and together they composed the letter to be dispatched to her renegade sister.

Dear Frida,

Papa gave me the assignment of telling you that for God's sake he doesn't have to give you "permission" since it is a long time since you asked him for any "permission," but he begs you not to implicate him in any more scandal and disgrace.

Now you can't go back. That scandal would be much worse for Papa than your marrying your Poet-Prince, whose work, thank goodness, he respects highly. By the way, he says he would rather have given the creator of The Father *a literary prize than his daughter.*[34]

The strange circumstances that led to the announcement were related many years after this by its author, the Austrian writer Hermann Bahr. In March 1893, on assignment for his paper, Bahr was in Berlin working on a series of articles on anti-Semitism. On his way home one night, inebriated after a merry evening, he encountered Strindberg. In the "confused, animated, somnambulist discussion" that ensued, Strindberg began to sing the praises of Bahr's "beautiful compatriot," Frida Uhl. Bahr's first thought was of Friedrich Uhl. He reflected that Uhl's brilliant theater criticism, appearing as it did in the *Wiener Zeitung*, had much less impact than the judgments of the competing drama critic writing for the more widely read *Neue Freie Presse*. In his less than sober state, Bahr had the foolish notion that an announcement of Frida's connection to the famous playwright might work in Uhl's favor. That night he sent a telegram to his paper saying Strindberg had become engaged to the daughter of "Councillor Uhl."

At the time, Bahr was a young, ambitious literary essayist and reporter who, only a month before, had been named theater critic for the Vienna-based *Deutsche Zeitung*. The appointment put him in direct competition with the drama critic of the *Neue Freie*

Presse, and perhaps this also lay behind the boyish joke inspired by the fortuitous meeting with Strindberg.

In recalling his prank, Bahr speculated about Strindberg's response.

> *Why didn't Strindberg deny it? Out of chivalry, so as not to darken Frida's reputation? Maybe but certainly not only because of that. He had, above all, a nearly mystical faith in fate, he saw in this newspaper notice an indication. If it was in the stars that this beautiful young Viennese woman was intended for him, then no retraction of the announcement would help. . . . Also she was very beautiful—she was so fair—a sun's ray lay on her southern visage.*[35]

Although Bahr contemplated the effects of his mischief on Strindberg alone, the published notice galvanized all three figures in the drama he had created. Despite Strindberg's secret engagement to Frida, a detail he had not revealed to Bahr, the young journalist's overweening assumption that he was responsible for pushing him into marriage was not entirely wrong. Until the notice appeared, the engagement, at least on Strindberg's part, was wearing thin and he was not paying it much heed.

For Uhl, the unexpected announcement confirmed his worst fears of the gossip and tattle of his fellow journalists in a city where almost everyone had something to hide. He had always felt that the irregularities of his family life would cause him trouble. His quick consent to the marriage was designed to avoid the threat of further revelations.

In Frida's case, the notice meant that the dreaded confrontation with her father could no longer be avoided. She dispatched a telegram to the paper denying the report, wired Strindberg that there was no longer any choice about asking her father for her hand, and wrote a long and candid letter to her father. After admitting to the engagement and explaining why she had kept it a secret, she described the nature of her attachment to Strindberg. She insisted that it was not passion that had impelled her, but "a sincere warm liking and honest admiration, with deep respect for the qualities of Strindberg's mind. I can learn a lot from Strindberg and I can be more for him than others can." There, simply put, was Frida's vision of marriage—intellectual stimulation, an opportunity for growth, and the possibility of being of use.

In the rest of the letter, Frida urged her father to forget about the obligation of a dowry, calling it a dreadful custom whereby parents sacrificed their lives for their children. To make her point, she quoted him against himself, letting him know how aware she was that he often did things out of "exaggerated propriety which you damn in principle." She reminded him that in a review of a play by Ludwig Fulda, he had written that the best dowry parents could give their daughters was a good education enabling them to earn money on their own.[36]

Frida's frantic telegram to Strindberg was answered with a cool reply. He cabled that his financial situation had not changed, and therefore he could not allow a newspaper notice to determine his future. He preferred the current state of affairs—an engagement without a contract.[37]

Frida was in despair when, that same day, she received Mitzi's letter with Uhl's grudging consent. Sending it on to Strindberg, she included a note suggesting that their financial difficulties might be resolved with the money promised for her trousseau. But, even at this impasse, with her father's wrath hanging over her, Frida allowed Strindberg an escape.

I am afraid you may not love me anymore and want to get your children back. If that is the case, be honest, I beg of you. I love you enough and desire your happiness, even at the price of mine. Say one word and I will deny the notice and everything will be as if there had never been anything between us.[38]

Strindberg's reply, despite his protestations of love, was concerned more with the insult to his honor than to the implications for Frida of the untimely announcement of their engagement. And he could not resist reminding her of the earlier incident, when she had offended him in the same fashion by attempting to pay for their meal at a restaurant. "Remember, my dear, that I am a man," he admonished her, "and that the code of honor for a man is not the same as that for a woman. Remember that noisy evening in the Sudermann place where you had almost lost me. . . ." Regarding the letter to her father, he was unwilling to write it until he was able to answer Uhl's "first and entirely justifiable question: Are you in a position to support a wife?"[39]

This stubborn response compelled Frida to act. Asking no one's permission, she cabled Strindberg that she was returning to Berlin. But when she arrived at the station, it was the Neumann-Hofers who greeted her. Strindberg was ill, they told her, and then, with some hesitation, informed her of his rumored connection with Dagny Juel. Shaken, but determined to hear the news firsthand, Frida sent a reproachful note to her errant fiancé. An answer came back from Carl Schleich, Strindberg's medical companion at the *Ferkel*, asking, with appropriate gravity, if Frida would visit the invalid.

Strindberg had broken off the affair with Dagny by this time, but the telegram announcing Frida's imminent arrival unnerved him. With the connivance of his friends from the *Ferkel*, he planned for their reunion to take place at a pseudo-sickbed, where he could count on her motherly sympathy. It was a stratagem he had once used successfully during his courtship of his first wife. The ruse had the desired effect. Seeing Strindberg ill, Frida was distracted by concern, and love was rekindled. When she returned to his room the next morning with her arms full of Easter blooms, she accepted his shamefaced admission of his affair with Dagny and his lame excuse that he had been under the influence of drink. She had herself, after all, consented to "any escapade" his heart desired. In return, grateful to be forgiven, Strindberg agreed to send the appropriate letter to Friedrich Uhl. Frida added one of her own.

Dear Best Father,

Many thanks for your lines that were more than a yes and make me so endlessly happy as only a poor maidenly creature can be—since in the last few days my friendly inclination toward my future husband has greatly increased. It is not surprising—the greatest genius that exists at the moment and a love equal to the spirit . . .

Dear best father, I think I am crazy with happiness. If only you were here—because now you are totally reconciled—even if you don't say so—with your daughter who sends many kisses.[40]

Since Mitzi had written her own conciliatory phrases at the end of her letter conveying Friedrich Uhl's consent, she and Frida were once more on good terms. Relieved that her troublesome sister was at last sailing toward the appropriate port of matrimony, Mitzi agreed to come to Berlin as chaperone during the remaining weeks. But before she got there the engagement was in trouble.

In the warmth of their happy reunion in Berlin, Frida and Strindberg became lovers. Soon after, Frida sent a frank letter to her fiancé asking him to enlighten her on a variety of sexual matters. Her candor awoke his darkest suspicions, and he retaliated by confronting her with a rumor—a rumor he claimed to have heard more than a month before from Neumann-Hofer—that she had had an affair with Sudermann. If it was true, he wrote her, he wished to break the engagement. To restore his sexual confidence, a second letter followed, filled with masculine bravado and unpleasant innuendo. It closed with a distinction between an *homme galant,* such as Sudermann, and the *homme d'honneur* he considered himself. The former, he explained, marries his mistress; the latter, never.[41]

Frida was frightened but held her ground. Before answering Strindberg, she confronted Neumann-Hofer. He swore that he had said nothing untoward about her friendship with Sudermann. But even after this reassurance, a more troubling question remained in Frida's mind. She asked Strindberg why he had held his doubts in abeyance until the crucial moment of her submission.

> *Of course, how you happen to wish to break our engagement today on April 16*—after all that has occurred—*for reasons you learned of on March 9 and that did not seem to bother you till now—that is a question of character that I do not wish to discuss, because what I am concerned with for the moment is to see that the insult you threw at me is taken back.*[42]

The forthright manner in which Frida dealt with the crisis calmed Strindberg, and they reconciled, but his fears had not been entirely laid to rest. Only a day or two later he could not resist baiting Frida once again by accusing her of posing half-nude for an artist of her acquaintance. When she denied it, he refused to believe her, saying that marriage had taught him about women's lies. Frida had had enough. "If this slap in the face was an insight into marriage," she wrote him, "I don't want to marry. Even if as a result I am faced with people's contempt and gossip. What do I care about the respect of the world, if I have no respect for myself."[43]

Mitzi, on the other hand, arriving at this disconcerting juncture, was very much concerned about "contempt and gossip." As Friedrich Uhl's representative, she had been given the mission of making sure the much-publicized engagement ended at the altar. She informed Frida of her alternatives: if the engagement was definitively broken, she would have to go abroad until the scandal had passed and promise never to contact Strindberg again. When Frida looked doubtful, Mitzi knew she had to take matters in her own hands. Serving as go-between, she effected a second reconciliation between her stubborn sister and her sulky fiancé. Frida was convinced to put the events behind her as the temporary aberrations of a nervous bridegroom, and Strindberg, impressed by Mitzi's psychological finesse, became the tender suitor once more. Marry soon, she advised them both, and fight after.

It was decided to hold the wedding in Helgoland, an island southwest of Denmark still in British possession, to evade the lengthy wait demanded by the Prussian bureaucracy. With its more relaxed laws regarding matrimony, Frida and Strindberg could marry as soon as his divorce papers arrived from Sweden.

The first part of her task accomplished, Mitzi tried to be positive in conveying her impressions of Frida's conquest to Friedrich Uhl. Strindberg was basically a distinguished man, she reassured her father. He was healthy, had no bad habits, was good-looking, with eyes the color of a bright morning at sea, and was said to have "lived like a monk" since his divorce. Then came the more disturbing message: although Strindberg was very productive, he was so helpless in practical matters, so shy and fearful of ridicule, that he could not deal with theater directors and publishers. For those reasons he had very little money, and Frida was already running around with his work.

A more pessimistic tone prevailed in Mitzi's letter to her husband. Strindberg was clearly a genius, she wrote, but she had the unsettling feeling he was on the verge of a breakdown, and she could not understand how Frida had the courage to trust him. His attraction to her sister struck her as primarily sensual rather than intellectual, while Frida's to him was "pure literary admiration and worshipful veneration of his spirit." Mitzi was convinced that Frida could not satisfy Strindberg intellectually, but, she admitted, no woman could. "His opinion of women is obviously the most limited imaginable," she wrote, explaining that Strindberg had told her that all he wanted was a wife who allowed him to love her and would not hate him for it, "since women hate men because they cannot be their equal." Despite her doubts about the success of the union, Mitzi tried to close her letter on a hopeful note by saying she believed Strindberg to be thoroughly honorable and decent despite his eccentricities and fixed ideas.[44]

On the eve of her marriage, Frida could not be as clear-eyed as Mitzi. She was too inexperienced to realize that although she was ready to dedicate herself to a genius, it was the troubled man described by her sister—poor, overwrought, with deep-seated suspicions of women—who would ultimately determine the character of the union.

With the engagement now official, gifts were exchanged. From Strindberg, Frida received a quill pen, writing paper, and a painting by her fiancé. The dedication read:

> *To Fräulein Frida Uhl from the painter (symbolist) August Strindberg. The painting is meant to depict the sea (bottom right), clouds (above), a reef (right), a juniper tree (above left) and symbolizes* Night of Jealousy.[45]

3

A Working Wife

THE WEDDING IN HELGOLAND was a simple affair conducted in the pastor's study with two laconic sailors serving as paid witnesses. Bride and groom were tense, and toward the end of the ceremony the proceedings began to take on a farcical tone. When the pastor asked Frida to swear that she was not carrying the child of another man under her heart, it was a thoroughly confused Strindberg who answered with great solemnity that he was not. Seeing her bridegroom's serious demeanor, at that very moment, Frida, to Mitzi's dismay, broke into wild, uncontrollable laughter as the service limped to a close. Recalling her behavior, Frida reflected later, "And my laughter? The laughter of a schoolgirl before she goes out into the world."[1]

The world presented itself soon enough: on her wedding night Frida was awakened by Strindberg's trying to strangle her. The bridegroom, emerging from a dream at dawn and confused by the new companion in his bed, had his hands firmly around his wife's neck before he realized what he was doing. His attempts to calm his terrified bride by explaining that his action had not been intended for her, but was a habitual response to his first wife, only made the situation worse.[2] During their courtship and engagement, Frida had managed to suppress the disturbing signs that Strindberg often confused her with Siri von Essen. Now she did not fall asleep for a long time as she faced how deeply affected Strindberg still was by his former wife. It was only a few weeks later, when the German edition of Strindberg's novel *Le plaidoyer d'un fou (A Madman's Plea)*, his candid summation of his first marriage, fell into her hands, that she understood the full extent of her situation.

The twenty-five-year-old Siri von Essen was married to Count Gustave von Wrangel, an army officer, and was the mother of a little girl named Sigrid when Strindberg, twenty-six, first met her in Stockholm in 1875. His friendship with the couple gradually evolved into a flirtatious foursome when Siri's young cousin joined the affluent aristocratic household and attracted the count's eye. Initially Strindberg could not reconcile his interest in Siri with his respect for her as a mother, but, as time passed and the count chose to look the other way, the inevitable transformation occurred from mother to lover, wife to mistress. Since Siri harbored a long-held ambition to be an actress—a profession not permitted the wife of a regimental officer—Strindberg offered the added attraction of a life in the theater.

Siri and her husband separated in 1876, but neither wanted to harm the other's reputation. Siri went to Copenhagen to desert her husband "officially," but kept her love affair with Strindberg from the public eye and maintained a cordial relationship with Von Wrangel. She began training for her new career by attending rehearsals and successfully auditioning for a place in the Royal Theater. Then tragedy intervened: four-year-old Sigrid died of tuberculosis. In December 1877, eight months pregnant with a child Strindberg was not entirely convinced was his because of the continued contact with Von Wrangel, Siri finally married her lover. The baby girl conceived out of wedlock was registered as being of unknown parentage and immediately given to a wet nurse. Two days later she was dead.

Against all odds, this marriage, begun under clouds of jealousy, tragedy, and guilt, was happy at first. The young and still-liberal Strindberg began married life as an enlightened husband, allowing Siri her independence, encouraging her to act, and even writing plays for her to star in. The publication of his novel *Röda Rummet* (*The Red Room*), a sardonic description of metropolitan life seen through the eyes of a young journalist, launched his career. But after the birth of two daughters, in 1880 and 1881, opportunities diminished for Siri. Two years later, when Strindberg and the family left Sweden to broaden his contacts, and a third child, a son, was born, Siri's chances for a career virtually disappeared.

Tensions grew as the Strindberg family found itself, in a series of French and Swiss boardinghouses, in uncomfortably close proximity to one another and in relative isolation from anyone else. Strindberg became abusive, accused Siri of drinking and flirting with women, and suspected her of infidelity with both sexes. His letters to friends in Sweden, particularly to the theater critic Pehr Staaff, were full of vituperative and mistrustful comments. "Never marry!" he advised Staaff. "The moment a man enters into matrimony both sexes become his wife's accomplices and he is condemned to the clown's role until death and immortality."[3]

At the same time, the unfolding marital drama became a fertile source for Strindberg's creative imagination. The guilt, anguish, and disillusionment of the later phase of his life with Siri inspired his three great naturalist plays and *A Madman's Plea*, all of them written in a fever of inspiration in 1887 and 1888. There was the fear of false paternity in *The Father*, the seduction across class lines in *Miss Julie*, and the revenge on the adulterer in

Creditors. The entire course of the marital crisis was explored in *En dåres försvarstal* (*A Madman's Plea*); the title conveyed the novel's ambivalent tone. The narrator conducts what he believes to be an objective study of his courtship and marriage in order to discover if his wife has been unfaithful. But Strindberg was really examining himself and the conflict that was tearing him apart: was he guilty as adulterer or was Siri to bear the burden as temptress? *A Madman's Plea* is a psychological tour de force, a depiction of the self under siege in which the narrator's mind becomes a permeable membrane mingling reality and fantasy in poisonous combination. Suspicion and delusion sabotage rational thought so completely that the ebb and flow of opposites—love/hate, mother/lover, real/ideal, madness/sanity—become impossible to resolve.

The price of Strindberg's experiment in self-disclosure involved exposing intimate details of what was clearly Siri's life. Despite the subjectivity of the narrator, the descriptions of the fictitious couple's adulterous courtship, the death of their firstborn, and, above all, the unresolved question of the wife's culpability left Siri exposed.

Strindberg had written the book in French for discretion and initially tried to keep himself from publishing it by sending the manuscript to his brother for safekeeping. But in 1893, pressed for money, he permitted a German translation.[4] With this decision, he put the travails of his first marriage in an explosive package that would continue to detonate throughout his second union. In her memoir, Frida recalled the shock of recognition that occurred when *A Madman's Plea* came her way before Strindberg could prevent her reading it. More threatening to her than his obsession with that past was the self-exposure at the heart of his genius. If her husband could write this way about his first wife, why should he not do so about the second?

I, myself, was at stake, the way I sat here and walked and breathed. Were the terrible accusations a reality or a desecration of reality by a fantasy that could reoccur any day and leave me soiled. For the first time I saw art as enemy and destroyer. I had eaten from the tree of knowledge and saw myself naked.[5]

Looking back at their courtship in the new light of *A Madman's Plea,* Frida perceived troubling parallels. Was Strindberg simply casting new actors in familiar parts from the earlier drama? Frida, like Siri, had already been a victim of his unfounded jealousy, and his affair with Dagny provided the guilt he inevitably associated with his first courtship. Even during their honeymoon in Helgoland, he allowed the *Schwarze Ferkel* temptress to disturb the peace.

Despite the travails of their wedding night, Frida and Strindberg had briefly experienced the happiness of newlyweds in their little white Helgoland cottage, with a veranda and garden, in the sunshine of May. Strindberg had resumed his creative routine of starting the morning with a solitary walk followed by three hours of work. Frida corresponded with publishers and theater managers. In the afternoons they strolled along the beaches in the fresh sea air. A cheerful weather report was sent by Strindberg to Mitzi: "Sun every day. Temperature: extremely serene. Little wind—mild. No magnetic disturbances indicated by the atmosphere."[6]

All too soon the mail boat brought news from the outside world. Adolf Paul, Strindberg's Finnish companion at the *Schwarze Ferkel,* seemed to think the bridegroom would wish to stay informed about Dagny. He related the devastating effect "Aspasia's" affairs were having on their mutual friend the young scientist Bengt Lidforss, who was in love with her. Strindberg could not resist the mischief of writing to a friend in Sweden and making sure that both Dagny's and Lidforss's families were notified about the goings-on in Berlin. After stating that he was now a happily married man, he described Lidforss as having been drunk for a month and ruined by "that damned woman Dagny Juel," who, he boasted, "was also my mistress for three weeks."[7]

Strindberg's intervention brought results. Dagny's sister went to Berlin, only to find that Dagny had become engaged to Przybyszewski. Lidforss responded with fury to Strindberg's meddling, but Strindberg replied that his letter had been well intentioned, adding self-righteously that not everyone "caught on her lime twig had the strength in their wings to break loose as I did!"[8]

These reminders of debauchs past shook his new equilibrium. Since writing always relieved his psychological stress, he suggested to Frida that they each compose a memoir of the period preceding their meeting. Strindberg's first lines did not bode well for Frida's peace of mind. "One was presented with the choice of killing a woman or being killed by her," he wrote. "I chose a third—I left. And my first marriage was dissolved." Fortunately, the exercise was short-lived, since Strindberg became even more agitated as he started to write about the "gallery of damned souls" at the *Schwarze Ferkel*.[9]

Frida's response to Strindberg's growing anxiety was to take charge of their immediate future. Grabbing at straws, she decided to respond to interest in her husband's work in England. J. T. Grein, founder of the Independent Theater in London, similar to the *Freie Bühne*, had made vague noises regarding a production of *The Father*. There was also the rumor that the young publisher William Heinemann was interested in a translation of some of Strindberg's poems. On the basis of these slim prospects, the ease with which the British Isles could be reached from nearby Hamburg, and her own fluency in English, Frida persuaded her husband to set sail for London. It was a decision that almost destroyed the marriage before it had fairly begun.

On the coal steamer on which they had booked passage for the two-and-a-half-day journey, Strindberg conversed animatedly with the captain about sea matters, while Frida was bedridden with severe seasickness. When they arrived at Gravesend, she was so weak they decided to remain there. The only room they could find had a big double bed, a form of intimacy despised by Strindberg, for whom modern marriage meant separate quarters. The two-bedroom system, he had once written, "keeps love alive and fresh so that the demonstrations of tenderness are only the result of deep inner feeling and not of a strong supper."[10] It was the first of a series of disagreeable accommodations Strindberg could not adjust to, and it became clear to Frida that responsibility for his well-being in these strange parts now lay in her hands. Desperate, she rented a second room for him, an indulgence they could not really afford.

After gaining her strength, Frida left her husband in his private chamber and went conscientiously off to London to reconnoiter as his agent. Once there, she discovered that Heinemann had never had any intention of publishing Strindberg's poems and the Independent Theater was ending its season. J. T. Grein greeted Frida with enthusiasm but confessed he had no money for a production of *The Father*. To deflect her disappointment and dismay, he offered her the use of his house on Warwick Street, Pimlico, for the month of June, while he was away on the Continent.

Frida returned to Strindberg discouraged but not defeated. Admittedly their circumstances were inauspicious. They had no home, little money, and few immediate prospects for the publication or performance of his work. More unsettling, Strindberg showed little inclination to make plans for their life together. Still, her youth and energy kept her optimistic. Surely their marriage would work out if she held to the task she had set herself.

The move to London did not make it easy. In Grein's house they were given two narrow rooms and the services of his housekeeper, but a heat wave carrying the stench of the local market sapped Strindberg's energy. The English cuisine of chops, steaks, and a leg of mutton on Sunday did not appeal to him. But what bothered him most was that in this densely populated city he knew no one and, worse, no one knew him.

Even an innocent Sunday excursion to the school Frida had attended in Hampstead was ill-fated. After walking a considerable distance in the heat, they came upon an inn. Strindberg was eager for some English ale. Disconcertingly, the innkeeper, standing at the door, asked abruptly, "Where did you sleep last night?" Unbeknownst to Strindberg, the query merely reflected compliance with a law demanding travelers be at least three miles from home if wishing service on a Sunday. Strindberg immediately assumed his honor to be at stake and raised his cane in a threatening gesture. "Drunk in the light of day" was the startled innkeeper's response, and slammed the door in their faces. "We strode back through the field like Adam and Eve driven from Paradise," Frida recalled.[11]

Their money was disappearing, the heat continued, and, with his declining physical well-being, Strindberg's creative energies failed him. He abandoned efforts to write and contemplated turning to science and the hypotheses he had been collecting for years in the green sack that accompanied his travels. Yet even this new project was insufficient distraction. Upon leaving Sweden the summer before, he had been unable to steer his life in a specific direction. The psychological crisis that had driven him to expose his family in *A Madman's Plea* had made him fearful of the further harm he might be driven to with his pen. Writing ten years later, he admitted to the self-disgust he felt at the rapacious use of others in his work.

> *What kind of profession is this: sitting here, tearing the skin of my fellow Man and then offering them the skins in the expectations they will buy them. Like the hunter, who in his hunger, cuts off the dog's tail, eats the flesh himself and then gives the dog the bones, his own bones. Running around and secretly extracting people's secrets, holding up his best friend's birthmark for ridicule, using his wife as a rabbit intended for vivisection, wreaking havoc like a Croat, knocking over, desecrating and burning and selling! Disgusting.*[12]

Frida had provided an escape from these disturbing conflicts, and her ambition and determination had amused Strindberg sufficiently to allow her a free hand. Now, in England, incapable of writing, unable to speak the language, and without friends or connections, he felt unmanned by his dependence on her. It was soon clear to Frida that Strindberg should not remain there, and she urged him to join Adolf Paul in Rügen, a bathing resort on Germany's Baltic coast. She would stay in England to further his cause and follow in a few weeks. With this separation and without the comfort of each other's physical presence, the acute insecurity of their life affected each of them, in differing ways.

Strindberg wrote to Frida that he feared he had overestimated himself in marrying her and "sooner or later" might leave her in distress. Calling himself a good-for-nothing with no energy to earn a living, he admitted that their springtime romance—"secunda primavera, alas"—had roused him briefly but the past still haunted and disturbed him.[13]

While Strindberg ruminated on retreat, Frida conceded to a growing passion. The intimacy of married life had deepened her feelings, and her letters betrayed a sensual attachment lacking earlier. After his departure, she wrote him, she had huddled in their bed, where she could still see the impression of his head and catch a last whiff of the fragrance of his hair.

> *August I love you — Now I can tell you. I never knew that someone like you existed. . . . And then I met you, got to know you, was angry sometimes, felt unhappy sometimes, loved you more and more, loved you with my entire soul, with all my spirit, loved you in total madness. . . .*[14]

Nevertheless, she did not lose sight of their straitened circumstances and reassured Strindberg that she was intent on procuring money for them from the fruit of his work.

Her plan was to write articles about Strindberg, contact people who had written enthusiastically about him, and begin translating his work with a Swedish collaborator. No sooner had Strindberg left for Rügen than she sent a postcard to his publisher in Stockholm asking for a copy of his early novel *Tjänstekvinnans son* (*The Son of a Servant*) to translate. But Strindberg's first letters were reserved and few. In a curt note he even admonished her for writing his friends regarding the disposition of his paintings without asking him first. Alone in England, Frida felt like a reprimanded child and wrote histrionically to Strindberg that she was prepared to leave him if he no longer loved her.

> *I spend my life breaking my head for your welfare, expending my energy, my time, my friends, my peace of mind for you. . . . Do you love me or not . . . ? If no, no. My God, just say it. I won't take revenge. I will step out of the role that I appeared to be destined for. Say it. Our paths will not cross again. If my heart breaks—my God it's already broken.*[15]

What Frida could not know was that Strindberg, instead of finding relief in Rügen, had been confronted with new worries.

On his arrival in Germany, he found letters from Siri demanding money owed the family. Worse, *A Madman's Plea* continued to bedevil his existence. Since no copyright agreement existed between Germany and Sweden, a Swedish weekly had begun reprinting it in serial form as soon as it appeared in German translation.

Strindberg wrote Frida that the scandal would prevent him from returning to Sweden for years. Cut off from his native country, unable to write, and forced to accept that Frida was keeping them afloat, Strindberg's doubts about the marriage increased. Then his mood gradually changed, his letters turned tender and conciliatory, and he begged Frida to join him.

It had become clear to Frida, however, that though Strindberg might look upon her task as an indulgent gesture to a young bride, their diminishing funds made her work on his behalf necessary. From Rügen, Strindberg had urged her to borrow money from her family, but she had adamantly refused. Now that her father had accepted her union and she was once more in his good graces, she would not give him the satisfaction of reviving his doubts about the viability of her marriage.

For a twenty-one-year-old, Frida had a heavy load to carry: writing, translating, and searching for possible backers. She made sure to meet the most important people in English theater at the time, such as Ibsen's translator, William Archer, and the prominent actress Elizabeth Robins. A closer friendship developed with the twenty-nine-year-old publisher William Heinemann. Unlike most Englishmen, the young man, whose father was German, spoke several languages and was interested in foreign literature. He encouraged Frida to pursue a project she and Strindberg had considered: setting up a small independent theater as a venue for his plays. She got in touch with a theatrical agent and sent Strindberg a tentative schedule for a September season. Delighted with Heinemann's apparent support, Frida reported to Strindberg that she lunched with the publisher regularly. Her candor did not make her distant husband happy. Strindberg was not entirely wrong in his suspicion that it was Frida and not his work that attracted Heinemann; in 1912 the publisher wrote to a friend that he had refused to publish Strindberg for twenty years and still saw no reason to change his mind. Nevertheless, Frida's instincts were not far off; four years later Heinemann, with Elizabeth Robins and William Archer, backed an independent theater. Frida was never given a chance to nurture the seeds she had planted for Strindberg in London, but her ability to discern the key voices in cultural politics was evident.

As the letters from Rügen continued to convey news of Strindberg's misery and self-reproach, Frida urged him to return to England. When even Adolf Paul wrote her of Strindberg's unhappiness, she answered that it was not only Strindberg's work keeping her in England, but also their future. "The way things stand now, only energy can save the situation and that is why I cannot leave the spot. I am following my honest convictions. If I am wrong I cannot help it."[16] Trying to entice her husband to return, she promised a house in the country and the company of such English colleagues as the writer Justin McCarthy, who had written the first article in England appreciative of Strindberg. Only reluctantly did she mention another alternative: Strindberg could go to her parents, who were currently making one of their joint appearances in the villa at Mondsee. At Frida's suggestion, an invitation from Maria Uhl was sent to Rügen.

Dear little son, offspring of my daughter's heart,

You may cross yourself—but don't be shocked—it is only your new Mama (mother-in-law is an ugly term and does not deserve to be used) . . . who invites you to your new parents. . . .

Your new father longs for your genius, I for your broken heart. We want to take possession of what belongs to us—each in his own way. Come and stay for as long as you wish and for as long as you like it here.[17]

Strindberg could not resist this siren song with its maternal notes. But, in accepting Maria Uhl's invitation, he disappointed Frida, who had been busy searching for quarters outside London. She was still living in the house of J. T. Grein, even though he had returned home, and she felt ill at ease in a bachelor's household. Yet she did not want to admit defeat by leaving England and returning to a poverty-stricken existence with Strindberg, especially not directly under the eyes of her parents. She was worried, too, that no money had been paid to his children, living with Siri in Finland. Her solution was to retreat to the convent of the English Ladies in Haverstock Hill. Only a year had passed since she had left it as a schoolgirl and she still considered it a safe haven.

Strindberg spent ten days in Mondsee without Frida. He was delighted by the warmth with which Frida's mother welcomed him, bridegroom and new son-in-law crossing their threshold without the bride. It did not take long, however, before he was caught in the web of conflict that was Uhl family life. Mitzi, trapped in her unhappy marriage, wrote Frida about the scene of Strindberg's arrival.

He seemed to believe that you would be here to greet him with us, which I can only explain by the fact that he has the wrong expectations of the relationship between our mother and her children, in other words that she, of course, would have invited you too, which, she, of course, did not. . . . He does not suspect that Mama expects compensation from sons-in-law and grandson for all the love that even the poorest is not denied in a marriage and that the daughter, as soon as she has delivered the son-in-law and grandson, is dismissed as superfluous.[18]

Mitzi reported further that Frida's mother had greeted Strindberg by saying "I welcome you. I am so glad that my daughters, these frivolous girls, find such good men." She warned Frida that she had better not give her mother "much time to empty her heart completely, since it can easily happen that she will paint you black and then [your husband] will see you as black." She added darkly, "I experienced something like this in my life."

But Strindberg was overwhelmed by Maria Uhl's warmth and approbation. Her religious zeal immediately brought back memories of his own mother, whose piety had influenced him profoundly as a child and whose death had blighted his adolescence.

The warm relationship with Mitzi that had developed before the wedding did not survive the visit. Expressing his negative opinions of women in her presence, Strindberg offended her, as she wrote to a friend, by trying to compliment her in a most peculiar, backhanded way. He explained to her that, for him, she did not actually exist, since no woman was clever and she clearly was. Therefore, he reasoned, she was not a woman, nor was she a man—she could only be nothing. Mitzi left Mondsee the following morning.[19]

Friedrich Uhl, elegantly attired, arrived a day later. Although Strindberg was not unaware of the ironies inherent in the meeting, he found the editor and theater critic a sympathetic if not a kindred colleague. He reported to Frida that her father had praised her writing efforts. "[He says] you have made a name for yourself as a writer in Vienna, that your articles are very good, your style is mature, you already have a personal voice, and you are an ingenious donkey. . . ."[20]

The two got along, but when Frida wrote her parents about

her retreat to the convent and her concern about Strindberg's children, Uhl became disenchanted with his newly acquired son-in-law. He questioned him about Frida's competence in handling his affairs, inquired who accompanied her to the theater, and raised doubts about Grein's reputation. He even intimated (mistakenly) that a theater Frida had referred to did not exist. In a situation uncannily reminiscent of the battle of the minds in *Creditors,* Strindberg became uncomfortable enough to ask Frida to come to Mondsee.

As the days passed, Uhl grew fearful of the small-town gossip aroused by Frida's absence and pushed Strindberg to *demand* her departure from England. When Strindberg replied that this was not how he dealt with his wife, Uhl countered that he would then exert his paternal authority.

In treating Frida as a child, Uhl was usurping Strindberg's rights as a husband. His son-in-law made him uneasy. The unorthodox manner in which he conducted his marriage to Frida threatened Uhl's overriding concern with decorum. More profoundly, his presence in Mondsee was an uncomfortable reminder to the ever-prudent Uhl that when it came to success as a writer, the reckless younger man was his superior.

Strindberg captured the source of Uhl's discomfiture in a brief but pointed dialogue in *The Cloister.* In that fictionalized account of the events in Mondsee, he has the editor ask Axel, Strindberg's fictional alter ego, if he has a secure income. When Axel replies that it is as secure as any a writer can have, the older man tells him he will have to do what others have done and write for newspapers. As Axel protests that no one will print his articles, the editor gives away his lifetime of compromises by saying, "Then write them so they will be printed."[21]

The peremptory tone Uhl had begun to take toward Strindberg left his son-in-law no choice but to insist that Frida return to restore his pride. He gave her a time limit, threatened divorce, and let her know that her role as his business manager had been no more than a temporary concession on his part.

When Frida still showed no signs of returning, Strindberg took it to mean their marriage was over. He dreaded going back to Berlin alone, he wrote in his next letter, but he could not reconcile himself to her "ambition," as he called her attempts to gain them a living. At the same time, he conceded that Frida had talent. "Now I've read your articles, with their colorful vibrant style, I'm aware that you are somebody and that I was wrong to tease you."[22]

Such a concession could not be allowed to stand, and a retraction followed. His acquiescence to Frida's wish to work and to write had been signs of weakness, he wrote her. Capitulation to her desires had led to her contempt for him. Why else would she not return? The letter closed with a reminder and a warning of how he had handled divorce before. "One dies of shame and comes back to life in order to avenge oneself."

In marrying Strindberg, Frida had escaped her patriarchal overseer, but her father had regained the upper hand. By playing on Strindberg's pride, he had once again arranged to rescind her modicum of freedom. Her faith that she could achieve a breakthrough for Strindberg in England may have been far-fetched, but the adventure of trying was more consoling than acquiescing in the slow slide into poverty her husband appeared to be bent on. Going back, she knew, would render her less useful.

There was no longer any choice, however, and Frida returned to Mondsee—but too late. The day before her arrival, Strindberg had departed so abruptly that Uhl feared he had committed suicide. After an apologetic message arrived from his son-in-law, en route to Berlin, Uhl determined to have nothing further to do with his troublesome daughter or her spouse. He made it clear to Frida that she was permitted only one night in the parental home before joining her husband.

In *The Cloister*, Strindberg recalled a surprisingly joyful reunion in Berlin:

> *When he came home, he found the door locked. With a presentiment, he knocked on the door and called out his name. As the door opened, his young wild one was in his arms and that seemed to him so natural and so simple as if he had left her alone for two minutes. Happy, younger, prettier, he had her again and no accusations, questions, or explanations were uttered, only "Do you have a lot or little money?"*
>
> *"Why do you ask that?"*
>
> *"Because I have a lot and I want a festive dinner in Berlin."*[23]

With their meager resources which consisted of the money remaining from Frida's trousseau and the few royalties that had been sent to Berlin in their absence, they rented a small attic flat on the Neustädtischen Kirchstrasse. Once settled, Frida worked hard to promote Strindberg among German publishers and continued writing articles for the *Wiener Zeitung*. Strindberg, however, could not bring himself to write and devoted his time entirely to his scientific interests. In their garret he set up apparatus for his unorthodox chemical and alchemical experiments, by which he attempted to prove that sulfur was not an element and that gold could be made from new combinations of copper and sulfate of iron. Their little domicile filled with fumes as their pockets emptied.

Adding to their diminishing financial prospects, *A Madman's Plea* continued its destructive course. An anonymous complaint by "a German mother" had led to the banning of the book under the *Lex Heinze*, a new law initially designed to control the activities of pimps and prostitutes, but now increasingly used to censor anything that smacked of "immorality." Not only was Strindberg's book seized, but he was to be brought to trial. The case, scheduled for the spring, felt to him like a replay of the horrors of the *Married* trial years before.

Strindberg's collection of short stories titled *Giftas (Married),* which had been published in Sweden in 1884, reflected the early, happy period of his first marriage. Through a variety of characters, men and women, upper and lower class, Strindberg celebrated the marital state while openly acknowledging its dilemmas. His stories dealt fairly with such issues as women's desire to be equal partners, the changes brought about by the arrival of children, and the gradual replacement of romantic illusions by sturdier realities. Unabashedly, he emphasized the role of sex as a crucial bond. Yet even here, in this paean to contentment, he could not resist provocation by referring to the celebration of the Mass as "an impudent deception practiced with [commercial wine and wafers] which the parson passes off as the body and blood of Jesus of Nazareth . . . the rabble-rouser who was executed over 1,800 years ago."[24]

The edition was seized and the author was accused of "blasphemy against God or mockery of God's word or sacrament," a charge accompanied by the threat of two years of hard labor. After some fearful months spent under the cloud of possible imprisonment, Strindberg was finally convinced by Karl Otto Bonnier, his publisher's son, who came to see him personally in Switzerland, that he should return to Sweden for trial. He was exonerated in Stockholm, but the acquittal did not prevent him from being branded an *enfant terrible.*

The accusation of blasphemy had served only to cover up the real source of the furor surrounding *Married*: the book's advocacy of a more open-minded attitude toward sex and marriage. In 1886 a divinity teacher named John Personne published a pamphlet titled *Strindberg, Literature, and the Immorality of Schoolchildren*, suggesting that Strindberg's books led young men to masturbate and consort with prostitutes and declaring Bonnier no better than a woman running a brothel. The right-wing press joined Personne's bandwagon, as did five Swedish publishers, who resigned from the publishers' organization that Albert Bonnier headed. For many years thereafter it was difficult for Strindberg to have his books published or his plays produced in his own country.[25]

The bitter aftertaste of the trial, which Strindberg felt had been partially instigated by the Swedish Society of Married Women's Property Rights, could be sensed in a second volume of marital tales, published as *Married II.* This was no longer a celebration of the marital state, but a harsh critical assessment, which concluded with a story clearly intended as a rebuke to Siri. Titled "The Breadwinner," it took place in a boardinghouse abroad where a hardworking writer is driven to suicide by the neglect and contempt of his wife. Strindberg's older daughter, Karin, remembered that the second volume of *Married* became "an incurable cancer" in her parents' domestic life.[26]

DESPITE THE LACK of money and the impending legal difficulties in Berlin, Frida was not discouraged as long as she could contribute to their life. It was only after discovering in early October that she was pregnant that she began to lose heart. If they could barely survive themselves, how could they manage with a child? Her suggestion that abortion might be the only solution brought on a crisis. Woman as mother was Strindberg's ideal. His longing for his own mother had never ceased and he sought the maternal in all his wives. Siri had first attracted him as a mother, and Frida's pregnancy gave her an appeal that transcended her role of breadwinner.

There seemed to be no way out of their plight. Strindberg was furious, Frida desperate. They fought bitterly, and when Strindberg began to resort to accusations that had more to do with his first marriage than with the present crisis, Frida could take no more. She fled to Mitzi in Vienna and wrote Strindberg that she was prepared to divorce. The letter closed with a bitter reminder: "My name is not Siri von Essen, but Frida Uhl."[27] Years later she described how the suspicion aroused on her wedding night that she would be shackled to Strindberg's memories of Siri had begun to come true.

> *In his eyes, I wore the clothes of his first wife and acted, so he said, as she would have acted. And he hated me then, as he hated her, imputed and forgave crimes that I had never committed, and loved me again immediately—as he had loved her. That was the worst. Sometimes, I no longer knew, was it actually me that he loved and hated, or was it still the other one, still her, only her. Or was it just a poet's vision stripped from her and given me to wear? Or did he need hate to love?*[28]

In Vienna, Frida saw a doctor about the possibility of an abortion, but, overcome by the strong attachment she still felt for Strindberg, went no further. Strindberg, on his part, was so unhappy to find himself alone that he sent telegram after telegram begging Mitzi to convince her to return. Once again her sister was instrumental in sending Frida back into Strindberg's arms. She let him know Frida's terms. His wife, she wrote him, was still willing to go anywhere with him if he would stop mistrusting and persecuting her. However, they would have to live somewhere other than Berlin, which was too expensive. If Strindberg could not agree to these requests, Frida was ready to divorce and accept the blame on grounds of desertion. She asked only that he relinquish all rights to the child, and, most important, that he never write a book about her.

Strindberg answered eagerly. "Can I come as soon as possible to Mondsee or Dornach or somewhere near Vienna? I leave Berlin gladly."[29]

4

A Country Wife

FRIDA AND STRINDBERG WERE reunited in Brünn, Moravia, a provincial city not far from Vienna where living was inexpensive and distant relatives could be counted on to care for Frida if necessary. Compared to the joyful reunion in Berlin only two months earlier, this one, on the platform of a provincial railroad station, was subdued but no less emotional. Strindberg recalled that Frida greeted him by burying her nose in his coat collar like a child and kissing the seam "in order not to show her feelings because she was always embarrassed by them."[1]

The apartment in Brünn was smaller than the one in Berlin: two rooms, one dark, the other with a view of a factory. The kitchen was shared with the landlady, a widow with several children. Frida now did all the housework and their poverty increased as royalties, commissions, opportunities for new productions of Strindberg's plays diminished with word of the indictment of his book.

Strindberg devoted himself entirely to writing about science. He had much to say, but these attempts by a nonscientist were unlikely to make money. Nevertheless, Frida threw herself wholeheartedly into assisting him with *Antibarbarus,* a polemic against what Strindberg saw as the barbarous methods of modern science. In the form of four letters about chemistry from a teacher to a student, he elaborated on his theory of the transmutation of elements. Writing in Swedish during the day, he worked on a German translation with Frida in the evening under the light of their single petroleum lamp.

Although he had always been interested in science, had integrated it into his fiction, and by 1890 had begun seriously to study the latest literature in chemistry, Strindberg could not depart from his own philosophical constructs. In his letter accompanying the first sixteen pages of *Antibarbarus* for consideration by Bonnier, he referred to the manuscript as a "natural-scientific-philosophical work."[2] Unable to assess the book's scientific value, the publisher sent a rejection and, adding insult to injury, reminded Strindberg that he still owed him money.

Without an advance for *Antibarbarus,* Strindberg and Frida found themselves almost penniless. No choice was left but to retreat to the place both Frida and her sister had tried to avoid for most of their lives—the little, isolated hamlet of Dornach, on the banks of the Danube between Mauthausen and Grein, where Cornelius Reischl, their maternal grandfather, had his estate. In a household where the number of servants outnumbered the inhabitants, and the surrounding woods provided ample supplies of venison, hare, and pheasant, the couple could not be too much of a burden.

Frida and Strindberg stopped briefly in Vienna en route to Dornach, but Friedrich Uhl, still furious about Strindberg's precipitous departure from Mondsee, would not even permit an overnight stay with Mitzi. Taking some refreshment in a café before traveling on, Frida and Strindberg encountered Paul Schlenther, the director who had been instrumental in producing Strindberg's plays at the *Freie Bühne* in the optimistic season of Strindberg's first arrival in Berlin the year before. Schlenther recalled that

Frida looked pale and exhausted, but Strindberg, "smiling at the prospect of paternal delights to come, drank, like Bacchus, one punch after the other as he took his blessed wife from one country to the next."

Even though they traveled third class from Brünn to Amstetten, in Upper Austria, they arrived with too little money for the porter and none for the one-hour trip by sleigh and ferry to Dornach. The porter was paid by the sleigh driver, the sleigh driver by the ferryman, and the bountiful Reischls took care of the last debt as their granddaughter and her famous husband landed, virtual beggars, on their doorstep.

In the spacious Dornach house they were given their own roomy quarters and had to socialize with the family only at meals. Since the land belonging to Reischl extended for more than an hour's walk in all directions, the estate was almost completely isolated. Only a quarry and a few small farmhouses lay nearby. Connections to the outside world were maintained by the twice-daily delivery of letters, newspapers, and other necessities brought across the river by the ferryman in one of Reischl's old leather hunting pouches.

At the start, Strindberg had no trouble with the family. Grandmother Reischl paid him little attention, and Maria Uhl addressed him with the respect and admiration that had marked her attitude to him since their first meeting. The grandfather, who was happy to have someone new to talk to, engaged Strindberg in political discussions stimulated by the periodicals and newspapers showered on the household by Friedrich Uhl. Strindberg deferred to the old gentleman, refused to be drawn into arguments, and did nothing to threaten Reischl's complacency. When they played an occasional game of chess, Strindberg made sure his host won.

Having adequate living space for the first time in their married life, Frida and Strindberg found life together easier and more harmonious. Strindberg set up his scientific apparatus and happily explored the natural wonders of the countryside. To Reischl's surprise, his guest also found much to absorb him in a collection of books the old man had taken in payment from an impoverished creditor. When Frida and Strindberg were alone together in the evening, with only the sound of the river's wild current penetrating the silence, they continued their collaboration on *Antibarbarus,* and, according to Strindberg, with the specter of immediate poverty behind them, Frida became more pliable, even "humble," as she gave in to her expectant state.

Distant though they now were, the contacts in Berlin still held fast, thanks to Strindberg's voluminous correspondence. Soon after his arrival in Dornach, he sent Bengt Lidforss, the young Swedish scientist whom he had been so eager to rescue from the clutches of Dagny Juel the summer before, the completed sections of *Antibarbarus.* Lidforss wrote to Strindberg with enthusiasm that the book was bound to be a success "despite one's professional reservations. . . ."[3] He agreed to smooth out the German translation and arranged for it to be printed by a Berlin publisher.

Christmas passed peacefully. When the large household staff was invited for the annual gift giving, Strindberg insisted on making his own contributions of silver coins and tobacco. Then he and Frida withdrew to celebrate alone under the tree Frida had smuggled into their rooms. Strindberg was given a new quill pen, oil paints, and a bottle of Swedish punch; he bestowed upon Frida a small pencil portrait of himself at thirteen drawn by his brother Axel. Frida recalled that after Strindberg turned down the lamps, they experienced a sense of peace that had long eluded them.

It was as if, suddenly, the moon, the night and eternity had entered the room. Behind the glowing tree, the river landscape shone with a magic clarity. The glitter of the little flames was reflected in the silvery mirror of the water until they went out and left us in the dark, alone with the moon and the shimmering current.[4]

As the new year began, however, and Strindberg's relationship with Reischl became problematic, he began to feel his dependence and isolation more keenly. Although he had tried not to raise the ire of his host, he was often provoked by questions from the old man, who had no understanding of what he was about. Dissatisfied with Strindberg's answers regarding his scientific experiments, Reischl began to suspect he was harboring an interloper and needled him about the financial prospects of his scientific endeavors. Strindberg felt trapped, until through the agency of fate he was shown the door.

As the date for the hearing of *A Madman's Plea* approached, a bailiff arrived in Dornach to give Strindberg his summons. Strindberg did not respond, having decided to follow a lawyer's suggestion that, as a Swedish writer, he was not legally liable for a translation in Germany. Here was the weapon Reischl had been looking for. No respected notary could permit someone in trouble with the law to live in his home. He made up his mind on the spot: Frida might stay out her pregnancy, but Strindberg would have to leave. Desperate, Frida turned to her grandmother for clemency.

A solution was found in the form of a small house adjacent to the Reischl property. Referred to as the *Häusel*, or little hut, it had been acquired by Frida's grandmother with the profits of her dairy. Though she used it to stable a recalcitrant donkey named Lumpi, she agreed to evict the animal in favor of the outcasts. Both Frida and Strindberg were delighted. Humble though the dwelling was—the walls were damp, the windows small, the roof covered with straw, and water had to be hauled from the river—

they had regained their privacy. And the *Häusel* was beautifully situated, directly on the riverbank, with a tilled field on one side, the remains of a garden with an ancient pear tree on the other, and the woods behind.

The thick walls and small windows reminded Strindberg of buildings in a cloister complex and in the attic he furnished his own monk's cell with his laboratory equipment and library. An accomplished painter, he began a series of canvases to cover the walls and, with Frida, painted the window frames and doors, planted roses and clematis around the entrance, and seeded the garden.

Yet these idyllic days were invaded by old enmities. Just before moving into the *Häusel*, Strindberg had made a brief excursion to Berlin to read the proofs of *Antibarbarus*. While there, he sought out old acquaintances from the *Schwarze Ferkel*, but the bohemia he had known had moved elsewhere. Dagny and Przybyszewski, now the central figures, held court in their small apartment on Louisenstrasse. Lidforss, he discovered, was still very much in Dagny's thrall, and Strindberg was not made welcome. He returned to Dornach uneasy about possible repercussions from these encounters with the past, and his fears were soon confirmed. *Antibarbarus* was to appear in May, but on April 13 Lidforss printed a prepublication review in the Swedish newspaper *Dagens Nyheter*. Instead of reflecting the enthusiasm he had expressed earlier, it was a devastating critique of Strindberg's scientific method, a calculated revenge, perhaps, for Strindberg's misguided attempt to separate him from Dagny the summer before.

With the birth of their daughter, Kerstin, on May 26, any possibility of a peaceful domestic existence for Frida and Strindberg came to an end. Kerstin was a sickly child, and soon enough Strindberg was shunted aside as Frida's mother and grandmother, as well as the local midwives, descended upon the *Häusel* to offer advice. Diapers and laundry hung in every room. Strindberg took refuge in his monk's cell, where a surly maid served him poor coffee and worse food.

As Kerstin's health worsened, Frida took little notice of Strindberg's misery. Finding herself without milk after a month, she frantically sought a wet nurse in the neighborhood, but to no avail. Fearful of asking her father or grandfather for help, she finally turned to Mitzi to finance a trip to Vienna, where, at last, a suitable woman willing to come to Dornach was found.

Frida's worries about Kerstin's survival were further compounded by pressure to have her baptized. Since there was no Protestant clergyman in the neighborhood, and Frida, a freethinker, saw no need to have Kerstin baptized in the Catholic church, rumors grew around Dornach that the Devil was playing havoc with the unbaptized child. Trying to force the ceremony, Cornelius Reischl threatened banishment once again, and Strindberg took note of the irony inherent in this replay of the Thirty Years' War. Frida, however, realized she would have to accommodate the family on which they were dependent, and finally agreed to the baptism, to Strindberg's disgust.

Amid these crises Strindberg felt increasingly isolated, though as he was struggling with his domestic difficulties in Upper Austria his reputation in Paris was growing. A long, appreciative article on his work had appeared the previous autumn in the *Revue des Deux Mondes*, and now the young actor and director of the *Théâtre de l'Oeuvre*, Aurélien Lugné-Poe, had decided to stage a production of *Creditors* after a season of performing Ibsen. The successful premiere of the play on June 21 encouraged Strindberg to take control of his destiny. He began to plot a getaway by reopening a correspondence with Leopold Littmanson, an old friend from his youth who had married a wealthy Frenchwoman and lived in Versailles.

"I'm writing to you to find out if you are alive and would like to put me up over the summer," Strindberg wrote. "So I can learn to speak French as well as a Swede can."[5] In another letter he wrote sardonically that happiness was "to sit in a cottage by the Danube among six women who think I'm half-mad, and to know that in Paris, the headquarters of the intelligentsia, 500 people are sitting in a theater quiet as mice and foolish enough to expose their brains to my stimulation."[6]

July brought further word from Paris. A young German publisher named Albert Langen wanted to publish *A Madman's Plea* in French and was eager to meet the author. But it was only toward the end of the summer, a hot summer, a summer punctuated by domestic pressures, that Littmanson proffered the longed-for invitation. On August 21, Strindberg departed for Paris, promising Frida it would be only a brief stay with his friend in Versailles.

After her husband left, Frida felt the need to defend his departure to her sister. Had he not gone, she wrote her, the difficulties of their existence in isolation from the world and amid the family would have done him in. They were hard enough for her to bear.

Yes Mitzi, these are my dreams of freedom . . . to sit in hated Dornach, without good clothes, without books, without a husband. I've come very far in a year. . . . [Strindberg] waved, laughing, but moved and sad, as his ship passed the little house and when I no longer saw him, I ran into his room, threw myself on the bed and cried. The baby began to howl just then and this time I paid it no attention. I was angry at the poor little thing, angry for five seconds. It didn't bring its father and me together, instead it separated us. And now I am a straw widow. That could be fun, but not for me.[7]

It was only two years since Frida had completed her schooling, but love, marriage, and devotion to an impoverished genius had done their work. From the rare and privileged position of a young woman exercising a profession in a world capital, she had ended up held fast by poverty and motherhood in a place so provincial her father had never set foot there again after negotiating his unfortunate marriage.

Yet in the same letter she made clear what still bound her to her difficult husband. She conveyed to her sister the excitement of being in intimate contact with a superior mind. Strindberg, she wrote, had once spoken to her of the inadequacy of the human brain. He complained that it was insufficiently developed to cope fully with the messages from without or within. But the thrill for Frida had been to observe the superhuman effort Strindberg dedicated to overcoming this failing as he mastered the impressions crowding in upon him.

Although Strindberg had made his escape from Dornach, he seemed reluctant to enter Paris and spent his time in Versailles, writing to Frida that big cities would be the death of them. After meeting Albert Langen, however, and two of his friends, an elegant Dane who went under the name Willi Gretor, and Gretor's secretary, the young German writer Frank Wedekind, he cheered up considerably. Langen was eager to make plans for the French edition of *A Madman's Plea*. Gretor waxed enthusiastic about the paintings Strindberg had brought to Paris, and even offered Strindberg an apartment of his in the suburb of Passy, rent-free until the beginning of October. Once again at the center of an adoring coterie, as he had been at the *Schwarze Ferkel*, Strindberg began to feel at home in Paris and picture life there with Frida. It gave him pause. "... Let us settle down in a village close to Paris," he wrote, "one that is simple and concealed ... and make a rule never to go into society alone. Emancipation is unknown here and an emancipated woman means a prostitute."[8]

The letters between Frida and Strindberg during this separation reveal how differently each of them viewed their future. Frida, left alone in Dornach, was determined to resuscitate the career Friedrich Uhl had bestowed on her *faute de mieux*. It had given her a feeling of self-worth at the very beginning of her adult life, and now she knew it would be the saving of her. She began writing reviews for the *Wiener Zeitung* again and told Strindberg she was working twelve hours a day.

. . . I have rediscovered the sense of myself I had as a young girl and my love for my profession. . . . I have made my plan. By November I will have earned . . . what I need to pay all the debts and to travel. Once and for all: I won't abandon my child. She is my whole life. . . .

Now I am once more who I was. I recovered my firm unyielding will, my love for work. That's what keeps one from sinking. I am going to be a journalist again, speaking with her own words. I am certain of serving as the Paris correspondent for at least two newspapers.[9]

Strindberg replied in his own vein by expressing his satisfaction with Frida's concern for Kerstin. How, he asked her, could she reconcile these family feelings with her desire to work for newspapers? He followed with a description of *his* expectations of their life together. She would be a mother, a household manager, a woman whose talent for writing might be indulged between family tasks. Her ambitions, he told her, in as many inventive ways as an inventive man could think of, would be untenable if they were to stay in Paris. It would lead to disorder in the household (if not abandonment of the family), and would contribute to the temptation of the tavern. It was not justified by her profession, which was a useless one anyway, since the German press could pick up information from the French papers just as fast and no one learned anything from reviews (he certainly hadn't).[10]

Despite his reservations, when Strindberg received money from Gretor for some of his paintings, he asked Frida to come to Paris, but a cautionary preface accompanied the invitation.

Dear little martyr,

Even though

you, at 22, entered your twenties just two years ago,

you, instead of vegetating there, spent sixteen hours daily the entire winter aestheticizing with your novels,

you have experienced the most beautiful thing of all—childhood and motherhood,

I have never worked, thought, suffered, and, at the same time, had such pleasure as I have had, from your beautiful state as a young mother,

everything that you bring out in your letter is false,

I am telegraphing you 250 francs so that you can come here to torture me and make me happy.[11]

Paris was too tempting and, choosing to ignore the implications of Strindberg's polemic, Frida took the money he sent her, left Kerstin in the arms of the wet nurse, and brought with her to France what Strindberg had asked for—torture and happiness in equal measure.

She found Strindberg in excellent spirits and comfortably settled in the elegant apartment in Passy lent to him by Gretor. Once again he amazed her with the range of his enthusiasm, the degree of his response to his surroundings. Paris had stimulated him to write essays on everything, from the nature of the modern to the possibilities of flight, with a pace he termed the tempo of the future. To walk through the city with Strindberg, she wrote Mitzi, was to possess it more surely than the princes and grand seigneurs who owned the great houses they passed.

Strindberg's new friends delighted her also, particularly Langen and Gretor, who were both in their twenties and gave her much courtly attention. Unlike the habitués of the *Schwarze Ferkel*, these were men-about-town, wealthy young dandies who gambled in Monte Carlo, drank champagne at Maxim's, and kept boxes at the theater and the opera. In her letter to Mitzi, Frida made special note of the elegance of Gretor's gloves and the style of Langen's spats. Respectable people, she wrote, had always made her anxious, but here in Paris respectability seemed to be of little concern. Both she and Strindberg sensed something questionable about their benefactors, but for the time being the pleasures of being in Paris together overrode all suspicion.[12]

Gretor was an enigmatic character, physically handsome, despite a decided limp; aristocratic in bearing and dress, although no one knew exactly where his money came from. He attracted many members of the foreign colony in Paris. Wedekind was so intrigued by Gretor's contradictions—the combination of a generous nature and a complete lack of scruples—that many years later he made him the central figure in one of his plays. The German art critic Julius Meier-Graefe remembered Gretor as an extremely talented and amusing presence, who alternated between the personae of painter and art dealer in order to move easily among the denizens of the Latin Quarter and those on the Right Bank. "Even when he betrayed people, he gave them what they needed" was Meier-Graefe's summation of the strange appeal of this con man.[13]

There was a great deal of truth in Meier-Graefe's statement. Strindberg, Frida, and Langen were all affected by Gretor. By purchasing Strindberg's paintings, he had enabled Frida to come to Paris, and, less than a year before, he had inspired Langen to enter publishing.

Langen had arrived in Paris from Cologne with a considerable inheritance and the intention of enjoying a few *Wanderjahre* before settling into a profession. Gretor advised him on how to use his wealth with élan. He offered him the apartment of his mistress on the elegant Boulevard Malesherbes, helped him furnish it in the best taste, and sold him a collection of old masters to match. He also introduced Langen to the Scandinavian writers and artists in Paris, including the Norwegian Knut Hamsun, whose first novel, *Hunger,* published by Samuel Fischer in Germany, had been a great success.

At the time Langen met Hamsun, the writer had run into some trouble with Fischer. An unfortunate article had appeared intimating too close a connection between Hamsun's work and the novels of Dostoyevsky. Fischer decided not to publish *Mysteries,* Hamsun's most recent novel, even though it had already been translated into German. To help a fellow Scandinavian, Gretor gave Langen the German translation to read, and the young man's response was immediate. He bought the rights from Fischer and decided to make *Mysteries* the first book to appear under his own imprint as publisher. In December 1893 a notice was placed in the trade paper of German book dealers announcing the establishment of Albert Langen Verlag, founded "to make talented Scandinavians, as well as French, accessible to the German public."[14]

Langen, who was to be a great publicist for his writers, tried to put Strindberg in the limelight after meeting him in Paris. He had a French paper ask him for an article on Alexander Dumas's play *The Wife of Claudius,* in which Sarah Bernhardt was currently starring. As Langen had hoped, Strindberg's piece piqued Bernhardt's interest, and she invited its author to view a performance from her special loge. Langen was sure Bernhardt would ask her guest backstage after the performance and he tipped off the press about the possibility of an intriguing encounter between the notorious Swedish playwright and Paris's reigning star.

To make the most of the opportunity, Langen arranged a grand pre-theater dinner for Strindberg, with several journalists among the guests. Frida recalled that amid the elegance and glitter of the evening, Langen amused himself like a small child by throwing lighted cigarettes to his dog to catch. Refusing to sit by and watch, Frida, with her usual lack of inhibition, applied one of these glowing missiles to Langen's hand. "You'll never make it in Paris this way," he told her. She responded with amusement: "We will, Herr Langen, we will. But obviously on the Left Bank."[15] After the dinner, Strindberg never showed up in Bernhardt's box. Aware that he was being used, he went out for a beer with Frida instead.

Langen was not discouraged. If Strindberg could not serve his immediate purposes, perhaps Frida would. She was, after all, well connected in the theater and a linguist. He asked her to help him translate the work of the French playwright Henri Becque, and Frida, unable to resist the opportunity for additional income, agreed. Each day that Langen appeared at the apartment in Passy to work with her, however, Strindberg paced back and forth in the adjacent room like a caged lion. Finally, he could not resist repeating to Frida the equation of emancipation and prostitution. For two days they did not speak, and Frida wrote to Mitzi about her dilemma.

I love him in a way I will never be able to again—from day to day I love him more. But when he restricts my freedom, he is no longer the lover, but the enemy, and still he has a certain point. A Strindberg should have so exalted a position that the wife he chooses for himself should be there only for him. But what if he goes under? Perhaps it would be better for him to die in the way he chooses to. But does it have to be like that?

As a matter of fact, perhaps he is right, maybe an erotic spark is always present when a man meets a woman, a woman a man. Maybe there is something erotic about working together and it makes itself felt between young Langen and me. But, Mitzi, if one takes heed of all the maybes, does one still dare to breathe in this world?[16]

Frida was right that Strindberg wanted her "to be there only for him." He could not give her the freedom she wanted, even if it cost them their survival. As soon as any threat of sexual competition arose, as it was bound to with Frida's male colleagues, his ego, at once proud and fragile, could not permit it.

At the end of the second day of silence, as Strindberg sat sullenly alone at the Café de la Paix, he was greeted by old friends, the Norwegian artist Fritz Thaulow and his wife, Alexandra, the sister of Oda Krohg, who lived nearby in Dieppe. They invited him to dinner and, when he replied that he was in Paris with his wife, urged him to bring Frida along. Alexandra Thaulow recalled his response:

"She is very nasty, she steals my thoughts and she writes books. She is a devil."

We had heard that he was married to an Austrian and were very curious after hearing this description. As we approached the hotel, Strindberg said. "Let me go ahead and tame the wild beast."

We waited patiently expecting an alarming creature. What a surprise. . . . Strindberg was accompanied by a poor, small, pretty, dark-haired woman, her face and eyes showing signs of tears. She didn't look more than seventeen or eighteen. She had been sitting alone the whole day waiting for him. Now she was smiling with delight to be going out with him and his friends.[17]

There was forgiveness and reconciliation, but the good fortune bestowed upon them by Langen and Gretor began to unravel. Langen had discovered that a number of the paintings sold him by the Dane were fakes, and both men had left town to settle their differences elsewhere. Meanwhile, the luxurious apartment in Passy was seized by creditors, and Frida and Strindberg escaped to two sparsely furnished rooms in the Hôtel des Américains on the Rue de l'Abbé. They discovered that Gretor was a pseudonym for Willy Petersen, the son of a wealthy industrialist in Copenhagen who had already run through the fortunes of a few other young men before Langen.

Choosing to ignore the fact that, with the departure of their two patrons, the possibilities for a viable existence in Paris had also disappeared, Strindberg and Frida continued to enjoy the city. Seizing precious time together before having to face the future, they strolled through the Luxembourg Garden and browsed among the bookstalls. But the idyll ended more abruptly than expected when a telegram arrived informing Frida that Kerstin's wet nurse, insulted by Grandmother Reischl, had left the child. Frida was instructed to return to Dornach immediately. Because Strindberg had an important appointment on the day of her departure, he could not see Frida to the train. Theirs was a casual farewell on a traffic island in front of the Printemps department store. Strindberg leaped on an omnibus and waved goodbye. Neither of them had any idea they would never see each other again.

5

Betrayals

It was with feelings of savage glee that I turned homeward from the Gare du Nord where I had parted from my little wife. She was going to our child who had fallen ill in a distant land. So now I had accomplished the sacrifice of my heart. . . . Restored to the world of the free, I became aware of a sudden expansion of myself. . . .[1]

IN 1897, STRINDBERG IMMORTALIZED Frida's departure in the very first sentence of *Inferno,* the semiautobiographical novel of the two years following their abrupt separation. They were the very same feelings conveyed to Frida less than two weeks after she left Paris. "Why this wild joy when you left?" But in his letter he added: "And the remorse that followed, and the regret."[2] Their marriage had reached an impasse: Strindberg could no longer endure the isolation and enmity of Dornach; Frida and Kerstin could not survive the insecurity and poverty in Paris. Hence Strindberg's "savage" and "wild" feeling of relief that circumstances had momentarily released him from this cul-de-sac.

Once alone, he spent seven days in Dieppe with the Thaulows and then returned to the Hôtel des Américains. He set up his chemical apparatus and began devoting himself to the experiments begun in Dornach and which he now hoped would launch him as a bona fide scientist. His social life consisted of almost daily contacts with an international group of artists that he had been introduced to by the Thaulows. To Frida, however, he complained of loneliness and the temptation of the tavern, so hard to resist without her.

Frida arrived in Dornach to find Kerstin healthy, rosy, and content in the arms of Maria Uhl and Grandmother Reischl. It was left to her to go to Vienna to bribe and cajole the offended wet nurse to return. When she came back with the woman in tow, the *Häusel* was no longer warm enough to live in. As autumn deepened and cold mists rose from the Danube, Frida was forced to retreat to the big house, a daughter once more and the least important member of the matriarchy.

Distance made Strindberg circumspect, and in a letter to Frida he tried to understand the contradictions in their marriage. How was it that they both loved and hated each other? How to explain that he loved her for her faults—her frivolity, her lack of awareness, her instinctual life bordering on the vegetal? In the same bemused tone, yet betraying a certain unease, he asked why their "dirty acts" seemed clean and pure to him, while those of others seemed filthy. Sentimental memories followed, of days in Dornach with Frida in a Japanese hat among his cucumbers, a morning in Paris when, like two students, they had gone off to the Panthéon and the Bibliothèque Sainte Geneviève, and Frida, looking like a young girl, had made him feel old.

Having momentarily let down his guard, he closed with the usual warning: "Don't make a fool of your husband. Jealousy does not exist for me, but disgust, hatred, and revenge. . . ."[3]

The next day he made a few wistful suggestions that she

return. "Why should I lure you here? Would your presence give me courage and strength to act? Perhaps. With you gone I lost interest in everything."[4]

The minefield of contradictions these letters implied was nothing new for Frida; she had learned to navigate this territory before and their warmth offered her the illusion of safety. So safe did she feel that, when Strindberg continued to harp on his loneliness and poverty, she decided to return to his side. It was now possible for her to come back to Paris, she wrote him, since Kerstin was well taken care of. Working with Langen and other publishers, she could contribute to their common welfare. But Strindberg's resentment of his dependence on her was the explosive she had overlooked. It blew up in her face with a little help from his other family, in Finland.

Strindberg's first response to her offer of comradeship was predictable. It could mean only one thing, he wrote her, the desire to consort with unmarried men.[5] The next letter, however, set out to destroy a marriage he could no longer handle. "Do you act consciously and by design or is it your immoral nature that compels you? In London you established your reputation by dining in public with an unmarried man, and you a young wife; in Berlin you are notorious, in Vienna as well and you made a fine beginning in Paris. . . . At this moment," he concluded, "I am possessed by a single emotion, just one, the last: to defend my honor, take my revenge, rid myself of what is degrading. . . . Find someone else!"

This was no longer a case of misunderstanding, but a deliberate and brutal blow. How could Frida defend herself against these fabricated accusations of betrayal? A clue to Strindberg's vicious onslaught lay in the postscript. "My divine insouciance led me into a marriage where I was treated as a beggar, lower than a servant, and to the point where my children curse me."[6]

What Frida could not have known was that Siri had been desperately pressuring her former husband for support. The guilt this engendered was transformed into anger at Frida, in the hope, perhaps, that the drastic nature of his attack would cause her to abandon the hopeless enterprise their marriage now appeared to be.

More profoundly, Strindberg could no longer cope with Frida's erotic appeal. Her visit to Paris made it clear that motherhood had not diminished the attraction of his young, headstrong, ambitious wife. He had been tortured by her meetings with Langen, and when Frida suggested their resumption, Strindberg felt trapped. Not only did Frida's sensuality seem to him to invite attention from other men, but it also awakened his own ambivalence about sex. He had always feared the loss of self inherent in the power of eros. *A Madman's Plea* had recorded the alternating feelings of sexual attraction and repugnance in his first marriage, and in *Inferno* he wrote of "the feeling of spiritual purity, of masculine virginity," that filled him as he lay alone in bed after Frida's departure.[7] Prefacing his second letter with the warning that he was "prepared to risk everything," he gave in to the sexual denigration of Frida brought on by his own anxiety. He called her, among other things, "the dirtiest human creature I have ever known," and told her to "go your dirty way to the life you seek in the gutter." Nor did he hesitate to add that her mother, too, had called her a prostitute.[8]

Frida was distraught, but kept hoping the letters were a momentary aberration, and Strindberg would soon regain sufficient composure to rescind his maniacal accusations. It was not until Friedrich Uhl joined the fray that separation became inevitable. On November 15, the editor of the *Wiener Zeitung* received a letter from a Mr. John Swanljung, Siri von Essen's lawyer. He wrote to ask if the Honorable Friedrich Uhl would advance the 2,100

Swedish crowns in child support owed by his son-in-law to the family now living in Finland. Everything about the letter seemed designed to infuriate Uhl. It alluded to his "comfortable circumstances," drew attention to the three children's misery, and suggested that there would be satisfaction in saving his son-in-law's honor.

Confronted yet again by threats of scandal and debt, Uhl rejected all involvement. He did not even deign to write to Frida or Strindberg. He sent a magisterial and sardonic response to Maria Uhl. He had never shirked his duty as a father, he declared, but he did not consider himself obligated to the children of another father. In fact, Siri's plight was an embarrassment. "August could have shown more consideration for me," he concluded.[9]

This turn of events produced the crisis Frida feared—another duel of pride between father and husband—and yet it also brought relief. Grieving over Strindberg's hateful letters, she thought she understood the source of his attack: shame at his exposure to Friedrich Uhl. Frida felt compassion for her husband, but now both he and her father barred the way to his side. To her family, honor and patrimony appeared to be at stake. Uhl demanded that no scandal, particularly one caused by the irregular life of a son-in-law, mar the celebrations planned for his seventieth birthday; Grandmother Reischl required assurance that the family fortune would not be dissipated by the obligations of a destitute spouse. Maria Uhl delivered the ultimatum: Frida was to leave her husband or depart from Dornach with her child.

Before yielding to this pressure, Frida begged Strindberg to retract the harsh words he had written her, but he answered by telling her to "be humble, repent," and change her conduct. He then listed his requirements for her behavior should she wish to return. Besides the obvious strictures on flirting and going about by herself, he insisted that she never see Langen or Gretor again.

There were also professional demands: she was no longer to promote her German friends, since they were unpopular in Paris, and instead of "contributing to dubious journals," she was to dedicate herself to translating his work. He was not the same person he was, he reminded her at the close, and would continue to "regard her with disgust."[10]

Frida had very little choice. To survive she had to throw in her lot with her father, who continued to pay her monthly for her reviews and articles. She put Kerstin in the permanent care of her mother and relinquished the rights to her inheritance from her grandparents to assure the child's security. Divorce proceedings began and she moved into a family apartment in Vienna to become, as journalist and translator, the sole wage earner of her husband's second family.

As Frida tried to pull her life together, Strindberg was being lauded in Paris. On December 11, *The Father* received its long-awaited French premiere at the *Nouveau Théâtre*, one of the largest in the city. In response to enthusiastic critics, the play was performed ten nights running and was subsequently mounted in other cities, but Strindberg, too lethargic to fight for his share of the profits, received only 300 francs from the producer. In his self-destructive mood, he took little pleasure in his momentary celebrity, refused to meet well-known people clamoring to see him, and addressed his correspondents in the new guise of mendicant and beggar. Proceeding doggedly with his chemical experiments, suffering from the psoriasis that emerged during periods of stress, and abandoning efforts to earn enough money to live on, Strindberg was in a sorry state as the year ended. When his friends from the Scandinavian community saw him so reduced that he could not even attend to his chapped and bleeding hands, they started a subscription, enabling him to enter the Saint-Louis Hospital for treatment at the beginning of January.

Not long thereafter an inaccurate report of his condition appeared in the Austrian papers, awakening pity in Frida, but suspicion in Friedrich Uhl. Determined to hold her to the divorce, Uhl reminded his daughter that she had already been dismissed in Strindberg's letters. Did she want to risk another humiliating rejection in person? When she stubbornly insisted that Strindberg needed her, Uhl wired French colleagues for an accurate report of his son-in-law's condition and cold-bloodedly informed her of the true state of affairs: her husband's illness was minor and did not require her presence.

Frida remained in Vienna, but could not resist reopening the correspondence with Strindberg. It was a somewhat chastened spouse who replied, asking for pity for his lonely Christmas and admitting that it would have been better had he not shared his life with anyone, since the contrast with his present existence was too cruel. He invited Frida to correspond with him.

She promptly made the mistake of sending Strindberg money, only to have it sent back. His role of beggar had become essential—a mendicant could be neither husband nor father. Nonetheless, a desultory correspondence continued, and by the end of January Strindberg was asking Frida if she had the courage to visit him, and begged her to give their marriage another chance.

Unsure, Frida hesitated, and Strindberg retreated. By mid-February, the verbal abuse had begun once more. In April, Strindberg could not resist avenging his honor at the expense of his father-in-law. Having convinced himself that his poverty was not shameful, he accepted financial help from his friends as long as it was provided with discretion and dignity. When Knut Hamsun arranged a special benefit performance in Berlin, however, Strindberg took offense. He placed an announcement in the Scandinavian newspapers saying that the money would go to his children,

Kerstin included. Friedrich Uhl, convinced that Strindberg had deliberately intended to ignite a rumor that the editor in chief's granddaughter was living in poverty, was furious. "Was that Strindberg's revenge," he asked Frida, "since old Uhl didn't lay out the money for the other children?"[11]

Strindberg's provocative gesture persuaded Frida that reconciliation was impossible. She accelerated the divorce proceedings and broke off the correspondence for more than a year with a candid farewell written in April 1895.

> *. . . Our marriage was a failure. But believe one thing of me, for your sake, not mine. I never did the terrible things you accuse me of. I sinned from pride, stupidity, from a lack of charity, I mishandled you, to put it simply. But I did not betray you, I did not damage you.*
>
> *I would rather die than become your wife again. As combatants, we are too unequal. You would kill my soul which is only beginning to recover in peace and in the love of my child. . . . We are each other's destruction.*

Frida's readiness to concede her faults while at the same time insisting on her innocence testified to a clarity of vision she had managed to hold on to. Strindberg had attacked her on all sides. He had accused her of adultery, impugned her motives in wanting to help him, disparaged her intellect. Now she was left with the child he had so urgently wanted her to bear. Her letter put a brave front on all she had suffered, but at its close she acknowledged that Strindberg was the survivor.

> *It is sad for love to end this way. Sad like the autumn that strips the trees and allows the flowers to die. Will there be another blossoming? I believe there will be for you—a tree full of strength with a heart incapable of being broken.*[12]

In the year Frida and Strindberg were without contact, their separation went forward. To spare him scandal, and no doubt her father as well, Frida settled for an annulment rather than a divorce, on the basis that her marriage to a divorced man was illegal in Catholic Austria. This tactic, designed to ease the process, did not prevent Strindberg, in moments of high dudgeon, from accusing Frida of denying her daughter's paternity.

On receiving some papers in connection with the annulment in May 1896, Strindberg reopened the correspondence, inquiring about Kerstin and the size of the debt he owed her family. Frida answered in the same tone as the year before, blaming herself for having been far from an ideal wife, but insisting, as she always had, on her autonomy. She closed on a generous note.

> *Believe me August, now you will have no more devoted and sincere friend than the one who lacked the qualities to be your wife. Whatever happens, you can count on me.*
>
> *You owe no one anything. As far as the child is concerned, I told the judge and repeat to you that I neither want nor will accept any support. I will earn what is necessary with my work. And in the worst of circumstances my family will stand in for her.*[13]

Alas, by refusing Strindberg the opportunity to pay his debts, the abuse resurfaced, exacerbated by a frantic letter from Frida in response to an article in the French papers confusing Strindberg with his nephew Nils Strindberg, who was about to embark on an expedition to the North Pole.

"You cannot abandon the child," she wrote, and unwisely added "I will stop you by force."[14]

"What is it to you," Strindberg answered, "since you have dissolved our union? You don't want me to die, but you want me to suffer. . . ." And then he revealed once again his unholy alliance with Maria Uhl by adding, "It is the demon that possesses you and that your mother has divined, calling you a race of vipers."[15]

IN THE SUMMER of 1896, four years after her stay with the Porges family when she was just out of school, Frida returned to Munich, a twenty-four-year-old divorced mother hard pressed to make a living. Albert Langen, who had moved his publishing venture to the city the year before, had invited her to assist him in promoting the French dramas he wished to see performed in Germany.

"Too heavy," Heinrich Porges had prophesied on hearing of the young Frida's engagement to Strindberg years before. And so it had been. Frida had fought for and lost that relationship at great cost. When she arrived in Munich, almost two years had passed since she had last seen Strindberg. She was no longer the high-spirited girl he had courted so ardently in Berlin. But she was young, resilient, and, if nothing else, Friedrich Uhl's parsimony, his insistence that she fend for herself, challenged her to begin anew. Munich was a good place to do so.

"Everything that was young and hopeful and wanted to spread its wings in the field of art gathered in Munich during those . . . years as if by appointment," the playwright Max Halbe recalled of his move to the Bavarian capital in 1895.[16] His first play *Jugend* (*Youth*), a naturalist drama of adolescence, had been one of the big successes of the memorable Berlin season of 1892–93. Now the word *Jugend* seemed to be on everyone's lips in Munich. A magazine by that name dedicated to all that was new in the arts made its first appearance in the city on New Year's Day 1896, and soon thereafter *Jugendstil* became the term for the radical art nouveau style in which the weekly was designed. The artistic ferment could be felt most keenly in Schwabing, Munich's Latin Quarter, where contributors to *Jugend* and other young artists and writers had formed their own bohemian community.

The city's artistic vitality had encouraged Langen to embark on an additional venture. While living in France, he had been struck by the exuberance of Paris's satirical magazines—provocative publications thriving in the absence of censorship in France. Controls were still in place in Germany, but Langen decided Munich was the place to test the censors. Dissent and provocation already marked the atmosphere of a city divided between the liberal, anticlerical government of Prince Regent Luitpold and an increasingly conservative and vocal Catholic majority. On April 4, 1896, the first issue of Langen's *Simplicissimus*, named after a picaresque hero of a seventeenth-century novel, appeared on the newsstands in Germany and Austria. Following its French models, the new magazine was printed in a handsome large-size format with color illustrations. A talented group of Munich artists had been recruited to contribute cartoons lampooning the military, the clergy, and, above all, the "*Spiesbürger,*" or bourgeois philistine. Writers were invited to contribute poems, stories, and prose pieces that would live up to the first issue's slogan to "strike the lazy nation with hot words."

More mischief to come was promised by the poster promoting the magazine that appeared all over Munich that summer of 1896. It depicted a spirited and well-built Devil so absorbed in reading *Simplicissimus* that he pays little heed to the beautiful woman pulled along in his wake. The mismatched duo might have been a prefiguration of the affair between Frida and Frank Wedekind that began shortly after her arrival in the city in the fall.

Wedekind had left Paris for Munich hoping to find support for the publication or performance of his plays. In his early thirties, he settled in the city just as *Simplicissimus* made its debut. An illustration for his short story *"Die Fürstin Russalka"* (*"The*

Duchess Russalka") decked its first cover. The image of a pensive maiden gave no clue to the satiric contents within. By making his heroine a pious and naïve noblewoman, Wedekind sent out a tongue-in-cheek warning that radical thinking had infiltrated even the bastions of the aristocracy. After reading Ibsen, Tolstoy, Nietzsche, and Sudermann, Wedekind's duchess feels impelled to cut her hair, loosen her corset, dress as a man at an Artists' Ball, and write learnedly about women's rights. At last she is saved from these "confused drives that go against nature" by the traditional fulfillment of motherhood. Her savior, however, is no bourgeois, but a political radical.

In *Simplicissimus,* Wedekind satirized stock responses to women's emancipation, but in his plays he offered his own solution to the relations between men and women: the glorification of sex. By the time he came to Munich he had already written the two sex-driven dramas that would establish his reputation many years later, *Frühlings Erwachen* (*Spring's Awakening*), dealing with sexual repression, and *Die Büchse der Pandora* (*Pandora's Box*), exploring its unbridled release. Both celebrated the sensual and the physical with a degree of frankness that seemed to militate against their ever being performed in public.

Spring's Awakening, which was written in 1891, drew on the adolescent sexual confusion that had driven two of Wedekind's schoolmates to suicide. The play not only explicitly acknowledges all aspects of the teenage characters' sexuality from homoeroticism to incipient masochism, but also demonstrates their innocence in contrast to the self-serving and, in some cases, fatal responses of their parents and teachers.

Wedekind settled in Paris in 1892 to live out the dream of personal and sexual freedom he had harbored in his youth. The writer Lou-Andreas Salomé observed him in his habitat when she met him there in 1894.

One was sure to find him in a café in the Latin Quarter where he wrote poems at night on the sticky marble tables by the door. . . . Being at that time without an income or a place to live more or less, he sat between the grisettes not without some hope that by the time the café closed and they had filled their purses sufficiently one of them would good-naturedly take him home for shelter, to breakfast, and a little tenderness.[17]

In his diary he kept a graphic account of his encounters with the women of the *demimonde*. He was as candid about his own physical capacities, predilections, and shortcomings—the adjustments required by his false teeth, for instance—as he was about the variety of pleasures offered by Rachel, Alice, Henriette, and several others. Sometimes, after divesting them of their diaphanous petticoats, ribbon-trimmed chemises, and neat laced bootees, he was given to carrying his scantily clad companions about on his shoulders. On other occasions he would have them don his clothes and amuse him by telling him stories of their trade.[18]

If Strindberg's tendency had been to punish women for what he believed was their wanton nature, Wedekind celebrated them for it. In the erotic opportunities of Paris's *demimonde*, he sought the utopia of his fantasies, a world where submission to sensual pleasure outside bourgeois considerations of "love, fidelity, and gratitude" had its own justification. His gradual recognition of the impossibility of that ideal was the subject of *Die Büchse der Pandora* (*Pandora's Box*), which he subtitled *Eine Monstretragödie* (*A Monster Tragedy*). Lulu, his heroine, who embodied Wedekind's vision of primeval innocence joined to unrestrained sensuality, is gradually destroyed by her lovers. Each of them has a far more distorted view of sex than she, and her downfall concludes with her murder by none other than Jack the Ripper. (The infamous criminal was still active in London as Wedekind wrote his last act.)

When Wedekind met Langen in Paris in 1894 and presented the newly minted publisher with his *Monster Tragedy*, Langen was not enthusiastic. It was the ubiquitous Gretor who intervened. He encouraged Wedekind to transform the play into two independent dramas—*Der Erdgeist* (*Earth Spirit*) and *Pandora's Box*—and then convinced Langen to reconsider. As Gretor had hoped, the publisher was sufficiently intrigued by the revision to at least take the risk of publishing *Earth Spirit*. The play was the first book by a German writer to appear under Langen's imprint, and assured its author a degree of notoriety when he moved to Munich in 1896.

Once settled in the city, Wedekind was soon a regular fixture at the parties of the younger members of the Porges family—their daughter Else and her husband, Max Bernstein—who were now at the center of Munich's artistic life. Under the pseudonym Ernst Rosmer, Else wrote plays, libretti, and music criticism, while her husband, aside from a flourishing law practice, was a drama critic. At one of their festive occasions, Frida and Frank Wedekind were reintroduced. It was inevitable that Frida would sense another opportunity to be of use in this bright and ambitious, but poor and insufficiently appreciated playwright. The eccentricity of the young writer's appearance, his fabled "six or seven beards," apparently did not put her off.

Max Halbe recalled his first opportunity to compare the man with the hirsute myth.

Faced with the reality, I did not find the description particularly exaggerated. Even if there were actually only three or four or five—two long grown-out mutton chops ending in a point, a mustache and a goat's beard reaching nearly to his chest—the whole actually appeared like a pile of black beard and gave those who encountered him the impression of a Magus, a Magician, a Wizard, or a member of a circus. The impression was reinforced by the downright flashy elegance of this strange apparition's outer appearance since with his yellow-checked trousers, he wore a gray morning coat, a shiny new top hat and his hands were covered with yellow kid gloves.[19]

Wedekind's deliberately cultivated antibourgeois stance was not without an element of self-promotion. To protest conformity in appearance, he indulged in self-display, to subvert polite discourse, he resorted to scandal-provoking innuendo, and to expose sexual hypocrisy, he flaunted his own promiscuity. When the "strange apparition" appeared at parties, he assumed the role of *Bürgerschreck* (disrupter of polite society) to the hilt. His favorite persona was that of a rude Casanova asking young unmarried women if they were virgins, and wives how many times a week they slept with their husbands.

After Strindberg, Wedekind's more open attitude toward sex—if crudely expressed—must have seemed liberating to Frida, but her young admirer was no more interested in emancipation than her husband had been. Strindberg's exclusionary tactics had depended on old theories of biological difference—it was not "natural" for women to live as men did—whereas Wedekind took the more radical but no more enlightened approach of singing the praises of the flesh at the expense of the mind. "A woman who earns her living through love is far higher . . . than one who lowers herself so far as to write feuilletons or books," he wrote before meeting Frida.[20] And by looking at women through a sexual lens exclusively, he refused responsibility for their vulnerability—emotional, social, or economic. He had successfully suppressed all bourgeois concern for the safety of the gentler sex in a world where unprotected women were fair game.

Wedekind's devotion to the role of provocateur had its roots

Maria and Friedrich Uhl
as newlyweds.
Courtesy of the Weyr archives.

Wyndham Lewis's poster for the Cabaret Theatre Club at the Cave of the Golden Calf, 1912. *Courtesy of the Division of Rare and Manuscript Collections, Cornell University.*

Frida, age twelve, in Mondsee. *Courtesy of Strindbergsmuseet, Stockholm.*

Christian Krohg's *August Strindberg*, 1892, oil on canvas. *Courtesy of the Norsk Folkemuseum, Oslo.*

Frida, age eighteen.
Courtesy of the Weyr archives.

Caricature of the *Freie Bühne* in the magazine *Kladderadatsch.*

Mitzi and Rudolf Weyr.
Courtesy of Strindbergmuseum, Soxen, Austria.

Edvard Munch's *Zum Schwarzen Ferkel*, 1893, pencil, private collection. Left to right: Gunnar Heiberg, August Strindberg, Sigborn Obstfelder, Munch, Holger Drachmann. *Photo: Munch Museum, Oslo (Svein Andersen/ Sidsel de Jong).*

Frida with Kerstin and Max Friedrich, c. 1904. *Courtesy of The Royal Library, Department of Manuscripts, Stockholm.*

Th. Th. Heine's poster for *Simplicissimus*, 1896. *Courtesy of Museum für Kunst und Gewerbe, Hamburg.*

Kerstin Strindberg, in her early twenties. *Courtesy of The Royal Library, Department of Manuscripts, Stockholm.*

Frank Wedekind in Paris. *Courtesy of the Münchener Stadtbibliothek-Monacensia.*

Augustus John leaning against a gypsy caravan, 1909. *Courtesy of Michael Holroyd.*

Arnold Genthe's portrait of Frida, 1915.
© Museum of the City of New York.

Augustus John's *The Way Down to the Sea*, 1911, oil on canvas, private collection.
Photo: Envy Creative Ltd., Newbury, Berkshire.

Frida with "Ali," in the 1930s. *Courtesy of Albert Bonniers förlagsarkiv, Stockholm.*

Max Friedrich Strindberg, c. 1960.
Courtesy of Kristof Sulzbach.

in a family very much like Frida's. His father, too, had first espoused and then betrayed the liberal principles of 1848. Dr. Friedrich Wilhelm Wedekind was a disappointed veteran of the revolution in Germany and left Europe in 1849 to set up his medical practice in San Francisco. Through shrewd real estate speculation during the Gold Rush, he became a rich and established bachelor, a respected member of the small immigrant community. At forty-six, he met the twenty-year-old Emilie Kammerer, a professional singer and dancer from Germany, who had come to San Francisco after performing in South and Central America. In California, she had married an improvident innkeeper and supported him by performing in a Melodeon, a variety theater with a somewhat unsavory reputation.

It was as a courageous, lively, and talented performer that Emilie Kammerer first attracted Dr. Wedekind, but after she divorced her first husband to marry him in 1861, he reverted to the traditional moralist he was. Not only was she to give up her career, but they were to return to Europe, where her unorthodox early life would not reflect on his choice.

Benjamin Franklin Wedekind, as Frank was originally named, was born in Hannover in 1864, the second of six children. On returning to Germany, Dr. Wedekind, who was sufficiently wealthy to give up his medical practice, involved himself briefly in the political battle against Prussian unification but soon abandoned it as a hopeless cause. By the time Frank was eight years old, his father was in full retreat from the active life and had retired to the neutrality of Switzerland, where he purchased Schloss Lenzburg, a medieval castle high above the small town of the same name in the canton of Aargau. With this move, he also inflicted his withdrawal on his family. Though the children went to the village schools, the anomaly of their residence, three hundred and sixty-five steps above the town, separated them from their peers and made them feel like outsiders. At the same time it encouraged an unhealthy hothouse atmosphere in the castle itself, where the tension between the parents set the dominating tone.

As the years passed, Dr. Wedekind increasingly withdrew from family life. Disagreeing with his wife's liberal and open-minded upbringing of the children, he spent most of his time in his own quarters concentrating on an eclectic collection of antiquities. By the time Wedekind was a young man, his father had transformed himself from a believer in liberal ideals, a freethinker capable of admiring an adventurous woman, to an authoritarian figure ruling his family from a distance. The contrast between his mother's life-affirming colorful past and the deadly isolation and social constraint of the existence his father had forced upon her pointed the way to Wedekind's desire to goad the class he stemmed from.[21]

Enfants terribles such as Strindberg and Wedekind, men who thrived on provocation and had troublesome reputations regarding women, had a dangerous appeal for Frida. On the one hand, her own adventurous spirit was affirmed and excited by the element of risk. But there was a deeper and more destructive aspect to their allure. Brilliant, self-absorbed, ambitious men for whom women were dispensable, shared qualities with Friedrich Uhl. They were men given to abandoning women, just as her father had virtually abandoned her when she was six years old. The unfortunate attraction for Frida of those most likely to leave her was the challenge of keeping them from doing so. Inevitably, all of her resources—maternal concern, professional assistance, and feminine charm—would not be enough. As the specter of desertion returned, she learned to resort to a more drastic arsenal to keep a restless lover from moving on.

DURING THAT SUMMER of 1896, as Frida began a new life in Munich, Edvard Munch reencountered Strindberg in Paris. In the lithographic portrait he made of him there, he captured the sharp, wary glance of the public man with seething private obsessions. Strindberg's powerful head, with its great crown of hair and prominent forehead, was framed by Munch with a series of agitated lines emanating from a schematic nude.

The image was prophetic—in June and July of 1896, Strindberg suffered the worst of the persecution complexes that had plagued him since he had begun to live alone in Paris. His renewed contact with Munch brought news of the *Schwarze Ferkel* circle and the tragedy that had just befallen Przybyszewski. The Pole's former mistress, Marta Foerder, who had borne him three children, the last one of which had been conceived after his marriage to Dagny Juel, had committed suicide. When Przybyszewski was arrested for her murder immediately thereafter, both Strindberg and Munch were willing to offer assistance. Once he was released, however, Strindberg became possessed with the idea that the Polish writer had come to Paris to torture and punish him for his long-ago affair with Dagny. The attacks began with the hallucinatory sound of Schumann's *Aufschwung*, a piece Przybyszewski had often played at the *Schwarze Ferkel*. Strindberg then experienced strange and debilitating physical sensations, caused, he believed, by some sort of gas apparatus set up by his enemy and capable of harming him through the walls of his bedroom. He even wrote enigmatically to Frida, "Do you know the key to that fatal enigma, our divorce? The vengeance of Aspasia! To destroy us both."[22]

Strindberg had seen only too clearly that Przybyszewski's fate could be his own. The possible tragic repercussions of abandonment and betrayal were before his eyes, and to exorcise his own guilt he needed to make an enemy of this doppelgänger.

Soon after these episodes, Strindberg fled from Paris to the

Thaulows in Dieppe, and then to the care of a doctor in Sweden. There the attacks abated somewhat but he began to feel persecuted by the doctor himself. Before the situation became acute, Frida, writing from Munich in mid-August, invited Strindberg to come to the Danube to visit Kerstin and Maria Uhl. This letter seemed to ease Strindberg's guilt. Salvation, he wrote to a friend, was to be found through "work without honor or gold, duty, the family, consequently—woman, the mother and child."[23] In *Inferno* he recalled that the invitation had brought him back to life and he waxed nostalgic about the landscape of Upper Austria.

It was in a mellow mood that Strindberg returned to the scene of his marriage, and, for the first month there, believed that if he became reconciled with Frida's family and their child, Frida might eventually reappear. Using the intimate *Du* once again, he wrote her the letters of a spouse reporting on the outcome of family quarrels, asking her to send him books from Munich, expressing his delight with Kerstin and signing them "Your Husband (in expectation)."[24] When, in late September, Frida wrote that reconciliation was no longer a possibility, Strindberg began to experience his symptoms of persecution once again. But by this time he had become close enough to Maria Uhl and her twin sister, Melanie, for them to offer him the consolation and advice he longed for. In encouraging him to read the work of his fellow countryman, the eighteenth-century mystic Emanuel Swedenborg, they provided Strindberg with an imaginative framework in which to effect his own healing.

What appealed to Strindberg, with his bent for self-chastisement, was Swedenborg's explanation that hell was here on earth and all suffer punishment to atone for the sinfulness of mankind. In his mind, and with a little help from Dante, Strindberg was able to superimpose Swedenborg's description of hell on the Danube landscape. Accompanied by his own Beatrice—two-year-old Kerstin—he passed through an inferno of his own making in the river gorge at the nearby town of Klam. He glimpsed the presence of a punishing god in the threatening forms of overhanging rocks, felt the heat of hellfire in the flames emanating from a blacksmith's shop, and heard the eternal cycle of suffering in the repetitions of a mill wheel's rotation. Salvation, after such a journey, was symbolized by the figure of the Madonna at the other end of the gorge. Although his delusion that he was being harassed and pursued by his enemies did not cease immediately, he had been given the vision of some form of transcendence that he held on to for the rest of his life.

The modicum of peace he had gained and the warmth of his mother-in-law tempted Strindberg to remain in the vicinity for a few more months. Devoted and attentive as Maria Uhl was, however, she remained at the behest of those who supported her. Old lady Reischl and Friedrich Uhl were watching Strindberg from afar, threatened by every report of his ex-son-in-law's strange behavior. Once again the chatelaine of Dornach saw the threat of the legacy hunter, and the editor in chief the possibility of shameful public exposure.

At the end of November, Maria Reischl wrote to Mitzi about how dependent Strindberg had become on Maria Uhl. She had to accompany him as he moved from place to place pursued by his fears. Worst of all, since Strindberg had no money, Maria Uhl was paying for everything. "He will also suck me dry if I let him" was Maria Reischl's prognosis.[25]

Not long after this letter was written, Friedrich Uhl officially requested that Strindberg leave, hoping thereby to expunge him from his family forever. But the bond that had formed between Strindberg, Maria Uhl, and Kerstin proved far stronger than the tie to Frida. By pointing the way to his recovery from the guilt and mental anguish that had plagued him since the breakup of his first marriage, Frida's mother had moved Strindberg's life in a new direction. He departed for Sweden at the end of November, but leaving the haven on the Danube was a wrenching break. As soon as he arrived in Skurup, near Malmö, he began writing letters to Maria Uhl almost daily, addressing her as "Mother" and signing himself "Your son." Kerstin also received delightful letters.

Maria Uhl felt a deep emotional tie to her son-in-law. Her marriage had provided no comfort and her daughters had been taken in hand by their father. This time she was determined not to give up the long-dormant feelings of maternal affection awakened by Strindberg and Kerstin. Her missives to Sweden made sure the flame was kept alive, and she kept their unusual epistolary attachment a secret from Frida.

"Your postcard," Strindberg wrote in one of his earliest letters, "so loving and with such beautiful words, as if from a better world, melted my sick heart completely."[26] A week later, her descriptions of life with Kerstin brought another poignant response. "Your painterly letters make me feel I am living with you . . . see you both, hear you both, and suffer that my soul cannot be with you completely."

At Christmas, reading Balzac, Strindberg was overcome by forgiving thoughts of Frida. It would do Frida good to read Balzac, too, he wrote Kerstin. "Mama will meet herself there and also August-Papa and it is always good when bankrupt souls meet."[27] But in Maria Uhl's new ménage, there was to be no room for Frida. Using Strindberg's own words, she wrote him that her daughter had, indeed, become a "complete bankrupt." But the rejection she hoped to elicit from Strindberg did not happen. Instead he became instantly concerned.

What you write me about Frida makes me ill. Does she have the same unlucky star I have? And has it knotted our destinies together? Let her come to Klam and refresh herself with the child, the fountain of youth.

Then he added, aware of the slightly illicit, covert nature of the bond between him and his former mother-in-law, that if Frida returned home, the intimacy of their correspondence would have to be sacrificed.[28]

Threatened by the possibility of losing her close relationship with her ex-son-in-law, Maria Uhl questioned Strindberg's concern and implied that a more appropriate response might be the expression of pleasure at his former wife's downfall. Her correspondent bristled and asked scornfully if Maria Uhl really wanted him to be happy about Frida's misery. "You don't really mean that. Even from the selfish standpoint, what can her bankruptcy help me, bankrupt as I am."[29] And although Strindberg seemed to acquiesce by adding that he was resigned never to see Frida again, Maria Uhl's tactic had alerted his acute psychological antennae. He admonished her for "playing Providence."[30]

At this first hint that Frida was in trouble, Strindberg began to have visions. She appeared before him constantly, and he caught glimpses of her on every street corner. He begged Maria Uhl to find out if she was sick in Munich. But Maria Uhl deflected his inquiries, and Strindberg felt paralyzed. "Is it my duty to look for Frida?" he asked rhetorically. "But, in fact, I don't know what I will find."[31]

By the beginning of February, Strindberg had begun to make plans for writing *Inferno.* Naturally, Klam's river gorge was to be the setting for his hell; Kerstin, his guide. He wrote Maria Uhl that what he would like best would be to return to the Danube for two months in the spring and write his book with Kerstin at his side. He promised Kerstin to put on his "seven-mile boots and fly through night and wind and ice and snow. . . ."[32] The more Maria Uhl wrote him about the delights of the little child, the more Strindberg longed to see her.

But it was not to be. Maria Uhl bowed to renewed pressures from Maria Reischl and Friedrich Uhl, and in early March Strindberg was forbidden the reunion. The decision to deny Strindberg access to his child for the sake of Reischl's fortune and Uhl's pride was the turning point in the life of Frida and her daughter. Had Strindberg been allowed to return to Dornach everything might have worked out differently for them both. Strindberg's immediate response was scathing:

> *Everything in Dornach is enchanting, but the logic is divine. A mother wants to reconcile her two children, a religious act we heretics allow priests to perform. In Dornach it is called pimping. In our parts, we call tearing a marriage apart a crime, and it is referred to that way in the Holy Scriptures as well. But to tempt or force a woman from her temporarily poor husband to find a rich one for her—that is pimping.*
>
> *So no child, no wife, no homeland. Good. But to lose the child, that is the most painful.*[33]

Even with the ban on his return to Austria, Strindberg continued to worry about Frida. She appeared to him in many visionary guises—dressed in a brown or white habit, her face suffused with tears.[34] At last in mid-July, Maria Uhl's comment that Strindberg should be happy to be ignorant of Frida's fate, led him to demand an explanation. He urged Maria Uhl to be candid. He was ready, he told her generously, to offer consolation if necessary.

The next day he asked again. "Ultimatum: If she is alone and unhappy, I will write her a word of comfort. If she is happy and not alone, I only need to know where she is living so as not to fall into duel-complications. . . ."[35]

Whether out of fear or thwarted love, Maria Uhl misled Strindberg. But perhaps Strindberg had already guessed the truth. In one of the last of his inquiring letters he mentioned a final prophetic vision: "My dreams and suspicions have shown me for a long time: an abandoned mother with a child." Strindberg's claims that he was a seer were not unwarranted. In July 1897 Frida was alone and unhappy, *and* awaiting the birth of an illegitimate child.

WEDEKIND'S ATTACHMENT TO Frida was his first liaison with a woman of his own class, albeit a woman who, by virtue of divorce, was no longer subject to its restrictions—paternal or otherwise. Frida was young, appealing, sexually available, and, if no longer innocent, not yet a *femme du monde*. And she was well connected with the theater world Wedekind was anxious to break into.

Although he was kept busy by *Simplicissimus*, Munich proved less hospitable to his work than he had expected. The theaters there were either sponsored by the ducal court or dedicated to popular entertainment, and each had its own rigidly specified repertoire.[36] When even a new theatrical enterprise refused to continue with contemporary fare after the failure of plays by Halbe and Gerhart Hauptmann, Wedekind decided to try his luck elsewhere. In late 1896, he left for Berlin, with Frida at his side.

For Frida it was a frighteningly familiar second act. Not only was she returning to the German capital with another poverty-stricken playwright unable to overcome resistance to his controversial plays, but also she was pregnant. When she had discovered her first pregnancy, by Strindberg, two years earlier, she knew it meant financial disaster. There seemed to be no solution but abortion, and it was only at the last minute that she had decided against it. Carrying Wedekind's child put her in an even more precarious position. She could not marry immediately, since the annulment of her union with Strindberg was not yet official, and what little extra money she made was sent to Dornach for Kerstin. There is no evidence that Wedekind convinced her to keep the child, but during that winter and early spring there were plans for marriage. Frida was introduced as his bride, and the prospect of a Strindberg/Wedekind union was common gossip in Munich.

After arriving in Berlin in January, Wedekind wrote enthusiastically to his friend the composer Richard Weinhöppel, of the exciting possibilities his alliance with Frida seemed to promise.

> *From the moment I stepped on the platform of the Anhalter Bahnhof in Berlin, I really felt new life in me and today I am a new man. Dear good Frida. A big heart is really no small thing. I may have to change my whole outlook. Eh bien—I have twice as much faith in the success of my trip. If someone can lighten the hundred visits required for such a result it is Frida. If someone can mint pure gold from the ten years of my work it is Frida.*[37]

A friend of Wedekind's seeing "the beautiful Frida Strindberg" on his arm in Berlin noted the advantages for the playwright. In a letter written in February Wedekind referred to Frida as his fiancée, but by April he was sending billet-doux to another woman and disingenuously writing "You can see . . . that I'm playing a double game—but which of us doesn't?"[38]

Frida returned to Munich in the spring. By June the couple no longer seemed to be in touch, and in July Wedekind wrote to a friend that he had never taken their relationship seriously. He had sympathy for Frida's plight, took some of the blame, but saw no way to stand by her.

The threat of entanglement was one of the themes explored by Wedekind in *Der Kammersänger* (*The Chamber Singer*), a play written the summer Frida was expecting her child. Gerardo, the singer of the title, is the kind of professional success Wedekind dreamed of being, but he also possesses the "brutal intelligence" with which Wedekind knew he was pursuing his own goals. In his hotel room, departing for his next engagement, Gerardo is accosted by Helena, a married woman and a "dazzling beauty" with whom he has conducted an affair. She tells him he must take her with him. The arguments Gerardo musters to escape alone do not convince her and, melodramatically, she pulls a revolver from her muff and shoots herself. With this mad gesture she succeeds in derailing Gerardo's career.[39]

On August 21, 1897, Frida's son by Wedekind was born in Munich and given the name Max Friedrich. "Max" was in gratitude to Max Halbe, who had been a supportive friend through the hard time after Wedekind's departure. By September, without having seen the child, Wedekind was living with his sister Erica, an opera singer, in Dresden. Writing to his mother from there, he assured her he was no longer connected to Frida. "First of all she isn't rich," he began. "Second, I am definitely not engaged, third, I am no longer involved with her at all. I would never marry her, nor she me. We had enough of each other."[40]

Frida had to make the difficult decision of how to present Max Friedrich to the world. With the advice of Max Bernstein, but without an official baptismal certificate, he was given the last name of Strindberg. By the letter of the law a child born within nine months of a divorce—and Frida's marriage was annulled only in May 1897—could still be considered a child of that marriage. She believed she was saving her son from the stigma of illegitimacy, but his confused identity was to cause lifelong problems for mother and son.

Frida had not begun her affair with Wedekind as an act of bohemian rebellion. As she later wrote her son, she had assumed they would marry. It was only as a divorced unwed mother—an outsider in bourgeois society and released from its imprisoning issues of respectability—that Schwabing with its bohemian sexual mores, beckoned as a haven and alternative way of life. Like the experimental circles of Kristiania and Berlin, the bohemians of Schwabing were young artists and writers enjoying a few years of impoverished freedom before settling down to a bourgeois existence. According to Theodor Lessing, a journalist studying in Munich in the 1890s, it appeared as if all Germany were experiencing an "erotic awakening" as parents began allowing their daughters to go to the big cities to study. "In Munich," he observed, "they ended up in the dionysiac atmosphere of Schwabing and there they expended the passions that had been suppressed for centuries. . . ."

The queen of this community and a good friend of Frida's after Max Friedrich's birth was the Countess Franziska von Reventlow, whose strict upbringing in an ultraconservative aristocratic household in Lübeck had made a rebel of her at a very young age. Like Wedekind's fictitious Countess Russalka, it was her reading of Ibsen that encouraged her to reject the passivity with which other aristocratic daughters accepted their fate. "It seems to me that a new world of truth and freedom opened up for me when I became familiar with Ibsen," she wrote. "I want to go out into life and live in the name of these ideas, living at home my wings are cut."[41] After a brief marriage, she took up a bohemian existence in the tolerant atmosphere of Schwabing.

Franziska learned to survive with little money. Among other odd jobs, she worked as a translator from the French for Langen and as a contributor to *Simplicissimus*. It was her satire of the Last

Judgment, in which she depicted God as relying on a ruthless state prosecutor to determine the eternal destinies of mankind, that led to the magazine's first confiscation. She also wrote a series of light novels, the most famous of which was a roman à clef dissecting Schwabing society.

Together, Frida and Franziska experimented with new forms of existence. During the course of one severe financial pinch, Franziska even managed a dairy shop, where she and Frida assumed the roles of merry bohemian shopgirls, receiving deliveries at four in the morning and ladling out the milk to their Schwabing neighbors. As long as the establishment was in existence, it was the place to go for a "milk cure."[42]

In Franziska, Frida had before her an example of a woman willing to take all the risks of bohemian life. Her friend refused to marry or take on any relationship demanding fidelity. In her letters and diaries, she acknowledged her desire and need to experiment widely with a variety of lovers. She did not defy convention for its own sake, she wrote one of them, but only to live according to her own needs. "There are few who want to be that kind of lover," she told him, "because I do not know constancy, only lust, desire, and retreat. It may appear that I make sport with those who inspire those feelings, but these three emotions have their sport with me."[43]

Franziska also had an illegitimate child, but her response to his birth differed from Frida's. She insisted the boy was to be hers alone, refused to name the father, and was determined to bring him up herself. When her friend the poet Rainer Maria Rilke, received a photograph of her clothed in a white gown and holding her newborn child, he wrote her that she had made a poem of her life. Who was to pay for that poem was another matter. Enthusiastic as the men might be about the erotic daring of these rebellious aristocrats, upper-class divorcées, artists and actresses, most did not recognize that sexual freedom demanded other forms of equality as well. Without the protection of a permanent partner and often with the burden of an illegitimate child, a sexually emancipated woman had to fend for herself financially and was easily exploited. As the main translator from the French for Albert Langen, Franziska was responsible for eight books in 1898 alone, besides contributing cartoon captions and pieces for *Simplicissimus.* Many of her translations were best-sellers. And yet she was continually hounded by creditors and forced to take on menial jobs she hated.

Frida could not follow Franziska's example in so decisively rejecting society. There was one crucial difference between the two women that could not be overcome. The rebellious countess was an aristocrat. No matter how outrageous her behavior, or how complete her break with her family, she would never lose the status of her class. It gave her a freedom her friend could not claim. Frida, although estranged from her father, depended on him for economic survival. And she suffered from her awareness that her fall from grace reflected on him. She was still the daughter of a newspaperman who lived in the public eye and had taught his daughters that there was no greater sin than to sully his name.

Frida remained in Munich, residing in a little lakeside house in the suburb of Tutzing, while Wedekind pursued theatrical possibilities elsewhere. His career took a gradual upturn in November, when he gave a reading in Leipzig and as a result was hired as secretary, actor, and director by Carl Heine, founder of the new Ibsen Theater. On February 25, 1898, the premiere performance of *Earth Spirit*—indeed, the first full performance of a Wedekind play—took place under its auspices.

Having gained confidence after traveling with the Ibsen Theater troupe, Wedekind was tempted to return to Munich in the spring of 1898. The director Georg Stollberg, who was forming a new repertory company committed to contemporary drama, had invited him to work as a director and actor. He also promised him a Munich production of *Earth Spirit* in October.

However, returning to Munich meant overcoming the disgrace of his abandonment of Frida, particularly in the eyes of the Porges family. With this in mind, Wedekind went to visit Frida immediately upon his return—seven months after the birth of their son. With cool detachment, he described his first view of the child in a letter to Carl Heine's wife, Beate, in Leipzig. "His mother undressed him on the couch and presented him with the same pride a jeweler makes as he brings out the wares in his cases. At the same time, her eyes looked fearfully at my lips, in case I had something to complain of. Frankly, I found nothing."[44]

By July, he was describing a new intimacy, writing to Beate that he had gone to Tutzing on his birthday to have lunch with "my little boy . . . in the circle of my family, if I am allowed to put it that way." His attentive behavior, he added, had led to his forgiveness by most of Munich society—even the mother of Else Bernstein had sent him a greeting.

When Beate Heine inquired further into this sudden flowering of a family instinct, Wedekind was more candid, admitting there was no hope of marriage between two people so ill suited. He was keeping up the appearance of reconciliation only in order to repair his reputation.

For a whole year I was considered a non-person who had left his beloved in the lurch and, especially now, I cannot afford this sort of reproach.

The only good thing is the distance that lies between us, everything else is sad, or bleak, so that it will not be easy to hide it from the world. I have, by the way, no reason to blame anyone. The situation is like that of a play. If a play is properly thought out, no matter how bungled the execution, something can always be done with it. If it is falsely thought out from the start, then nothing will come of it.... With great care, circumspection, and consideration, I am steering my boat between the cliffs and the whirlpool. For the moment I can do nothing better, since I have so much else to do.[45]

Wedekind was no less honest about his motives with Frida, but what she focused on was that she could still be of use to him. The more cynically Wedekind treated her, the more of a martyr she became. His rejections only brought out new protestations of her concern. When Wedekind became ill and refused her attendance at his sickbed, she wrote Max Halbe of the extremes she was willing to go to keep her lover from distress.

If I ever made a sacrifice that he should give me credit for, it was not that I often ran around hungry, like an abandoned child, with my child in my body, in order to give him the last bite, nor everything else—the torment of all those years—but the moment he waved me from his sickbed and I, smiling and making some banal remarks so as not to upset him, left.[46]

But the very same letter revealed that Frida's pride, negated in her emotional dependence on Wedekind, survived in her passion for her work. Frida adopted a different tone when, with self-assurance, she asked to review one of Halbe's plays and proudly told him she had received a commission from a French paper to write a series of articles on theater outside France.

Wedekind's ambivalence and Frida's torment ended on October 29, 1898, the night of the Munich premiere of *Earth Spirit*. The production was not a success; the curtain came down to jeers and catcalls. As Wedekind emerged from the theater, a lawyer was waiting to warn him of his imminent arrest. He was not to be apprehended for the sexual content of his play, but for an insult to Kaiser Wilhelm II that had appeared in *Simplicissimus.* In its third year, the magazine had grown increasingly blatant in its social and political criticism. Several issues had been confiscated in Austria or were refused sale in Prussian railway stations. The restrictions themselves then became the butt of jokes. A cartoon depicted Austrian soldiers slashing *Simplicissimus* posters in a frenzy while, unnoticed, a little red bulldog (in its first appearance as the magazine's mascot) watered their well-tailored trousers. When the weekly was removed from the kiosks in Prussian railway stations, Langen launched a questionnaire asking what the purpose of the railroads were. "Do we buy a ticket to get from place to place," it inquired, "or does the railway system watch out for our mental health while traveling?"[47]

Making light of the state visit of the Kaiser to Palestine in one of the autumn issues of 1898 had more serious consequences. Accused of lèse-majesté and threatened with incarceration were the *Simplicissimus* cartoonist who had made fun of the Kaiser's mission; Wedekind, who had satirized the monarch's posturing; and Langen, as the owner of the offending publication. Wedekind, at least, had taken the precaution of publishing his poem under a pseudonym, but the manuscript, which Langen had promised to destroy, was found on the *Simplicissimus* premises during a police search.

Wedekind had no choice but to leave Germany immediately. And yet the *Bürgerschreck* could not depart without celebrating the memorable night in which his two literary personas—scandalous playwright and provocative poet—were momentarily joined. He drank the night away with friends and in the early-morning hours, accompanied by Langen's deputy editor and the ever devoted

Frida, made his way to the railway station and departed for Switzerland. Frida was left behind to send on the baggage and take care of Max Friedrich. She was also to look after Wedekind's brother Donald, who, talented though he was in writing and music, lacked the ambition of his older sibling. In 1895, he had also begun writing for *Simplicissimus* and translating for Langen. With his brother's departure, Donald briefly took over his job as Stollberg's director. Soon he was also replacing him at Frida's side.

WHILE FRIDA'S DISASTROUS relationship with Wedekind was coming to a close, Strindberg was living in the Swedish university town of Lund, after a break of nine months in Paris. Throughout this time, he wrestled with the memories of their courtship, their short-lived marriage, and the intrigues of her family, in the two autobiographical novels, *Inferno* and *The Cloister*, and three plays, *To Damascus I* and *II* and *Advent*.

In reanimating the past, Strindberg was exploring his own destructive ambivalence and in each of the re-creations of the crucial years with Frida, he came around to some recognition of his own culpability. At the end of *Inferno*, the work written closest in time to the experiences it relates, he blames himself for the marital tragedy. "Which of us was responsible for the rupture? I was, I who had murdered my own love and hers."[48]

The real Frida is hard to find in these efforts. Strindberg was scrutinizing himself in the various guises he gave his "Frida" character. He was not exploring her feelings about the miseries of a poverty-ridden pregnancy or the stress of an overbearing family after childbirth. They were irrelevant to a Swedenborgian self-examination intended to determine the precise nature of his own guilt. In the *Damascus* plays Strindberg gave these experiences a mythic dimension, transforming them into a spiritual pilgrimage in which his alter ego was chastened and enlightened. Their tone is one of confusion, questioning, doubt, and muted redemption.

In calling his alter ego The Stranger, in the first two parts of *To Damascus,* Strindberg indicated that he was incapable of entering the lives of others. When The Stranger says to The Lady, the character based on Frida, "Life is a toy to us writers," he is offering the key to his own existence. The Stranger continues: "I was born melancholy, yet I've never been able to take anything seriously, even my own sorrows. And there are moments when I doubt that my life has any more reality than the things I write."[49]

Inspired by his awakening love for Harriet Bosse, Strindberg drew on his memories of Frida for the last time in 1901. Since the first intimation that he was attracted to the actress occurred while she was rehearsing the role of The Lady in *To Damascus I,* he was driven to write a third part of the play, one that would deal with the temptation to love once more. In the first act of *To Damascus III,* The Lady is still reminiscent of Frida, but in the second she has obviously metamorphosed into Harriet. The Stranger greets her by saying, "Are you here again? The same and not the same. You have become as beautiful, as beautiful as the first time when I asked you, may I be your friend. . . . But why did you kiss me then, why did you have to?"[50]

The most delightful glimpse of Frida as Strindberg remembered her can be found in the advice he first gave to Harriet about playing The Lady. "I had imagined the character as a little lighter," he suggested, "with hints of mischief and more outgoing. A little of Puck!"[51]

6

Cads and Cabarets

The intervention of the German justice system had made the break with Wedekind definitive, and Frida's feelings for his younger brother, Donald, a troubled young man still finding his way, had been more maternal than passionate. A year after Wedekind left Munich, she decided to give up the little house in Tutzing where she had lived during Max Friedrich's infancy, send the child to join his half-sister in Dornach, and look for further possibilities of making a living.

Frida was only twenty-seven, and her prospects now uncannily mirrored those of Sudermann's Magda. Like his heroine, she had become "the kind of creature that stumbles around the world, unprotected, like a man, with only her hands to rely on for work. . . ." Her first step was a brief trip to London in late 1899 to revive the contacts she had originally cultivated for Strindberg. It was a good beginning. By renewing her acquaintance with William Heinemann, she became his agent for the German editions of Heinemann books.

From London she gratefully answered a letter from Mitzi, revealing how precarious her existence had become.

I thank you from my heart for your letter. Even if I never see you again, it was a comfort to me to know that you, who, well into my life, I loved most on earth, is not my enemy. . . .

Next time I am in Vienna, I intend to find a lawyer: all the papers for the children have to be put in order. Every inheritance that comes my way during my lifetime or after my death must be given completely over to them. I don't want anything else in the world, except what I earn myself—but for the children everything that can protect them from a life such as mine. . . . I have done the children too much harm, particularly Kerstin, not to want to make up for it now—as much as I can.[1]

She confessed that these new resolutions regarding the children had been prompted by ill health, the discovery of a problem with her heart. "It does not mean that everything has to be over soon, only that everything could be over soon, and with my life, probably will be over soon." She asked Mitzi if she would intervene and ask Rudolf Weyr to be the children's guardian, should the worst come to pass.

Frida did not dwell on this troubling secret, which she begged Mitzi not to reveal to anyone, but went on to matters of business. Telling her sister of her contact with Heinemann, whom she called her best friend in England, she mentioned that two of his books would be perfect subjects for feuilletons. Would Mitzi write them under her own name if Frida sent her the material? This way the books would get publicity, Mitzi would earn some money, and Frida could begin to repay a long-standing debt, owed her sister since the impoverished years with Strindberg. She closed the letter with the sad acknowledgment that their communication had to be kept secret by family demand. "I told your husband in Vienna that I haven't seen you, that you want to know nothing about me; that you passed the severest judgment on me years ago."

Mitzi was ambivalent about the sister she had once viewed almost as her own child. After the disagreeable encounter with Strindberg in Mondsee and the drama of Frida's flight to Vienna with thoughts of an abortion, her involvement with the troubled couple had lessened considerably. In 1894, when Frida was waiting out her pregnancy in Dornach, Mitzi wrote dismissively to a friend about the fate of women intent on marrying "geniuses." For a long time, she had disagreed with many aspects of Frida's life, she explained, and had decided it was useless to give unheeded advice.[2]

Although Mitzi had reopened the correspondence with Frida, she had no choice about following her father's lead in minimizing the contact. She had remained close to Friedrich Uhl, also wrote for his paper, and often accompanied him to the theater. But there was a deeper reason for keeping her distance from Frida: Mitzi did not want to reveal that she was living on the edge of a precipice herself. Since 1898 she had been secretly separated from Rudolf Weyr.

While the good daughter was still caught in the trap of Uhl's overriding concern for respectability, Frida was free to improvise her new existence. In London she ran into the Danish writer Holger Drachmann, who had been a member of the *Schwarze Ferkel* circle in Berlin, and his friend Conrad Pineus, a Swedish art collector and dealer. By this time Frida must have devised a public persona that made a virtue of her anomalous position—a middle-class woman traveling alone and seeking work. Her manner impressed Pineus. He wrote in his diary, "A most remarkable lady. If I say that her views were the opposite of the ordinary bourgeois, I have certainly not said too much." Drachmann was equally admiring, Pineus noted, and the two gentlemen spent a great deal of time squiring Frida around London.[3]

It was an excellent moment to have reencountered Drachmann, since Frida was going from London to Berlin for the debut of German cabaret. Drachmann had been the first to urge his fellow-writers in Denmark and Germany to follow the example of the French in founding their own ventures of this kind. Since the mid-1880s, the *Chat Noir,* the pioneering cabaret, founded by the failed art student Rudolf Salis in Montmartre, had been one of the great attractions for foreigners in Paris.

At that time Montmartre was on the outskirts of Paris. Behind the houses on its narrow, winding streets, inhabitants still kept pigs and chickens. Initially the *Chat Noir* differed little from a number of small taverns in the neighborhood, until Salis invited the *Hydropathes*—a group of poets and musicians who met regularly for joint entertainments—to assemble there. The local patrons, including a residential criminal fringe of petty thieves, pimps, and their women, supplied a certain frisson for the newcomers, and soon the explosive combination of the raffish clientele and the irreverent poets began to attract an audience.[4]

The poets and musicians transformed the *chanson,* which had its roots in medieval songs of social comment, into an expressive medium for relating dark tales of urban life. They impersonated the inhabitants of the underworld, sang the laments of a prostitute, imagined the vengeful dreams of a pimp and the thoughts of a criminal condemned to die. The artists who patronized the tavern took the old tradition of shadow puppets—silhouetted figures manipulated behind a lighted screen—and transformed it into a cinemalike medium so sophisticated and expressive that it was capable of presenting such elaborate performances as Caran d'Ache's *L'Epopée* (*The Epic*), a narrative of Napoleon's campaigns presented in two acts and fifty tableaux.[5]

Amateur recitals gradually evolved into more structured programs of songs, monologues, and shadow plays, but the emphasis on informality and improvisation remained. Salis played *conférencier,* or master of ceremonies, and introduced the mix of spontaneity, provocation, and topicality that would come to define cabaret. He claimed to find his material while sneaking "around during the day, the way cats do on the roofs at night," and promised his audience to mock and unmask all he discovered.[6]

Strindberg was so entranced by the cabaret in the summer of 1894 that he suggested to his friend Littmanson that they start a *Chat Noir* of their own. In a letter to Frida he described how he would paint the walls, put on one of his pieces as a shadow play, and perform on his guitar.[7] Wedekind, who had always been attracted to circuses and vaudeville shows, saw new possibilities for theater in the cabaret's sophisticated recasting of popular genres. When he returned to Germany from his years in Paris, he regaled Frida and their friends in Munich with tales of the exciting performances he had seen in French cabarets. His descriptions fell on fertile ground in Munich, a city of literary entrepreneurs eager to find a way around censorship and officially sponsored culture. Inspired by Wedekind, one of the most enterprising of these amateur impresarios, Otto Julius Bierbaum, a poet and former editor of the *Freie Bühne*, took up the cause of cabaret in two books. In the novel *Stilpe,* written in 1897, the eponymous hero dreams of founding a cabaret where "art, [now] a bright slightly glistening web in a corner of life, could be thrown like a golden net over all people. . . ."[8] Three years later, Bierbaum adopted a more practical approach in his introduction to the anthology *Deutsche Chansons.* The collection was intended to demonstrate that the seeds for German cabaret already existed in the poems of nine of his contemporaries as well as in his own. "Applied lyrics" was the term he invented to justify the cross-fertilization of two cultures—literary and popular—long held to be separate spheres in Germany. "Today's urban man has cabaret nerves," he asserted, and added, prophetically, that if artists wanted to have an effect on life, they would have to negotiate with popular culture.[9]

Bierbaum's book was an instant best-seller. It also convinced one of its contributors, the Baron Ernst von Wolzogen, a composer of light verse and plays—and a good friend of Frida's from Schwabing—that the time had come to move from theory to reality. A group of investors in Berlin was ready to take the plunge, and all of Munich's literati, including Donald Wedekind and Frida, came to the capital to support the long-discussed experiment. Unfortunately, Wolzogen was the wrong pioneer.

French cabaret depended on the intimate connection between performers and audience. The democratic mix of Montmartre—artists and writers mingling with the urban poor amid middle- and upper-class onlookers—was the key to its style. Wolzogen, although planning to perform as the master of ceremonies, wanted to avoid direct intimacy with the audience. He named his cabaret experiment *Buntes Theater* (Colorful Theater), but added the term *Überbrettl* (Above the Boards) to indicate a variety show with superior fare. Looking back, he admitted that, as an aristocrat, he wanted to avoid contact with the masses.[10]

The first night, January 18, 1901, was a formal occasion, with women in evening dress and men in top hats. Wolzogen dressed with equal elegance and played the host in a setting resembling an early-nineteenth-century salon. Unlike the amateur participants at the *Chat Noir,* members of Wolzogen's troupe were primarily professional actors and singers. They lacked the spontaneity of the artist-performer. To show that he was aware of this departure from the French model, he gave a special introduction to a number recited by the poet Hanns Heinz Ewers. Unfortunately, the subject of the verses the live artist chose to recite—a dung beetle ennobled by the acquisition of money—hardly seemed to justify

Wolzogen's overture. Nevertheless, the recitation brought in something missing from the rest of the evening—scandal—and Wolzogen was grateful. "The earthshaking evening arrived," he wrote later, "in which Hanns Heinz Ewers openly said '*popo*' on my little stage at the Alexanderplatz! Berlin was carried away and the slim Rhinelander, covered with dueling scars, was crowned lion-king of the zoo!"[11] The young poet with the dubious distinction of using the colloquial term for derrière on stage for the first time was also Frida's latest lover. Wolzogen was dismayed and warned Frida that behind Ewers's façade of "the completely harmless young man. . . . there hid a very dangerous rascal," but to no avail.[12]

Ewers, who was the same age as Frida, had a reputation for scandalous behavior even before his uncensored recitation at the *Buntes Theater.* Indeed, it may have been this aspect of his history, rather than his somewhat meager poetic accomplishments, that prompted Wolzogen to invite him to join the cabaret. The scars on Ewers's face suggested participation in the aristocratic dueling fraternities at the university in which he had studied law, but, in fact, his lack of fencing skill had never gained him full membership. His apprenticeship as a junior lawyer proved equally unsuccessful: he was dismissed in 1897 after being sentenced to a month's incarceration for swindling members of a spiritualist circle. During these turbulent years he had liaisons with several women, and the erotic poems he published explicitly describing these encounters led to his being fined for circulating lewd literature. A heavy smoker and dedicated drinker, he also experimented with hashish and opium. Giving his reputation yet another twist was his affiliation with the periodical *Der Eigene,* advertised as "the world's first homosexual periodical."[13]

After her intimacy with Wedekind, Frida was not intimidated by Ewers's desire to shock and provoke. He appealed to her as a dynamic presence at the center of the new cabaret experiment. Their affair lasted only a few months, but during that time Frida was caught up in the intrigues, gossip, and free living of a theatrical entourage.

Wolzogen, who appreciated Frida's warmth and Viennese charm, was disturbed by what he saw as her gypsy existence, motivated by "literary-erotic curiosity." Unlike the liberal Pineus in London, who had admired her courage in improvising an independent way of life with little precedent, Wolzogen viewed her current existence as unwholesome and inappropriate. As for her affair with Ewers, he saw it as a symptom of her destructive obsession with "the werewolves of literature."[14]

But in the end, Ewers did Wolzogen more harm than he did to Frida. When a part of the troupe went on tour, Ewers was left in charge of those remaining in Berlin. On Wolzogen's return, Ewers took this rump cast and left to create a competitive venture. His was not the only one. Within the year, less ambitious but more authentic cabarets were springing up all over the city in bars and taverns, and both Ewers, reciting his poems, and Donald Wedekind, performing his brother's songs, were among the most active participants in such cabarets as Hungry Pegasus, the Silver Punch Bowl, and Seventh Heaven. By the end of 1901, more than forty requests had been received by the Berlin municipality for permission to open a cabaret.[15]

Contributing to the excitement, only a few months after the opening of Wolzogen's venture, was the debut of a cabaret much closer to the French style. What distinguished the *Elf Scharfrichter* (Eleven Executioners) in Munich from Wolzogen's undertaking were the amateur performers—artists, writers, musicians, and a lawyer—and the biting, mordant tone of the entertainment. Each night, the entire group—masked, robed in red, and carrying the ax of their purported trade—entered in procession singing of their intention to put the philistine on the block. Wedekind, who had returned to Munich after serving his prison sentence in a military fortress, joined the *Scharfrichter* troupe a few weeks after the first night and was soon the most popular German *chansonnier.* Playing the guitar, he sang songs based on his own erotic and perverse poems in a harsh, deadpan style that later inspired Bertolt Brecht.[16]

The first two years were the most intense and exciting for the cabarets in Berlin and Munich, and there were many exchanges among the founders, writers, and performers. Wedekind made guest appearances at Wolzogen's *Überbrettl,* Bierbaum wrote material for the cabarets in both cities, and Donald Wedekind promoted his brother's songs in smaller venues in Berlin. Frida had ties to all the participants during this time and was a member of the bohemia spawned by the cabarets. After performances, the actors, writers, musicians, and their entourage retreated to the Café des Westens on the Kurfurstendamm, where discussions went on till dawn.

Although it was Wolzogen who had invited Ewers to join in the planning for the *Buntes Theater* in 1900, and thus launched his career as a cabaret performer, Ewers continued to treat his supporter badly. After having betrayed him by defecting with some of his actors, Ewers continued to advertise this mutinous troupe as the *Buntes Theater.* When Wolzogen protested, Ewers conducted an ugly press campaign, accusing his former patron of attempting to quash competition, before he finally agreed to drop the name. Ewers's defection and double-dealing, the growing number of imitators of his pioneering enterprise, and Wolzogen's inability to keep his expenses down finally led to the disbanding of the *Buntes Theater* in May of 1902. Soon after, Ewers also left Berlin. With the major players of the cabaret scene taking their leave, Frida followed suit and returned to Dornach, to renew ties with her children after a long absence.

During the years in Berlin, Frida had led an intemperate life, unencumbered by children or a judgmental mate. She returned to Dornach exhausted, dissatisfied, and filled with self-reproach. To Kerstin, who had not seen her mother in several years, she appeared a stranger—a distracted, impatient woman with untidy hair and ink stains on her fingers. When Frida laid eyes on her eight-year-old daughter, she was shaken by her close resemblance to Strindberg. The visit was not a success, but the ice had been broken, and when Frida returned at Christmas, a chance discovery brought Strindberg nearer.

Rummaging through old possessions in the attic of the *Häusel,* Frida came upon Strindberg's letters to Maria Uhl. For the first time she understood how much her mother had concealed from her. In the letters she found a changed man, one more tempered, forgiving; a man who was willing to chide her mother for gloating self-righteously at her daughter's misfortunes. When Frida confronted Maria Uhl with her find, her mother desperately tried to make amends by giving Frida the letters to keep, but her daughter never forgave the betrayal.

As for Strindberg, Frida was so overwhelmed to discover he had been anxious about her that she forgave him almost everything. Finding the letters at this disheartened moment in her life was an unexpected chance to make her own peace with the past. She was moved to write her former husband a candid and emotional summation of all that had happened since their separation. It was her first letter to him in five years.

August, I saw you the last time in this life in Paris (8 years ago!) as the trees in the Luxembourg turned gold. . . .

For five years I thought I had been banned from your heart and your life. And for that reason I considered myself cursed, hated—lost, lost. To discover that you loved me, offered me forgiveness, reconciliation . . . not to have known that and to discover it now . . .

What an agony!

What a comfort!

I left you eight years ago, but I was not at fault. I would have come back to you. Your letters made me believe I was despised. I revolted—family, friends, all of them urged me to separate from you. You weren't there. Oh, had you come back, had I seen you. But I was alone in my bitterness. . . .

She knew he was married, she continued, and loved another. Since their destinies were no longer linked, she could write the "naked truth" without fear of oppressing him. She confessed that "loneliness, life, and youth" had left her the mother of "a poor little orphaned boy." The more she apologized for her own actions, the more she idealized Strindberg. In the course of the letter he was transformed from the husband who had abandoned her into the only great and noble creature she had met in her miserable life. "I bless you that you are the father of my child," she wrote. "Past and future, I owe to you. There is no one else in the world I can thank for an hour of pure joy."

In reading of Strindberg's attachment to Kerstin, Frida was led to believe she could share her worries about the child's future. She revealed the secret of her own medical problem and begged Strindberg to stay in touch with Kerstin. "She has your strength, your brain, your beauty, and a little bit of the good heart I had once," she told him, and added that she had taught Kerstin to love him and had promised her that her father would not forget her.

By the end of the letter Frida had come so far in her self-abnegation that she conceded to Strindberg that he had, indeed, foreseen the wanton woman she now believed she had become.

August, death would be sweet for me if it could expiate my life. But I was not common. I did not leave you to sell myself as you said. I never sold myself: No. No. I gave and I gave more than I had the right to give. And I see more, even more. You did me wrong and yet you were right. What wasn't true before, happened. Now I ask myself if you saw it, why did I not see it myself? Is it possible that it was already true and only my nerves were too coarse to recognize it?[17]

Frida was writing to Strindberg after four years of bohemian existence following Wedekind's departure. They were difficult years, far removed from the troubled, yet essentially innocent time of her marriage, when she had been young and hopeful and had loved her husband and believed herself loved in return. By exonerating Strindberg and blaming herself, she could erase the unacceptable reality that his rejection of her, which had brought her to her present plight, had been irrational and beyond her control. The new scenario, with its glorified image of her former husband, was her own creation, but it was a vision she could call upon for sustenance when necessary in the years to come.

7

Lost Bacchante

MITZI WEYR'S DEATH FROM a blood clot after a secret abortion took Frida back to Vienna in April 1903. She returned to comfort her father, and he, in turn, aging and in forced retirement, welcomed the reconciliation.[1]

Friedrich Uhl, so protective of his status in Vienna from his daughters' turbulent lives, had been forced out of his job by an oversight. He had failed to catch a skeptical phrase in a Christmas article published in 1899 referring to the birth in Bethlehem as "a pious legend." In earlier days this formulation would scarcely have caused a ripple, but now it fed into the new imperial politics. After the decimation of the Habsburg family by suicide, assassination, and the firing squad, the aging Franz Josef was saddled with the conservative and pious Crown Prince Franz Ferdinand as his successor. Uhl's subtle editing, honed to the emperor's requirements throughout many years, may not have been to the crown prince's liking. When a highly placed member of the clergy complained about the Yuletide piece, the crown prince asked the emperor to retire his faithful editor of thirty years, and the old ruler, unwilling to battle his harsh nephew on this issue, consented.

Uhl, seventy-five, left his post reluctantly, though he continued as the paper's chief drama critic. When a fellow-journalist arrived to offer condolences on Mitzi's death, he found Uhl sitting in his dressing gown in his bachelor quarters reading the day's theater news as usual. "You see this is how I am," he told his visitor, who found it difficult to reconcile Uhl's stoicism with his devotion to a daughter he had appeared to love as much as he loved anyone.[2]

Frida's irregular life had contributed to her estrangement from Mitzi, but it was Uhl who had insisted his older daughter have limited contact with her outcast sister. Mitzi, too, had been the victim of Uhl's obsessive fear of scandal. In a letter to a friend, Mitzi's husband had called his wife's death "the sacrifice of a mad father."[3] Was he referring to the pressure on Mitzi to keep the failure of her marriage secret, just as Uhl had done all these years? Was the reconciliation with Frida an implicit acknowledgment of his role in the loss of Mitzi? Whatever the reason, Frida had to live with the terrible irony that Mitzi's death was the price of her return to her father's good graces, her hometown, and a more secure position in society than she had enjoyed in years.

Despite his age, Friedrich Uhl was still very much in the center of Vienna's theatrical life. Early in his career as a drama critic, he had stressed the importance of staying in touch with the next generation. True to his word, he became a supporter of Arthur Schnitzler, Vienna's most controversial young playwright in the 1890s, declaring him "a great talent." Schnitzler often called upon Uhl for comments on the drafts of his plays, and, in a diary entry, recorded meeting Frida soon after she arrived in Vienna. "Was at Uhl's, whose daughter has just died. He was with Frida Strindberg, his other daughter, and he embraced me."[4]

By introducing Frida to Schnitzler, Uhl put her in touch with the writers and poets of her generation who had brought a distinctly Austrian style to maturity. In the early 1890s, Hermann

Bahr, the journalist who had written the fateful premature announcement of Frida's engagement, had become the mentor and promoter of a group of young writers later to be labeled *Jung Wien* (Young Vienna). They met regularly in the Café Griensteidl, a *Kaffeehaus* near the Imperial Palace. Bahr, instead of recommending the naturalist style flowering in Germany, urged his compatriots to look beyond the realities of the external world to the manner in which they were apprehended. "The truth," Bahr explained, "is what each person senses it to be." Encouraged by these ideas, *Jung Wien* focused on emotional and sensual responses to life. Some members of the circle concentrated on the aesthetic heightening of experience, others on the effect of nostalgia, while Schnitzler explored the conventions masking society's sexual games.

Among those participating in the discussions with Bahr was the journalist Karl Kraus, who, although in his early twenties, had already emerged as a sharp and demanding cultural critic. Unlike the other habitués of the Griensteidl, Kraus was bent on reform. When the Griensteidl was razed in 1896, Kraus published a critical pamphlet titled *Demolished Literature*. He declared the work of *Jung Wien* to be made up of ". . . premature wisdom, megalomania, provincial girl, cravat, mannerism, false dative, monocle, and secret nerves."[5]

The response of the former Griensteidlers was not as subtle as their prose. In a diary entry, Arthur Schnitzler noted: "Yesterday evening in the *Kaffeehaus,* Salten [a writer who had been the subject of some particularly withering comments] gave the little Kraus [as Schnitzler always referred to him] a smack, which was greeted with satisfaction on all sides."[6]

Thereafter the Viennese literary landscape could be said to be divided into two camps. Both sensed a malaise beneath the charming surface of Austrian life. Those allied to Kraus were idealists who believed in a cure, while those associated with Schnitzler were skeptics with little optimism about, but considerable insight into, the human condition.

For most of the 1890s, Austrian authors had no choice but to publish with German firms, since ambitious literary houses such as those begun by Langen and Fischer did not exist in Austria. By 1899, however, the lively developments in literature had inspired a local publishing industry. The modest but prescient Wiener Verlag was founded to publish the works of members of *Jung Wien*, as well as foreign writers. Frida, with her contacts to Heinemann and Langen, was soon a valuable colleague, although she had no permanent home in Vienna. In order to be closer to the children, and because it was less expensive, she commuted from Amstetten, across the river from Dornach, to the Hotel Tegethoff on the Johannesgasse whenever she needed to meet people in town.

In the ten years during which Frida's life had taken her from Berlin to Munich and back to Vienna, she had witnessed firsthand the drastic effects of censorship. It had driven Strindberg into exile and Wedekind to prison. Now she began to work with a publishing house that challenged government restrictions. Sixteen years after its suppression in Norway, Wiener Verlag issued a German edition of Hans Jaeger's *Kristiania Bohème*. "Times have changed," the introduction read. "The authorities now know how to differentiate the tone of truth and art from that of mere sensation and realize that an artist is allowed to speak of everything that oppresses himself and others." The publisher's optimism was justified; the book was not censored.

Two years later in 1903, Wiener Verlag's editor, Fritz Freund, published Schnitzler's controversial one-act play *Reigen* (*Carousel*) after Fischer, Schnitzler's regular publisher, had refused to take the chance in Germany. In ten scenes Schnitzler depicts a round of sexual encounters between recognizable types in Viennese society (The Count, The Sweet Girl, The Husband, and so on), beginning and ending with the same prostitute. The sexual strategies vary with class and station but, with the exception of the prostitute, all involve pretense or betrayal. An Austrian newspaper declared *Carousel*'s ten "acts of conception" shameless, even though they were indicated on the page only by a dotted line, but the book was not seized. When the edition sold out, Wiener Verlag gained the wherewithal for more ambitious ventures.

Soon Freund was publishing elegant editions of other members of *Jung Wien* and launching a Library of Authors in Translation. It was under the aegis of this series that Frida collaborated with Freund on his most ambitious project: the publication of the works of Oscar Wilde, in ten volumes, the first complete edition in German.

Two years after Wilde's death in 1900, his estate was heavily in debt, and the memory of his disgrace was still powerful enough in England to deter publishers and theater managers from printing or producing his work. Under this pressure, Robert Ross, his dedicated executor, put the copyrights in sufficient order to enable publication abroad. Frida accompanied Freund to London in 1904 to negotiate with Ross, and subsequently translated two of the edition's key volumes—Wilde's *Salomé* and *The House of Pomegranates.*

Frida's advice on publishing was also sought by young writers, including the poet and essayist Richard Schaukal, who had just moved to the city. Her letters to him are filled with insights and maternal concern. She asks if she can introduce him to Wiener Verlag and Sam Fischer. "Publishers," she tells him "are a very unaesthetic necessity of existence." Wiener Verlag, she says, has ambition, and will get the best authors, but she warns Schaukal to negotiate carefully. She sympathizes with the poverty of the poet and stresses her familiarity with it. "It is the same misery I observed in the two most important people that crossed my path."

One of the projects she proposed to Schaukal was an anthology of art and literature in memory of a young editor who had died suddenly in February 1905. The book would be to benefit his widow—the kind of mission that always aroused Frida's fervor. "There is so much misery in the world that one cannot help, that it is good to have an opportunity where one can," she wrote him.[7]

She also formed a productive alliance with Karl Kraus. After the fracas at the Griensteidl, he had spent a few years working as a freelance critic and editor, but soon chafed under the unspoken self-censorship with which journalists protected one another. With the fanaticism of the young (he was twenty-four) and the financial assistance of his family, he founded his own outspoken publication, *Die Fackel* (*The Torch*) in 1899.

The first issues were as hard-hitting and unforgiving as he had promised and attempts to silence him ranged from an actual physical attack to threatening letters, lawsuits, and, perhaps most devastating, deliberate disregard in the press. After the first quarter, he proudly published the statistics: "Anonymous slanderous letters, 236, anonymous threatening letters, 83, physical attacks, 1."[8] Since his research was thorough, his style a marvel of lucidity, and his aphorisms eminently quotable, he proved himself a man to be reckoned with as he exposed corruption in every aspect of society, most particularly among his fellow journalists. He soon became one of the dominant figures in Vienna's cultural life, and everyone from students to bureaucrats could be seen reading the pamphlet with the bright red cover, if only to discover who or what had been attacked.

Kraus and Frida were intrigued by each other. Kraus, a great admirer of Strindberg and Wedekind, was curious about her past, whereas Frida was attracted to the maverick and provocateur occupying the opposite end of the journalistic spectrum from Friedrich Uhl. Although Kraus, like so many men of his generation, publicly derided women with intellectual ambition, Frida's insights and experience were useful to him. She introduced him to her Scandinavian acquaintances, including Holger Drachmann, assisted him with material for *Die Fackel,* and supported the literary figures he admired.[9]

It was at Frida's urging that Kraus brought Wedekind to Vienna at a decisive moment in his life. In 1904, the first edition of *Pandora's Box,* the other half of Wedekind's *Lulu* tragedy, was published in Germany. It was confiscated immediately, and Wedekind and the publisher were accused of distributing lewd literature. Although the accusation was later rescinded, remaining copies of the book were destroyed. A private reading of the play in honor of Wedekind in Berlin inspired Frida, with Kraus's friend Robert Scheu, to suggest that a similar occasion be held under the auspices of *Die Fackel.*[10] She wrote to Kraus: "Scheu wants to dedicate an evening to 'The Box.' You should read, Hermann Bahr should speak." When Kraus questioned Frida's motives in this support of her ex-lover, she assured him that she had become "indifferent" to what had once gone on between them, but not to his work.[11]

Kraus, who had always been attracted to the theater and had attempted a career as an actor in the 1890s, not only was willing to support Wedekind, but also was inspired by Frida's suggestion to embark on a more ambitious homage than the one held in Germany: he would organize a private performance of the play with a group of actors and amateurs. He asked Wedekind to play Jack the Ripper and reserved for himself the small role of the exotic prince, Kungu Poti, one of Lulu's last clients; Tilly Newes, a nineteen-year-old Austrian actress, played Lulu. The night before the performance at Vienna's Trianon Theater on May 29, 1905, Frida wrote an encouraging letter to the youthful Tilly, calling her a "unique Lulu" and including a talisman as a token gesture of their shared enthusiasm for the play.[12]

The evening was a great success. As Wedekind wrote later to Kraus: "The performance represents without a doubt one of the most important moments in the development of my literary profession." Tilly Newes also received a letter of thanks from the author: "I must tell you how very happy I feel that I was able to see you and get to know you. That the public would not have taken in my abhorrent piece with such patience without your clever and, at the same time, Madonna-like acting, I have not the slightest doubt."[13] Other actresses had played Lulu before, but Wedekind had never been entirely satisfied with their interpretation. In Tilly Newes, he found the Lulu he had been seeking—both innocent and seductive. Within a year they were married.

Another writer to benefit from Frida's friendship with Kraus was Peter Altenberg, a great favorite of *Die Fackel*'s editor. Altenberg, who had created various personas for himself—holy idiot, clown, outsider, weak and melancholy creature— lived in a hotel, but his real home was the *Kaffeehaus,* in which, according to one of his poems, he found solace for a variety of his existential dilemmas.

You have worries, a few of these, a few of those—to the Kaffeehaus
She can't for some reason, even a rather plausible reason, come to you—
to the Kaffeehaus
Your boots are torn—Kaffeehaus
You have a salary of 100 crowns and spent five hundred—Kaffeehaus

You are a bureaucrat and wanted to be a doctor—Kaffeehaus
Inside you are close to suicide—Kaffeehaus
You hate and have contempt for people but still can't do without them—Kaffeehaus
You have no credit anywhere anymore—Kaffeehaus[14]

Altenberg's gift for capturing the mix of skepticism and sentiment that flavored Viennese urban life made him one of the few writers admired by both *Jung Wien* and Kraus's circle. When Frida organized a meeting to set up a public subscription for this seemingly poverty-stricken bohemian, members from both camps arrived to give their support. The poet sat humbly in a corner, striking a pose befitting his beggarly status, until one of his more fanatic admirers suggested that financial assistance might diminish the charm of his poverty. Cursing his supporter, Altenberg leaped up and proceeded to enumerate his needs, which included "an American rocking chair, a pension, orange jam, bouillon soup and filets mignon." (When Altenberg died, in 1919, it was discovered that he had squirreled away a considerable fortune.)[15]

This hilarious incident provided a lively scene in *Das Wort* (*The Word*), a play about Altenberg discovered among Schnitzler's papers after his death. The piece included a character modeled on Frida, who was given the unflattering name of Frau Flatterer. Although Schnitzler intended the play to be a social satire, his view of Frau Flatterer reflected some of his own prejudices. "There is something even more insufferable than a male writer, and that is a woman plying the trade," Schnitzler wrote of his creation.

Frau Flatterer was not a highly individualized figure, but some of her traits were familiar. Schnitzler described her as a woman in her mid-thirties, rather voluptuous, with fine facial features and somewhat pompously but not tastelessly dressed. She is a writer from Berlin eager to learn all she can about Vienna. On meeting the Altenberg character in the play, she, like Frida, is filled with a desire to help. But it was not only as a good-hearted benefactor of poor poets that Schnitzler saw her persona. Frau Flatterer is also a sensualist, who asks if there are "orgies" in Vienna and informs her companions at the *Kaffeehaus* that she always carries a tiger skin and thyrsus in her baggage so as to be ready to appear as a bacchante at costume parties.[16]

Schnitzler's picture of Frida revealed her anomalous position among Vienna's writers and intellectuals. Even though both *Jung Wien* and Kraus's circle were part of a literary bohemia obsessed with eroticism, their attitudes toward women were highly codified. The professional women they appreciated were actors, singers, or dancers, women whose careers were traditionally associated with sexual availability. And as Schnitzler so eloquently delineated in *Carousel,* a sexually viable women fit into a distinct category. She was either a prostitute, a working girl, an ingenue, a married woman, or an actress. She was not a journalist and publishers' agent, an organizer of public events, a divorcée with an illegitimate child, or a woman who was candid about her experiences among the bohemians of Munich and Berlin.

Frida never knew of Schnitzler's play, but she was a witness to the press campaign launched by Kraus in 1903 in praise of the sensually liberated (but not socially emancipated) woman. His hand-picked supporters on this subject were none other than Strindberg and Wedekind, who, for the next few years, debated in print their attitudes toward women and sex, attitudes that had determined Frida's destiny.

The catalyst was *Geschlecht und Charakter* (*Sex and Character*), a thesis written by the philosophy student Otto Weininger, which caused a sensation when it was published in Vienna in June 1903.[17] A fellow-student, the writer Stefan Zweig, remembered Weininger as an unprepossessing young man who "always looked like he had come from a thirty-hour train ride, dirty, tired, rumpled. . . ." Zweig was curious to meet him after hearing of his success but the lack of ease in Weininger's shy, introverted glance, his bitter mouth, his somehow unpleasant physical presence put Zweig off. It was only later that he understood how much Weininger suffered from an inferiority complex, sexual confusion, and the torment of someone who believed himself depraved.[18]

In his six-hundred-page tome Weininger drew on several disciplines, from biology to philosophy, to confirm, shortly before Freud, that women's sexual drives were as strong as those of men. But being a man of his time, Weininger retreated from the conclusion to which his findings pointed: women, therefore, were no more to be condemned for their urges than men were. Instead he postulated a new scheme of differences between the sexes. According to him, women were not just sexual beings, but sexuality defined their existence. Unlike men, who were only intermittently aroused and, therefore, capable of monogamy, women were in a constant state of excitation and, therefore, by nature polygamous. The differences did not stop there. Where men were free, conscious, rational, logical, and moral, women were enslaved, irrational, and amoral, and any interest they might betray in a spiritual or an intellectual life was motivated by the desire to please a man. A woman was a type and not an individual. Despite such statements as "the phallus is a woman's fate" and "an inferior man is still far higher than the most superior woman," and, most blatantly, "a woman is nothing," the book was published to considerable acclaim, and Weininger received enthusiastic fan mail from two leading men of letters: Strindberg and Kraus.

Strindberg wrote to Weininger from Stockholm that he was relieved to see the problem of women solved.[19] To Emil Schering, his German translator, Strindberg also expressed his fascination with the book. "Dr. Otto Weininger in Vienna has sent me *Sex and Character*, a terrible book, one, however, that has probably solved the most difficult of all problems.... *Voilà un homme.*" Coming from a man who celebrated, rather than decried, the sexual woman, Kraus's response was more guarded. "An admirer of women confirms the arguments of your contempt for women with delight," he wrote the author.[20] Kraus and Strindberg were odd bedfellows. Weininger's theory suited Strindberg's view of women as innately inferior; Kraus delighted in the young writer's recognition of women's intrinsic sexuality. But both men agreed that an organic difference made it "unnatural" for a woman to aspire to a man's world.

On October 3, 1903, the twenty-four-year-old Weininger went to the house in Vienna where Beethoven had drawn his last breath, rented a room, and shot himself. In the wake of his suicide, the press implied that the author of *Sex and Character* must have been mentally disturbed. Kraus, who knew of Strindberg's enthusiasm for Weininger, called upon him to defend the deceased against the slander. Eight days after Weininger's death, Strindberg sent Schering a manuscript titled *"Idolatrie/Gynolatrie"* and asked him to translate it and send it on to the publisher of *Die Fackel*. "I consider it a holy obligation toward the dead," he wrote. "(And wish no payment.)" He notified Kraus that the piece was coming and added, "I would appreciate your placing a wreath on the grave of the recently killed thinker for me. (Ten crowns are included for this purpose.)"[21]

Strindberg's essay was the lead article in *Die Fackel* on October 17, 1903. It tried to explain why most men lacked Weininger's courage in openly acknowledging that woman was "a rudimentary man." Such an admission, he pointed out, would interfere with a man's erotic attraction to a woman. This was followed by the conundrum repeated in his letters to Frida: courtship leads a man to "worship" a woman and thus gives her the illusion of superiority. Even the man believes it during this phase. The unfortunate result is that once the natural order is reestablished, a woman's primary aim is to pull the man back to the artificial situation of his wooing.[22]

Strindberg's second contribution a month later was the poem *The Dutchman (Upon a View of Lilith)*, which had been published in Sweden in 1902. He asked Kraus to print the German translation as evidence that he had preceded Weininger in recognizing woman's purely physical nature. It was the same hymn of praise to a woman's body Strindberg had begun to write while on his honeymoon with Frida in Helgoland.[23]

When it came to championing female sensuality, however, Wedekind was the ally of choice for Kraus, who praised Lulu as the ideal woman and published Wedekind's lubricious verses. A stanza from his poem "Confession," which Kraus printed in December 1904, read:

> *Love—now that brings no happiness on earth*
> *Loving brings envy and dishonor*
> *To be made love to in heat, with strength, and often*
> *That is life, that is happiness.*[24]

Happiness continued to elude Frida. Even as she gained respect for her cultural ventures, her love life approached the absurd. When she first returned to her native city, she formed an attachment to the writer and poet Werner von Oestèren, the offspring of a German actress and her wealthy Hungarian lover. Born in Berlin in 1874, Von Oestèren grew up in Bohemia and was a friend of the youthful Rilke. When Frida met him, he was considered an important new representative of German-Bohemian literature, having already published an epic poem, a play, a book of verse, and a well-received satire. An amateur actor, he had been involved with the popular Austrian actress Adele Sandrock and for a brief period had gone on tour with her, playing Armand to her Lady of the Camellias.

Von Oestèren shared a luxurious Vienna apartment with his mother and sister. The critic Franz Servaes remembered seeing Frida there during this liaison and, although Servaes found her appealing, his offhand comments about her give a sense of what she was up against wherever she went.

Taking part [in these social occasions] was usually the divorced wife of August Strindberg, the former Frida Uhl, who continued to bear the name of the great Swede proudly, despite the fact he had since been followed by Frank Wedekind with two illegitimate children [sic.] At that time she was in a relationship with Werner that could almost be considered legitimate. She had become pleasantly plump and was quite amusing.[25]

It was in the insecure realm of "almost legitimate" that Frida had learned to take measures. Von Oestèren, like Strindberg and Wedekind before him, had benefited from Frida's interest in furthering his career. But this time she was so determined to avoid another debacle that she tried to keep this lover under control by any means possible.

By 1905, when they had been together almost three years, the cozy atmosphere recalled by Servaes was a thing of the past. The relationship had degenerated to such an extent that Frida lodged a charge of "defamation of honor" against Von Oestèren. She was suing her lover for threatening remarks made to the detective tailing him at her request. Von Oestèren was purported to have said that if he chanced to meet Frida at the swimming pool, he would shove her off the edge without fear of the consequences. Leading politicians were his friends, he asserted, and, therefore, the press would render him harmless.

In the courtroom Frida said she felt justified in spying on Von Oestèren because she had supported him and he had taken advantage of her and betrayed her. In addition, she knew about his past. In 1898, while living in Prague, he had shot and killed his lover at that time. Although charged with murder, he had been released on grounds of insanity and thereafter spent some time in a mental institution. "Enough reason to have him followed," Frida said in self-defense. But Von Oestèren's lawyer insisted that the earlier incident—in which his client had been badly wounded—was common knowledge and not sufficient reason for hiring a detective. In fact, it had not been a good idea for Frida to bring up the old story at all, since he could now remind her that she had twice threatened Von Oestèren with a gun. She withdrew her charge.[26]

Frida's circumstances were beginning to take their toll. She was financially insecure and had no permanent home. Despite having given up her children to her mother's care, she still felt responsible for them, even though Maria Uhl continued to look to Strindberg as Kerstin's only real parent.

Strindberg had not seen Kerstin since 1896, when she was two years old, but his former mother-in-law had corresponded with him assiduously for a few years after his departure. Writing most of the time in Kerstin's voice, she exercised all the childish charm she could muster to keep Strindberg interested in his daughter. She sent shy kisses, embraced him with her "little arms," described herself as looking "just like my papali, but prettier," and let him know how much she missed him. She knew Strindberg remained emotionally attached to his little "Beatrice," who had accompanied him through his imagined *Inferno.* Whenever Strindberg became distressed by the annulment proceedings and seemed ready to put his life in Austria behind him, Maria Uhl assumed Kerstin's voice to draw him back.

Dearest, beloved Papali,

Please don't be angry. I am still here. Do you want to abandon me too? I think and speak about you so much, in the morning, during the day, and at night. I am as stubborn as you in loving. When I go past your little house, I still call "Papa come out, take your jacket, we are going for a walk." Yes, yes, I will remember that till I die.[27]

Strindberg could not resist these little notes, and the correspondence continued until September 1899, when Kerstin was sent to a small boarding school in the nearby town of Haag. Maria Uhl asked Strindberg if he would be willing to conduct the same exchange of letters through the headmistress of the school, but Strindberg adamantly refused. As she feared, the correspondence languished, but did not die out completely, even though in the spring of 1900 Strindberg met Harriet Bosse, married her a year later, and by March 1902 had become the father of Anne-Marie, his fifth child.

As Kerstin grew older and her grandmother read her the letters Strindberg had written to her in her early years, the child conceived an overwhelming love for the "invisible father who had disappeared, but, nevertheless, sent me the pulse of his being through a secret connection, like an artery bridging the distance."[28] From her own distance, Frida recognized Kerstin's intense feelings for Strindberg and, in 1904, began to write to him again for her daughter's sake.

Please answer her when she writes to you. She is ten, has great artistic talent, like you.

I don't earn enough money to emancipate myself completely from my mother. And Mother becomes more and more authoritarian and pious. I tremble that harm will come to her if her intelligence goes unappreciated.

For now please write to her—one line a month. So she knows you think of her—and so her love for you grows.

I know you have another child, but I am sure the mother won't mind if you are also good to the poor child who has your blood in her veins.[29]

In that same year, Kerstin went to her grandfather's house in Mondsee for the summer holiday. Now, as it had for Frida so many years before, the time had come to enter a convent school. Friedrich Uhl's housekeeper helped her buy and mark the school uniforms for her first year as a boarder in the Dominican Convent of the English Ladies in Upper Bavaria. There were other changes in Dornach. In December 1904, Maria Reischl died. Kerstin shed no tears at the loss. Her great-grandmother had often been unjust to her as the living reminder of Strindberg, whom the old woman never ceased to think of as a scoundrel.

Despite his growing silence, Kerstin continued to idolize her father. When Strindberg failed to write to his daughter despite Frida's begging him to do so, she feared her letters had been sent to the wrong address. In 1905 she sent a telegram to Schering asking where Strindberg was living. The translator forwarded the query to Strindberg, and the guilt engendered by his near-abandonment of Kerstin brought about a familiar reaction. In a letter to Harriet Bosse he maligned the victim of his actions.

We must take notice, this lady wrote me one year ago asking me to make you interested in her child, who, so it was claimed, had artistic talents, appealing to your feelings as a mother, etc.

Knowing the untruthful nature of this lady and her dreadful character as far as other things go, I tore the letter into pieces and didn't answer.

I have no scruples; ten years ago I was divorced from the girl, she was two at the time, and with no regret, because her nature was repulsive.[30]

In his next letter to Harriet, Strindberg asked her to ignore what he had written.

Max Friedrich's childhood followed the same pattern as Kerstin's. Maria Uhl cared for him in Dornach until, in 1902, age five, he also was sent to boarding school. His father was not heard from until 1903, when he sent a letter to Maria Uhl on the occasion of the little boy's sixth birthday. "To excuse myself," he wrote, "I can say only one thing, that for me all of life was only music for the future."[31] He enclosed a copy of the children's book, *Hänseken*, he had written several years before. It was an unfeeling gesture, since the book concerned a little boy rejected by his mother, who finds comfort elsewhere. Maria Uhl did not tell Max Friedrich who his father was until he was a teenager.

In December 1905, the eighty-one-year-old Friedrich Uhl, returning home from a trip to Italy, became ill in Mondsee. Frida was at his side when he died on January 19, 1906. Of all the losses she had sustained, the death of her father was the most devastating. Although he had turned his back on her when he believed the instability of her life threatened his own, he had also given her the gift of survival. She never ceased to admire him for his accomplishments and, soon after his death, she made sure his achievements were commemorated by completing the book he had been preparing for a German publisher. She reedited the selection of his dispatches, reviews, and memories of his journeys with the emperor through thirty years. When the editor questioned her about the relevance of some of the pieces, she answered, "Sometimes what a man loves is just as telling as what he achieves." The book, titled *Aus meinem Leben* (*From My Life*) appeared in 1910.

In the course of the following year, the antagonism between Frida and her mother flared into the open, no longer held in check by respect for Uhl. With the inheritance from her father, Frida had money for the first time in her life, and, after the years of financial hardship, she splurged. She bought herself an apartment in the most aristocratic quarter of Vienna, began to patronize expensive dressmakers, and moved up in society by becoming a friend of the emperor's mistress, the actress Katharina Schratt. Schratt, in turn, introduced Frida to members of the old aristocratic families connected to the Habsburg court, including Prince Fugger-Babenhausen.

For Maria Uhl, who had inherited the Mondsee villa, the death of her husband seemed to her to remove the last obstacle preventing Strindberg from visiting Kerstin. A month after Uhl's death, she wrote to Strindberg that it was her "heart's desire to reunite Kerstin with her father." She revealed her own continuing attachment to her former son-in-law by adding, "Will you also do me the favor of greeting me as you used to, with the honorable title of Mother or Grandmother?"[32] On February 22 Strindberg sent a wary answer asking for details, and a few days later Maria Uhl proffered an invitation to come to Mondsee for Easter.

Before receiving her reply, however, Strindberg, addressing Maria Uhl as "dear honored mother," as she had requested, wrote her early in March explaining why a reunion was impossible. Three marriages had complicated his life. He was divorced again, but lived in a "loose liaison" with Harriet Bosse, for the sake of their daughter, not yet five. He had thought a great deal about Kerstin.

The little one is tied to the fate of her mother and since I always expected Kerstin would have a stepfather, so I did not want to be mixed up in these unpleasant complications. Then I said to myself: Kerstin does not need me. In a few years she is grown up and enters life as a person in herself—what then is the point of a titular father? Why tear at the little one and her feelings. She has a brother that is not from me—Kerstin knows that. No, I cannot crawl back into this net. Through Kerstin, I will enter into indirect contact with her mother—I don't want to, I am not allowed to.[33]

Before Strindberg's sad reply arrived, two more letters were posted from Austria. Frida, having learned of her mother's invitation from Kerstin, tried to intervene by telling Strindberg once again how much Kerstin loved him; at the same time she dragged him back into her quarrel with Maria Uhl. "I beg you most humbly, write to her or see her. You can be quite alone. Don't punish the child because the mother has left you.... But without Grandmother for the love of God."[34]

On March 6, Maria Uhl also wrote Strindberg about how lovable Kerstin was and described her "artistic nature." She provided details about Friedrich Uhl's last illness (including a picture of him on his deathbed) and boasted about what he had left the family. At the close she gave her views of Frida. "... Always the same story—mainly that she is a poor child, she cannot help herself. Papa found the right word to explain her nature: she has no common sense, that is the problem, and what she does or does not do cannot be qualified." In closing, she added, "She has become old, is no longer beautiful...."[35]

Strindberg did not reply to either letter. Instead, he sent Kerstin a picture of Anne-Marie. Receiving the picture at school, she was deeply shaken. In the image of the pretty, well-dressed little child, she could see only a reflection of her own shortcomings. "That is why I am not where he is," she later remembered thinking, "because I am awkward and abandoned and entangled in problems, and because he has a wife who is completely different from my eccentric, restless, sloppy, rootless homeless mother Frida...."[36]

With Strindberg's silence, the battle between the two women intensified. Maria Uhl, without consulting Frida, began negotiations with a guardian to take Strindberg's place. Frida, in desperation, pleaded with him to intercede.

> *Only the most terrible despair makes me write these lines and address myself to you as a beggar, a beggar for the only thing in life that still exists for me—our child. The woman who calls herself my mother, after having ruined my life, is going to ruin that of my child.*
>
> *A guardian is contemplated who will control her fortune, her education, the prerogative of the father.*
>
> *On the pretext that your whereabouts are unknown.*
>
> *August, she wants to usurp my child. The same menace that formerly broke our union. The mother without a child, woman without a husband.*
>
> *Everything is in ruins, all is a deluge around me and the faith in your generosity is the only thing, the last rock of safety.*[37]

In the second part of the letter, Frida referred to Strindberg's autobiographical novel *Entzweit* (*Divided*), an early version of *The Cloister,* which had just appeared in German. She had not been portrayed fairly, Frida wrote, and he had thrown her to posterity, but she admitted the book revealed he had loved her. "That is the past . . . ," she concluded. "But save your daughter from an old woman who does not know what it is to be a mother."

When Strindberg still did not intervene, the struggle between mother and daughter over the issue of the guardian approached a climax. Maria Uhl had long held a pessimistic view of Frida's nature, and after her daughter's divorce from Strindberg, had considered Frida's way of life an affront to her own. She was devout, Frida was agnostic. After the failure of her marriage to Friedrich Uhl, she had retreated to a chaste life in the countryside, whereas Frida had held on to her urban existence and ignored all social conventions. Most important, whereas Frida had let Strindberg down, she had saved him. Now, in his absence, it was her duty to save his child.

When Frida realized that her mother was intent on depriving her of the only lasting family connection in her life—the children, offspring of the men who had built other lives with different women elsewhere—she began to despair. Suicide seemed the only way out of her isolation, and she wrote a departing letter to Strindberg, which was never mailed. It was a last attempt to understand the ambivalent feelings that still haunted her.

You will never again find a woman who understands you like me—I will never find a man who tires me less.

My child looks like you and I love her.

Sometimes it is as if I still love you, as if I am thirsty for your genius because no one else I have seen or spoken to has awakened love in me.

Your picture looks out at me and tempts me; it is a picture from the good hours of happiness but behind it lurks another face and I shudder—I never, never want to see you again.[38]

She began making arrangements for the financial welfare of her children by transferring to Kerstin the remaining income from Grandfather Reischl's real-estate investments, and, for the first time, contacting Wedekind regarding Max Friedrich. Writing to him through a lawyer, she told him she would no longer accept sole responsibility for the support of their child. Her language was harsh. "One doesn't put children in the world, so that the mother goes under in the process. Cursed be the man who forces a woman to rue the day she gave herself to him in love." From now on, she added, Wedekind would be responsible for his son's upkeep. And if he failed to do so, she threatened, his ten-year-old son would come to ask for it himself. Wedekind agreed to her terms to pay a certain amount each month.[39]

Frida's behavior became more disturbing as the year went on. Kerstin remembered being called to Vienna for a visit and then being sent back when her mother suffered an unexplained collapse. Frida took too many tranquilizing drugs, and her appearance became sloppier, her outbursts more irrational, her spending more rash. At some point she wrote a second, unmailed, suicide note addressed to Strindberg saying, "Have pity on your daughter—don't abandon her. Forgive me. I suffer . . . be happy." It was signed "The woman who is to die today" and dated "A day in the year 1907 after having taken sufficient veronal to kill myself."[40]

But Frida reconsidered and decided on a more public display of her despair. On New Year's Day, 1908, in a dramatic gesture, she fired a pistol at a reception given by Prince Fugger and his wife. A vivid report of the incident appeared in the papers.

The accusations on file against Mrs. Strindberg concern the following facts. Prince Fugger-Babenhausen, who succeeded his father in the spring, got to know Mrs. Strindberg in the society of Mrs. Katharina Schratt. Their acquaintance came to a close in an extremely alarming scene that occurred on New Year's Day in the Hotel Bristol and in which a loaded revolver played an important role. On that day Madame Fugger was in the Hotel Bristol with some friends. Suddenly, greatly agitated, Mrs. Strindberg appeared and began to utter a number of threats. When the Prince tried to go into the next room in order to bring a glass of water to the greatly agitated woman, Mrs. Strindberg pulled out a revolver and in the next moment, a shot rang out. In the police investigation, one could not be certain if Mrs. Strindberg had intended the shot for the Prince or herself. She claimed that the revolver had been loaded with a blank for this shot, although some of the other bullets that remained in the revolver's drum were not.[41]

No one was hurt, but by January 28, when Frida was summoned to a hearing to answer for her actions, she had fled to England. The public shooting had forced a definitive break with family and friends. Whether consciously or not, it had provided a way out of the tangled family web that had made an enemy of her own mother.

After Frida's departure, a warrant for her arrest was issued for extortion, embezzlement, and fraud. A Berlin actress claimed Frida had sold important paintings for her but had never given her the money. Dressmaking firms and department stores sought large sums of money owed them. Local food emporia joined the clamor for the payment of debts, as did the detective agency Frida used to keep an eye on her lovers. According to the barely hidden malicious gloating of the press, she had been given generous terms of credit because of her expensive clothes, her supposed income from a large inheritance, and her connections to Katharina Schratt.

Although she did owe money, the charges in the warrant were false, and Frida returned to Vienna to consult a lawyer. It was discovered that Von Oestèren not only had aroused her creditors after her departure, but also had placed the notices in the press regarding her supposedly false claims to money and connections. Her lawyer published a counterstatement, and the charges were dropped, but Frida knew that her life in Vienna was over.[42] Nevertheless, she sent a letter to Karl Kraus, the one man she felt she could trust, and related her story.

I don't know if you followed the Frida Strindberg case through the mud thrown up by the newspapers. I hope not because I am ashamed. If you have, please believe me, I did not leave here because of the . . . debts

I owed the dressmakers, but despite them. . . . I never had an argument with Prince Fugger, he never issued a complaint against me. I wanted to flee to him—that was all.

When I read the first reports in the newspapers, I came back here. At least they should tell me to my face that I have done worse things than to . . . creep away. I hate cowardice more than anything. That is why I can still cope.[43]

Kraus, who had no use for a publicly compromised woman, wasted no sympathy on Frida's plight and brutally replied that he had written her off. Swallowing her pride, she wrote once more. Abjectly agreeing that his rejection was "absolutely right," she nevertheless begged him for one last favor: the retrieval of a crucial item from her apartment, which had been officially sealed.

Before I injected the morphine, I took all of Strindberg's letters—four hundred in all—and packed them in a travel basket. It is in the kitchen by the window. On top of the basket is a label: "Strindberg's letters after my death to be held by Dr. Harnewolf, Vienna, for Kerstin Strindberg." It includes a box of Strindberg's letters, notices, books, that he left with my mother, a small box of Strindberg's books, a picture by Strindberg and a watercolor of Strindberg's oldest child.

I beg you please take all these things in my name for *August Strindberg. . . .*

No one but you will feel what these things are worth. I trust no one so completely as you. Save August Strindberg's property, if only for his sake.

I thank you in advance. I know you will do it.[44]

To his credit, Kraus did as she asked, and Frida, returning the favor, disappeared from his life. "Take my thanks. Once more I was irresponsibly stupid and shameless. Please don't be angry with me. I had been a ruin for a long time when you met me, and weeds grow on ruins."[45]

Despite the morphine, the public spectacle, the accusations, and the fear, the literary agent had not gone under. Frida did not forget to put in safe custody the piece of her past that she knew, already, was the most precious thing she owned.

8

Worshiping the Golden Calf

BOHEMIA WAS COMING INTO its own in London when Frida sought refuge there in 1908. Artists and writers rebelling against the many years of Victorian restraint were joined by enterprising foreigners and returning expatriates bringing new ideas from abroad. Among those arriving in England at about the same time as Frida were Ezra Pound, coming from America, Wyndham Lewis, returning after six years on the Continent, and Roger Fry, starting afresh at home after a stint as a curator at the Metropolitan Museum of Art in New York.

A sure indication of the shift in cultural attitudes was the banquet held toward the end of 1908 to celebrate the imminent publication of Oscar Wilde's collected works in English after the decade of silence that had followed his imprisonment and death. On this happy occasion, Frida's acquaintance Robert Ross, the executor of the Wilde estate, cited the importance of German editions in reviving Wilde's reputation. Frida had been one of his allies in that cause.[1]

Through Ross, the owner of an art gallery and a critic, Frida was introduced to the English art scene. Making herself familiar with the artists and galleries, she soon began to buy and sell art. With her highly developed cultural antennae, she proved so successful as an art dealer that one of her intuitive acquisitions brought a neglected artist a brief moment of national renown.

In the summer of 1910, while poring through work in a secondhand shop in New Oxford Street, Frida discovered a cache of rolled canvases that reminded her of Whistler. She bought about fifty, and sold them to a respected Bond Street gallery. Soon a rumor began circulating among London's art dealers that unknown Whistlers had appeared on the market. William Marchant, the owner of the Goupil Gallery, which had exhibited Whistler, was sufficiently intrigued to uncover the source and buy fifty canvases as well. Looking over his purchases, Marchant realized that the paintings were not by Whistler, but by Walter Greaves, who had been Whistler's devoted, if exploited, apprentice in his youth. Next, Marchant discovered the sixty-four-year-old artist himself, barely surviving on the drawings and portraits he peddled in the streets and pubs of Chelsea. In dire straits, Greaves had been forced to sell the precious canvases of his apprenticeship to a secondhand shop. The piquancy of Greaves's tale and the quality of the work convinced Marchant to mount an exhibition of the "Unknown Master."[2]

This was only the first of many ironies of the Greaves affair. Marchant had the paintings restretched, cleaned, lined, and framed. Their subjects were appealing ones—Whistlerian nocturnes, busy dock scenes, the back streets of Chelsea, and a spectacular crowd scene, *Hammersmith Bridge on Boat Race Day* (now in the Tate Gallery). Leading collectors and critics were invited to the private viewing on May 4, 1911, and the next day there was an excellent review in the London *Times.* The writer brought Greaves decisively out from under Whistler's shadow by declaring him an original artist, whose naïveté, as opposed to Whistler's "cosmopolitan cleverness," had its own appeal. Unlike his mentor, he wrote, Greaves was "a lover of things, not moods."[3]

Within a week, fifteen oils were sold, for a considerable amount of money, and Greaves's name was everywhere. Established artists helped him cope with his newfound fame, and he was pictured dining with art-world luminaries at an elegant restaurant. However, when one overzealous journalist suggested that Whistler had learned a thing or two from his apprentice, Whistler's disciples and official biographers balked. They launched a furious press campaign that burst the Greaves bubble. It had lasted a mere three weeks.[4] The unknown master faded from the news. Yet a year later, one of London's leading artists, Augustus John, was faithfully recommending him to his New York patron, John Quinn. "Greaves is a real artist-kid with Chelsea in his brain," he wrote him. "I shall never cease to appreciate his work—so unlike Whistler's at bottom."[5]

FRIDA HAD BECOME A great appreciator of Augustus John, ever since he seduced her when she appeared at his studio searching for Wyndham Lewis some time during 1910. It cannot have taken too long after her arrival in England for her to have heard of John. Only in his thirties, he was already a legendary figure. He was six feet tall, gracefully built, with reddish hair and, according to his aristocratic admirer Lady Ottoline Morrell, "beautifully-shaped eyes," gray-green in color. His hands, she added, "were more beautiful than any man's hands I have ever seen."[6]

John's mother had died when he was six, and the restrictions of life in a provincial town in Wales under the baleful eye of his straitlaced father led to the lifelong need to resist real or imagined control. The romantic garb, long hair, and occasional earring that he began to favor while still a student at the Slade School of Art in the 1890s were the first expressions of his rebellious spirit. The sartorial display as well as the bravura of his draftsmanship were much admired by his fellow-students, who were known to piece together the torn bits of his rejected work to keep for themselves. Although John married Ida Nettleship, a fellow-student at the Slade in 1900, he soon pursued the life his restless nature required. When Ida died in 1907, after giving birth to their fifth child, she and John had been living for several years in a ménage à trois with his mistress, Dorelia McNeil, who also had a child by John. The unorthodox family moved between Paris and London in a series of arrangements in which Dorelia and Ida sometimes shared a household while John sought ever-more-elusive liberties among itinerant gypsies and a number of other women who found his appetites irresistible. Flamboyant, gifted, notorious, a man who refused to be possessive or possessed, John was another brilliant bad boy Frida could not resist.

By 1910, John's bohemian entourage had grown more complicated. At the center was Dorelia, whom John called his "wife," although they never officially married. Her primacy was accepted by his other lovers, many of them artists' models and young working girls who floated in and out of their lives. He also had his followers—artists who admired him, benefited from his professional support, and sometimes formed their own amorous relationships with his women. Tensions, gossip, and jealousy were inevitable among these shifting alliances.[7]

Introduced into this extended family, Frida began to make trouble. She accepted Dorelia's preeminence like everyone else, but she considered John's way of life dissolute and his other women unworthy. Unlike them, she was concerned with improving his life and assisting him with his career. As always it was the possibility of being of use to a lover that ignited her passion, and she could not believe that John could have looked upon their relationship, too, as just another sexual adventure to be indulged in briefly and without consequences.

John sensed a threat to his freedom in Frida's concern for his well-being, but he had met his match. She would not accept rejection. The more John eluded her grasp, the more she pursued him. Annoyed but also flattered by this cosmopolitan woman's persistence, he allowed the chase to continue. For a while, her tenacity in playing the game of the huntress offered a certain degree of amusement.

John had become a successful painter as soon as he left the Slade, with yearly exhibitions and commissions for portraits. The flamboyance of his life was not reflected in his art, which was relatively conservative in subject matter and style, and by 1910 he was considered one of England's most important painters. When Frida began to buy his drawings and paintings, he did not need, nor did he welcome, her support, sensing that her acquisitions were yet another attempt to bind him to her. He refused to take her patronage seriously, and made fun of her efforts when writing to his much preferred patron, John Quinn.

Quinn was a wealthy, hardworking American lawyer who collected contemporary British manuscripts and paintings, and who had given John an annual stipend to have first choice of his work. In his letters to his benefactor, John regaled him with choice items from his bohemian existence, including numerous tales of the "mad Austrian" and her vigorous pursuit of his person. Quinn, greatly amused, wrote back, "Fornication with a lady who thinks she is a real lady is, after all, a rather expensive business."[8]

But after a while masculine glee over the "mad Austrian's" antics was a bit harder to muster. John, in the haphazard manner in which he handled his affairs, had submitted a large painting already promised to Quinn to an exhibition. Titled *The Way Down to the Sea*, it depicted four women (including Ida and Dorelia) and a little naked boy. For John, the exhibit was an opportunity to play a game with his patrons. He wrote Quinn that the collector Hugh Lane had offered him £500. Was Quinn still committed to his offer of £400? Quinn leaped to the bait and wrote John that he wanted the painting, and he enclosed a down payment of £100.[9] By the time Quinn's offer arrived, John had been put in an embarrassing position: he had received word that the picture had been sold. Assuming it had been bought by Lane, John attempted to placate Quinn by promising that the picture he was about to paint would be a better one. *The Way Down to the Sea*, he added for good measure, was not his best.

Unfortunately, Quinn's appetite had been whetted. "Damn Lane," he cabled, and added that he was willing to pay the higher price and was counting on John to secure the picture for him.

"Alas and a million Devils!" John wrote back, letting Quinn know that it was not Lane who had bought it, after all, but "the Austrian terror." He had asked her politely to give up the picture, but she had refused. For the first time, Frida is given a name in the correspondence.

> *I have had no end of trouble with that woman who is the walking hell-bitch of the Western World. She is the wife of August Strindberg—the Norwegian or Swedish writer—now a maniac I believe. She seems to have a lust for power and sticks at nothing to bring people under her sway. She's a dealer in works of art and a would-be appropriator of the bodies and souls of those that make them.*[10]

In September, Quinn arrived in London for his annual visit, and the "mad Austrian" more than lived up to his expectations. According to Quinn's diary, immediately after his arrival John informed him that he had just consented to visit the "Wild Woman," after four or five desperate letters begging for attention. Once the errand of mercy was behind him, John reported to Quinn that he had bitten the bullet and told Frida the relationship was over. This was the first act of the drama. The next day John learned that Frida had taken poison. Quinn, who was beginning to enjoy a certain relish in the proceedings, suggested they leave for France to escape.[11]

John agreed with alacrity and, to sweeten the occasion, proposed that two artists' models accompany them. But when they met at the station on the morning of September 6, Frida was there, revolver in hand. Quinn's diary notes for the day were agitated and fragmentary: "To station, John: woman; carnage."[12]

Frida followed them onto the boat at Dover, and, while John hid, Quinn, too curious to let the opportunity pass by, chatted with her on deck. He even promised to meet her at a café in Paris, an appointment summarily quashed by John. Not long after making themselves comfortable in Paris, the two men got word that Frida had attempted suicide a second time, in the very hotel in which they were staying. Borrowing the car and German chauffeur of a fellow-American guest, they fled.

Frida's fixation with John had begun to border on madness. The exaggerated dramas of despair to which she had always been prone were endemic in this relationship. Tracking down her lover, brandishing a revolver, indulging in near suicide, unaffected by shame or embarrassment, she had reached a state where anything was permissible to keep his attention. Much later, recalling the intensity of her infatuation, Frida still held to the delusion that John had shared her feelings.

For many years I was under the influence of a great passion. . . . He loved me as much as anything, but wasn't faithful for a day. A magnificent animal, but wild. Twice I took Veronal which harmed no one but me.

I don't know how often I wanted to die, and died in spirit. It destroyed me completely. I was dead for years.[13]

Despite his introduction to his formidable competitor for the picture, Quinn did not give up his quest for *The Way Down to the Sea* after he returned to New York. He badgered John to act until the artist cabled that the picture was definitively lost. Even his last-ditch appeal, offering Frida a profit of £200, had failed.[14] It was not money but John she wanted.

Six months later Frida's situation had changed. Money was exactly what was required for a project that would bring together all she had learned and absorbed since her arrival in Berlin twenty years before. The idea had come from J. T. Grein—the same man who had doused her hopes for a production of *The Father* at the Independent Theater eighteen years earlier. Grein, who now reigned over London's night life as the theater critic of the *Sunday Times,* had complained of the dullness of the city after dark in one of his columns in the spring of 1911. What was wanting, he wrote, was a French-style cabaret where "poets, dramatists, singers of a kind recite and create their fancies. . . ." Grein called for a man or a woman to take up such a project, which, he was sure, Londoners would welcome with delight.[15] Three years after her arrival in London, living at the Savoy—the hostelry at the center of the theatrical world—Frida answered the call.

As the preparations for the cabaret went forward, John faithfully kept Quinn apprised of Frida's financial troubles. He notified his patron that she had pledged her possessions, including "Quinn's" picture, as security.[16] Soon after, Frida wrote to John and asked him to negotiate the sale of *The Way Down to the Sea.* Her sentimental tone was a bizarre contrast to John's and Quinn's cold calculations. "In remembrance of the last dream and the last feeling that was in my life, I do not wish to harm anything of yours, if I can help it," she wrote John. A second letter followed saying it had broken her heart to part with the painting, and asking if an arrangement could be made by which she could buy it back within a year at a profit to the purchaser.[17]

John and Quinn debated strategies. John urged Quinn to give Frida no more than the original price, £500. Quinn suggested John treat Frida with "absolute, contemptuous indifference." He also sent John a clipping he had discovered regarding Frida's misadventures in Vienna. John's solution was to hand over the negotiations to an art dealer, who would be more professional in dealing with the tempestuous seller. At last, on November 27, 1912, Quinn wrote to John: "I closed with her and that ends it. I am now the legal owner of it finally and once and for all she is out of it for good. So to hell with her."[18]

The irony was that as Frida, John, and Quinn grappled over *The Way Down to the Sea,* the English art scene was changing, and, of the three, Frida was to be the quickest off the mark. At the end of 1910, two pioneers—the curator Roger Fry, by mounting his exhibition "Manet and the Post-Impressionists," and the art critic Frank Rutter, by defending it in his pamphlet *Revolution in Art*—brought the radical experiments of French art decisively before the eyes of the British public. Until then, new ideas about art had received little encouragement in England, since commercial galleries were cautious and the annual juried exhibitions unadventurous. Fry's large show, which included work by Cézanne, Gauguin, Van Gogh, Matisse, and Picasso, launched British modernism.

As further exhibitions of these artists followed, collectors began to acquire their work, and young artists avidly absorbed the lessons of the French. In March 1912, the Italian Futurist poet F. T. Marinetti and his entourage of artists—Boccioni, Carra, and Russolo—arrived for the first exhibition of the Futurists in England. Their manifesto, which demanded that tradition be swept aside to express the modern "whirling life of steel, of pride, of fever and of speed," as well as Marinetti's impassioned lectures and poetry readings in the same vein, added the element of revolutionary fervor to the modernist debate. Within two years, according to Frank Rutter, "London had painters as 'wild' as any in Paris." Against the background of these developments, *The Way Down to the Sea* was a very old-fashioned picture.

Absorbing these changes, Frida promptly commissioned three of the British painters sympathetic to French modernism—Spencer Gore, Charles Ginner, and Wyndham Lewis—as well as the innovative sculptors Eric Gill and Jacob Epstein, to decorate her cabaret. Her "rare discrimination in her choice of accomplices" was praised by the critic Ashley Gibson, who found Frida to be "an amazingly masterful, intelligent, and, in her way, fascinating Austrian Jewess of a certain age [whose] instinct had led her without fail to select the young men who mattered or were going to. . . ."[19]

Over the next few months, Frida formed a committee of journalists, writers, and artists, located an appropriately bohemian location—a large basement below a warehouse in a tiny cul-de-sac off Regent Street—and baptized her future cabaret the Cave of the Golden Calf. In April 1912, a *Preliminary Prospectus* was issued declaring that the cabaret would "do away with the necessity of crossing the channel to laugh freely and to sit up after nursery hours." It promised gaiety, but "gaiety stimulating thought." To make good on that pledge, fifty members representing literature, theater, painting, and music were to be admitted to the club at reduced rates. A varied program was planned, "offering free development to the youngest and best of our contemporaries and Futurists."

The use of Marinetti's term indicated that the establishment would be in the artistic forefront, as did the charming woodcut designed for the *Preliminary Prospectus* by Gore and Lewis. Their image of a belly dancer cavorting before a miniature calf, more farm animal than idol, combined the folkloric simplicity of Kandinsky's graphics with a Cubist rendering of space.

Gore had been responsive to Kandinsky's work since it was first exhibited in England in 1909. "The design is almost entirely one of color," he had written, "the forms scarcely explaining themselves and the color is so gay and bright, pitched in so high a key, as to appear positively indecent to the orderly mind of the Briton." The preliminary studies for Gore's wall panels for the Cave show him using precisely such "gay and bright" color patterns to set off a landscape of sea, sky, and undulating hills. Like Kandinsky, Gore used the motif of horse and rider—in this case, bareback deer hunters—to give his primeval setting a romantic air and dynamic focus.

Wyndham Lewis was asked to design the graphics for the cabaret's menus, programs, and announcements, as well as to paint canvases for the walls. The most belligerent and independent of the artists involved with the Cave, Lewis recalled his attraction to Frida's audacity, pluck, and enterprising spirit.

> *Strindberg, the Swedish dramatist, had a number of wives, one being a Viennese. [She was] a very adventurous woman (whose favorite remark, I recall was* "Je suis au bout de forces!"*; although often as I heard her say it, I never saw her in that condition, her "forces" being at all times triumphantly intact).*[20]

Lewis was a writer as well as a gifted artist. In the stories he published, he focused on marginal figures in society—innkeepers, the foreign inhabitants of boardinghouses, circus performers.

He described them as "primitive creatures immersed in life . . . the body was wild; one was attached to something wild like a big cat that sunned itself and purred." Frida's commission provided Lewis with a suitable context for the visual transcription of the "wild body" he was after. In the revelry that was the club's *raison d'être*, he had his subject; in the examples of the Cubist and Futurist works on view in London, he found his style. As Lewis wrote later, he was so thrilled with the commission that he would have worked for nothing.

To suggest an ambiance of intoxication and frenzy, Lewis created figures with masklike features and interlocking limbs. Emerging from shards of Cubist space and linked by the diagonal lines favored by the Futurists, they appear to be at the behest of forces beyond their control. On the poster Lewis designed to advertise the Cave, the letters themselves are caught up in the same manic rhythm that has the oversized dancer in its sway.

Unfortunately, between mid-May, when John wrote Quinn that Lewis was "thick with Strindberg (in his way)," and the opening of the cabaret in mid-June, Lewis had a falling-out with Frida and withdrew his wall decoration. Titled *Kermesse*, the Flemish term for carnival, it became instead the sensation of the 1912 Allied Artists Exhibition that opened in July. In his review, Roger Fry pointed out that *Kermesse*, "originally intended for the Cave of the Calf, the new Cabaret theater," made "all the rest of the pictures disappear. . . ."[21]

While Gore imagined the landscape and Lewis the inhabitants of the Cave, Ginner, Gill, and Epstein added the animals. Ginner's contributions consisted of wall decorations titled *Tiger Hunting*, *Chasing Monkeys*, and *Birds and Indians*. Epstein transformed the cellar's structural columns into the painted plaster totem poles described by Ford Madox Ford in his novel *The Marsden Case* as white caryatids with heads of hawks, cats, and camels picked out in red. The Cave's mascot, carved by Eric Gill of Hoptonwood stone or emergeng in relief on the club's sign, was no towering idol, but a sturdy, friendly animal, undeniably male, stretching out its head for a pat.

Tension grew as opening night approached. Diplomatic and easygoing as Gore seemed, he had difficulty negotiating Frida's temperament. "Days and nights I have spent arguing about the color of the walls and the ceiling," he wrote to a friend. "Most irritating thing I have ever had to do with." Nor was it easy to keep the motley crew of young artists on schedule. Ginner took long lunch hours, and Lewis, who had agreed to paint the drop curtain, did so only reluctantly and at the last minute. Gore's young wife, a dancer, was pressed into service to mix colors and stretch and size canvases.

Frida's planning was haphazard and her decisions improvised. Although performers had been hired, there was no master of ceremonies to hold the evening together. Yet luck was on Frida's side. Ten years before, she had given the young Norwegian singer and performer Bokken Lasson, a sister of Strindberg's friends Oda Krohg and Alexandra Thaulow, a letter of recommendation as a performer for Wolzogen's *Überbrettl.* The opportunity had launched Lasson's career, and by 1912 she had opened her own cabaret, a *Chat Noir,* in Kristiania. Flush with the success of her first season, she arrived in London en route to Paris shortly before the debut of Frida's enterprise. Frida declared her sent from heaven and begged her to perform as the mistress of ceremonies for the opening of *her* cabaret. Lasson consented, had her Pierrot costume posted from Norway, and set about assisting Frida with the preparations for the opening night. As she recalled, it was a daunting task.

At midnight, the day before the opening, we had a general rehearsal which was in a cave in the City. It was decorated with extravagance, but it lacked all kinds of things. It was naked and cold with no tables or chairs, with mortar and limestone dust everywhere. It looked like a construction site or a ruin. I could not imagine how this space could be ready to host a critical audience full of expectations the following evening. And even if I knew from my own experience that miracles could be done in twenty-four hours, I was quite nervous on behalf of Madame Strindberg. She hurried around among the craftsmen, talked seductively with them, gave instructions left and right, turned away unpleasant bills and had a fight with a furniture company in order to convince them to deliver chairs and tables in time, without cash payment.[22]

The kitchen, from which an advertised "artist's meal" was to be served, remained without gas and electricity. Somehow, with the bravura of the damned, Lasson and Frida opened the cabaret on June 26 as planned, hoping to placate the diners by extolling the "artistic" nature of a colorful but decidedly cold lobster salad.

When the public and the press finally entered the eagerly awaited Cave of the Golden Calf, they found themselves in a sophisticated ambiance. Under green-and-white-painted rafters hung with lantern-shaped lights, the space was set up as a theater with the audience sitting at little tables elegantly covered with white tablecloths. Surrounding them was the primitive world imagined in paint and plaster by Ginner, Gore, and Epstein.

A moment of suspense occurred when Lewis's drop curtain, not quite dry, stuck to the floor, but as soon as it was made to rise, the evening took off. There was singing by Bokken Lasson, accompanying herself on a guitar, there were dances to tunes of Grieg by an Englishwoman and more torrid fare by a Spanish dancer. An actor recited Oscar Wilde's *The Happy Prince*. At the close, a young man with a cockney accent delivered a "serio-comic homily" about the Cave and in true cabaret fashion mocked the participants by reminding everyone that Gore was the nephew of a bishop.

The following Sunday, Grein, in his column, heartily welcomed the cabaret, proclaiming that he had laid its "foundation stone" the year before, but that "a lady friend, a woman of many artistic tastes and connections" had taken up his lead. He praised Bokken Lasson's singing and, in particular, the impression made by the choreography of the Spanish dancer.[23]

In some ways the Cave was an ambitious hybrid. It was a cabaret, it was a restaurant with an excellent wine cellar, and it was a nightclub. Gypsy music (inspired by John) could be heard there as well as the dance bands that gave the patrons the chance to try the turkey trot and the bunny hug. Sir Osbert Sitwell remembered "a super-heated . . . garden of gesticulating figures, dancing and talking, while the rhythm of the primitive forms of ragtime throbbed through the great room."

Frida also organized a Cabaret Theater Club, a venture reminiscent of the one she had envisioned so long before when she wrote to Strindberg in Rügen. Every Sunday at 9:15 P.M. there would be an opportunity to see "a play of some ethical or literary value, which for one or other unfathomable reason has not been seen publicly. . . ." In its first season, the Theater Club offered plays by Henri Becque (whom Frida had translated), Dostoyevsky, Andreyev, Aristophanes, and Strindberg. Granville Bantock, one of England's leading composers and a member of Frida's committee, organized the music program, which included Pergolesi's little-known baroque operetta *La Serva Padrona*, Mozart's early singspiel *Bastien et Bastienne*, and Schoenberg's *Pierrot Lunaire*, which had its debut in Berlin in October 1912.

Wyndham Lewis's participation in Frida's enterprise attracted other members of London's literary bohemia, including Ezra Pound and Ford Madox Ford. In cabaret fashion, the writers also participated in the proceedings. Lewis and Ford created shadow plays, Katherine Mansfield performed a parody of her own devising, and Frank Harris demonstrated his skill as a reciter of Russian tales. Occasionally singers and dancers would emerge from the audience in the early-morning hours to give spontaneous recitals. By offering reduced prices to guests involved in the arts, Frida had made sure of the social mix that had marked the true cabaret atmosphere ever since the Montmartre "apaches" had first joined the artists and writers in high jinks at the *Chat Noir.* In Frida's version, London's *jeunesse dorée*—debutantes and Guardsmen—made merry with the bohemian avant-garde. Augustus John was not among their number, however. As he wrote in his autobiography, he never entered the place.[24]

Frida, nonetheless, kept track of John. She continued to admonish him for his affairs, his unsavory acquaintances, and his failure to be as great as she believed he could be. Still embroiled in the gossip of the John "family," she dedicated a sixteen-page epistle to her fear that "a silly Kensington girl" John had taken up with was setting him against her. She admitted that she had bribed the girl's mother to keep her daughter away from John—an action intended for his own good. "There was *nothing* to which I should not have forced myself to see you *once* again," she wrote to justify her action. "And to know that you would not be damaged by those people around you or by drink."[25]

By this time John had had enough. His replies to her letters were brief, cold, and dismissive, and soon after the mother/daughter episode, he broke with Frida definitively.

Cold, resolute, implacable, this time I succeeded in making my meaning clear. When at last she realized the truth—my truth, a sad transformation took place; her eyes previously a dark and lively brown, turned flat and leaden, her plump cheeks quivered, and her whole person seemed to sag: I was in the presence of a wounded animal, wounded, it seemed, unto death.[26]

John misjudged Frida. Death did not come into play. Her energies were too deeply engaged in the more immediate problems of the cabaret's precarious finances. Instead of pay, Gore had been given some John drawings, and Lewis, taking matters into his own hands, had made off with a day's income from the cash box. Later, he complained bitterly to Ford about what he had to cope with in the cabaret's administrative chaos. Ford, however, defended Frida eloquently.

> *Poor Madame S.—try to bear with her. She is trying to build up a Palace of all the Arts with three oyster shells and stale patchouli and sawdust and crème, the buttons off waiter's waistcoats, champagne corks and vers libre—which is what—including typewriters which go wrong and produce palimpsests—we are all of us trying to do in one field or the other.*[27]

In his inimitable style, Ezra Pound also expressed his appreciation of Frida's generous nature.

Whereas the Cave of the calf was started by FRIEDA.
"Are you any connection to THE Strindberg?"
responsus:
"Yess I ahm vun of his Wives"
and to me: "I needt money. I haff therefore dagen upp brosstiDushun in tdiss bardicular form."
I, then in the heights of Whistler and the refinements of Debussy, was unable to appreciate Frida.
... the only night club (one of the first in London) in which impoverished artists cd/ get into. Middle European acumen as to advertising value of Mr. Epstein, Frank Harris, etc. you cd/ even get eats fr free if you took 'em at Frieda's table.
... more brains than Gertie or Amy put together.[28]

The resounding popularity of the cabaret convinced Frida's committee to go on for a second season in the fall of 1913. To correct errors of the Cave's initial hasty construction, she renovated the premises and rebuilt the stage. Reconciled with Lewis, she added panels and screens by him and rented his latest version of *Kermesse*. The program was expanded still further. There were to be "Tango teas" in the afternoons, "Champagne Tangos" at night, and once a week a *"Cours de danse,"* with an instructor imported from Paris—"the teacher of La Belle Otero"—to give lessons in the Maxixe, tango, and waltz.

The Cabaret Theater Club became The Sunday Theater. Each Sunday would be dedicated to a different form of entertainment: cabaret, music, one-act plays, and special productions organized by a composer, writer, or artist to demonstrate different aspects of English intellectual life. In the program announcement for October and November, this translated into a performance of Joseph Conrad's "One Day More," a dramatization of his story "Tomorrow," written in collaboration with Ford; a "painter-poets night" featuring Wyndham Lewis; a "Soirée Paul Fort," an evening with the French poet making the rounds of cabarets from St. Petersburg to London with his repertoire of ballad-poems; and a "Georgian Cabaret" arranged by Harold Monro. Monro was the owner of the Poetry Bookshop—the scene of many readings—and the publisher of the avant-garde "little" magazine *Poetry and Drama*, which helped spread word of new literary movements.[29]

Monro's event, which had been scheduled for November 16, was postponed in favor of a more notorious performer—the Italian Futurist Marinetti. Returning to London for the fourth time in three years, Marinetti perceived that the Cave of the Golden Calf had become an essential venue for the avant-garde. The day after his lecture on *"L'art des bruits,"* which was followed by a "Futurist" supper, Lewis wrote to a friend that "Marinetti declaimed some blood-thirsty concoctions with great dramatic force."[30]

Unfortunately, the atmosphere at the Cave had changed by mid-season. Illegalities in the sale of food and drink led to police raids. There were feuds between the *patronne* and some of her customers, particularly the artists' models. Suspecting intrigues against her, Frida resorted to her favorite device of hiring a private detective, which only exacerbated the disagreements. Unscrupulous waiters began to pocket money, and funds were further diminished by Frida's frequent "scholarships" for artists. By February 1914, the Cave of the Golden Calf was forced to declare bankruptcy.[31]

Although the cabaret was no more, its influence could still be felt in that last spring before the war. The two artists who had been closest to Frida—Lewis and John—tried to set up similar establishments. With a little help from a well-heeled friend, Lewis founded the Rebel Art Center as a focal point from which to launch his own group of artists moving beyond Futurism. The entertainments he planned were very much like those at the Golden Calf—shadow plays, lectures by innovators in music, dances, special evenings, and, of course, a discourse by Marinetti.

John's Crab Tree Club opened in April, and the artists' models now flocked to this new bohemian center, but the atmosphere was rougher, particularly because the entertainment included boxing. It was described by the artist Paul Nash as a "place of utter coarseness and dull, unrelieved monotony. John, alone, a great pathetic muzzy god, a sort of Silenus—but also no nymphs, satyrs and leopards to complete the picture."[32]

DURING THESE HECTIC years in London, Frida made no attempt to contact her mother or her children, but, at the end of 1911, when she got word that Strindberg was ill with stomach cancer, she cabled him immediately: "Terribly anxious and sympathetic, please send news." Strindberg chose not to reply to this, or to her subsequent telegram on April 24. "I beseech you from a bruised heart to allow me to come to nurse and serve you."[33] Strindberg died on May 12, 1912. On May 19, when ten thousand people, including royalty and members of the Swedish government, followed Strindberg's coffin to the cemetery, neither Frida nor Kerstin was among them.

Kerstin had attempted to stay in contact with her father after Frida had fled to England in January 1908. She had written Strindberg several letters, telling him how much she wanted to hear from him. "It would be nice if you would come to know my thoughts and life," she suggested to him wistfully.[34] Strindberg's final response to his fifteen-year-old daughter was written on September 5, 1909.

My child,

I received no letter from Dornach. And I am so alienated from everything that has to do with Austria. To me it is like an old fairy tale, unbelievable but it was once true. . . .

Is the old grandmother still alive? Was she rich? Is Aunt Melanie alive?

I don't know anything and it is not my interest to know anything since all of it has become strange to me. I am sixty years old and live in a pension. But I am after all a writer and life for me is actually only material for dramas, mostly tragedies.

Stay well. And look upon me only as a souvenir.

Your father.[35]

Fighting back, Kerstin had replied, but to no avail.

You are no souvenir to me! Will never be! According to your letter you are asking for my life. But that you cannot take away from me. You are my father . . . even if far away from me. But to take away from the child the remembrance. No that is for me to decide. You remain my beloved old father.[36]

Even with this rejection, Maria Uhl still insisted to Kerstin that Strindberg loved her, and the child never ceased to worship him. His death before she had the opportunity to see him again was a personal blow from which she would never recover. The tragedy was compounded by events after his funeral. Greta, Strindberg's daughter from his first marriage, arranged to meet Kerstin in Munich in early June. It was Kerstin's first contact with Strindberg's family, and Greta treated her with great warmth, urging her to come to Sweden for a visit. Two weeks later, Greta was dead, killed in a railway accident at the age of thirty-one.

It was to be another year before Kerstin was able to travel to Stockholm. Young, shy, "a cloister girl," as she referred to herself, she ran into the machinations of a family dealing with the inheritance of a famous man. When she arrived, Henry von Philp, Greta's widower, came to greet her and dissuaded her from meeting the rest of the family. He suggested that she would not want to see the people who knew the scandals surrounding her mother. Kerstin meekly gave in, but she felt trapped as Von Philp entertained her a little too assiduously. Returning from one of their excursions, slightly drunk, on a foggy evening, Kerstin ran into a woman who looked vaguely familiar. It was her mother.

Frida had had no idea that Kerstin would be in Stockholm when she left for Sweden at the close of the cabaret's first season. Her purpose in traveling there had been to look after Kerstin's interests among the other Strindberg heirs and to ask for the return of some of her more intimate correspondence with her former husband.

Discovering Kerstin, Frida acted fast. She rescued her from

Von Philp's clutches, opened the door to her rightful inheritance by guiding her into the inner circle of Strindberg's family, but then abruptly departed. A telegram had arrived informing her that a crisis at the cabaret required her immediate presence in London. "After four years of absence, I saw my mother only three more times," Kerstin recalled.[37] This time it was to be eleven years before Kerstin saw Frida again.

As for Max Friedrich, Maria Uhl finally told him who his father was in 1912. The fifteen-year-old boy, hoping to find a sympathetic parent, traveled to Munich from his Salzburg boarding school to introduce himself to his father. Wedekind greeted him warmly, acknowledged his paternity, and invited him to share Christmas with his family, which now included his two daughters by Tilly Newes, Pamela and Kadidja. The Wedekind marriage was intact, but it had not been an easy one. Although Tilly Wedekind still appeared on stage, Wedekind was so jealous when it came to his young wife that he would not allow her to act with anyone but him.[38]

Max Friedrich already hoped to become a writer, and Wedekind was flattered by his son's reverence for his accomplishments. He offered him advice, provided recommendations, and encouraged him. The boy was thrilled to be able to correspond intimately with the man he first addressed as "Herr Wedekind." His letters to his father exuded warmth and appreciation, and he acknowledged that Wedekind was the first to bring real comfort into his adolescent life, the first to understand what he was about. Unfortunately, the contact had been too brief for Max Friedrich to understand what Wedekind was about. Their brief bond nearly ruptured when Max Friedrich dedicated a play to Wedekind which contained a barely disguised description of the jealous tensions he had observed in his father's household.[39] When Wedekind took it as an insolent reproof and threatened to break with his new-found son in anger, Max Friedrich wrote that he was "destroyed."

How deeply he was affected emerged in the next letter, in which Max Friedrich begged for love and forgiveness. "If you reject me, I am nothing. Take me into your love again. Let me know if I still have some value to you." To his signature he added "nearly in tears."[40] Although the two were ultimately reconciled, there was too little time for their relationship to recover the same warmth before Wedekind's premature death on March 9, 1918.

· 9 ·

In Exile

. . . I am bitterly sorry my dear, dear John that I could neither help loving, nor hating you—and that friendship and esteem and everything good drowned between those two feelings. The chief fault others had, who interfered with lies and mischief—the rest, I take it, was my fault—and therefore—I stretch out my hand to you in farewell. . . .

Good-by, John, I don't know whether you know how awfully good at the bottom of your heart you are. I know and that's why I write this to you.[1]

FRIDA WROTE THIS FAREWELL letter on board the R.M.S. *Campania* in September, having departed on one of the liner's last crossings to New York after the start of the First World War. John had been the second great love of her life and, just as she had with Strindberg, she sought friendship and reconciliation to overcome the bitter memory of rejection. "A noble epistle" was the way John referred to her letter in his memoirs. "In it I was absolved of all blame; all charges, all imputations were withdrawn; she alone had been at fault from the beginning; though this wasn't true. I was invested with a halo quite unnecessarily."[2]

Life in England had become more difficult for Frida after the outbreak of hostilities in early August. Although she was officially a Swedish citizen by virtue of her marriage to Strindberg, and thus not an "enemy alien," she was, nevertheless, subject to wartime restrictions. All foreigners in England had to register with the police and observe a curfew between 9:00 P.M. and 5:00 A.M.

Frida had been in England for six years but had never put down roots. She lived in rooming houses or hotels and made a "family" of friends, lovers, and the artists and performers she promoted. The cabaret had allowed for the mothering of protégés her nature demanded. But with the failure of that ambitious enterprise and the imminent dispersal of her companions by the war, she knew it was time to move on.

Frida was forty-two and still energetic. In London she had started from nothing and achieved much. Her commissions for the cabaret had resulted in the most avant-garde ensemble seen in London up to that time. The Cave of the Golden Calf, with its hedonistic and cultural diversions, had been a central gathering place and creative outlet for *les jeunes*, as Ford called the younger generation of artists and writers. In numerous novels and memoirs of the period, it was recalled with great fondness. When Pound and Lewis mischievously listed prominent figures in English society under the headings "blasted" and "blessed" in the first issue of their 1914 publication *Blast*, "Madame Strindberg" was among the latter.

Now Frida would have to attempt to be a creative patron elsewhere. Since a return to wartime Austria was impossible, the only real chance for a new life lay in neutral and English-speaking America. Friends returning from there encouraged her to contribute to the awakening interest in Strindberg on the other side of the Atlantic. Once again a chance to promote a genius—in this case, "her" genius—inspired her. With Strindberg's death, there was nothing to prevent her from taking up a mission of interpreting and defending him. She sent a proposal for an American lecture tour to an agency in London, and they recommended her to the J. B. Pond Lyceum Bureau in New York, the leading promoter of public speakers in America.

Her proposal was deftly framed—a careful balance between the titillation of the Strindberg myth of madness and misogyny and her own mission to "defy and fight the way history is written." She could offer the audience the viewpoint of someone who "knew a Strindberg that others never saw." The presentation was written in a sentimental, playful style intended to convince the people at the lecture agency of both the drama of her story and the fascination of her person. And although she claimed not to "overestimate" herself as one of Strindberg's critics, embedded in the hyperbole were some astute observations on Strindberg's methods.

No author, including St. Augustine and Jean Jacques Rousseau, has ever bared his own life and heart more completely than Strindberg does in his autobiographical work (and it is nearly all autobiographical). Unfortunately, he bared others, amongst them the bedmates of his choice, as well to profane eyes; and it was not exactly their charms that he recalled. . . .

Alas, one must have known him well to know, to understand and to forgive: In truth, the startling crime was nothing but unconsciousness.

She did not hesitate to dangle the possibility of other revelations.

I do not want to hold a lecture of Hero Worship. Far from it. Leave Heros and Gods to Priests. But leave Man to Woman.

I want to preserve Strindberg from the posthumous fate of Byron, Carlyle, and others—only I can.

To do this I shall also have to speak about the Great Power Behind the Veil, The Problem of the Sexes.

Maybe I shall tear down the Veil—further down even than Strindberg ever did. But shame was born out of Woman's fear. We are growing fearless. Maybe the audience will blush, but is not each wave of the blood, sign and maker of life?

She ended the proposal by admitting that she had never spoken in public. Then she added, with a certain insouciance, lack of experience did not seem to be an impediment for the women on trial for murder in two widely covered cases in France. Under stress, they had discovered hitherto untapped rhetorical powers. This provocative comparison paved the way for her closing flourish, one that may have eluded her prospective employer—but revealed her own ironic awareness of how she had come by her newest role. "Now to be eloquent on supreme occasions, it is—believe me—not always indispensable that one should previously murder. I fancy one might find the right word from heart to heart as well, had one just simply been killed oneself."[3]

The J. B. Pond Lyceum Bureau offered Frida a contract for ten lectures at $100 a lecture and passage to New York. The program was titled "Creators, *La Comédie Humaine:* Six Lectures by Madame Strindberg, Second Wife of the Great Swedish Poet-Dramatist." In the brochure she was introduced as "the daughter of Court Councillor Friedrich Uhl, Editor-Founder of the Imperial Royal Vienna Gazette." Her lectures were described as "unique in their kind because of the curious blending of the speaker's personality and her subject-matter. She has something to say which no other woman of the day can say, for she has plumbed the depths of European culture and stood on its heights." Aside from three lectures on Strindberg—"Strindberg the Man," "Strindberg and Women," and "Strindberg and the Intimate Theater"—there was one on the discovery of Walter Greaves, another titled "The Island of Bohemia" (Drachmann, Prszybyszewski, Wedekind, et al.) and, finally, a summation of her English adventures with Wilde, John, and Lewis.[4]

"It is high time for me to leave England," Frida wrote her British go-between, "for since you handed me Mr. Pond's amiable and flattering letter, I find myself 'lecturing' continuously—whilst walking in the streets, at night, in bed—so that grave doubts will certainly be raised before long, if not against my loyalty, at least against my peacefulness!"[5]

The lecture circuit in the United States was profitable. Professional societies, charitable organizations, and business clubs sought speakers able to combine fame (or notoriety) with a degree of showmanship. The cultural changes in Munich, Vienna, and London that Frida intended to describe in her talks were already affecting American society by 1914, but they would not yet have been obvious to Pond's establishment audiences. It was in Greenwich Village that young bohemians had begun to bait American "gentility" with the provocative magazines, little theaters, and sexual experimentation that had been the earmarks of Europe's cultural rebels.

Unlike the role she had played in London, where she had promoted local culture, in America she would be calling attention to creative achievements that had occurred elsewhere. This was a much harder task, and there was no Heinemann or Ross to direct her to those who mattered. In addition, Americans were particularly conscious in 1914 of their political distance from Europe. They did not want to get involved in the war. At its outbreak in August, President Woodrow Wilson had called it "a distant event, terrible and tragic, but one which does not concern us closely." Nevertheless, Frida counted on the lecture bureau to get her started and Strindberg to keep her going.

J. S. Pond handled the advertising and publicity very well. This was the first time Frida was the star, and she seemed to have as natural a knack for promoting herself as she had others. Her presence intrigued the press as much as her subject. The passion and intensity with which she pleaded the case of Strindberg led one reporter to describe her as a "living flame," while others could not say enough about her lively presence, energy, and sense of mission.[6]

The reports of the lectures themselves revealed a less subtle message than the one on which she had elaborated in her original proposal. "Widow Says Strindberg Did Not Hate Women," read one headline; in the article Frida was quoted as saying that it was only the "mannish" woman that aroused Strindberg's ire. "He wanted healthy souls in women," she explained elsewhere. And, pandering to her audience, "He would have admired American women, for they have healthy souls." In response to absurd questions, she betrayed her ready wit. When a woman asked if Strindberg's frequent references to cooks had a symbolic meaning, Frida answered succinctly, "They mean that genius is as greatly tormented by bad cooking as other mortals. Probably his motive was revenge."[7]

The publicity generated by Frida for Strindberg and his work led to a meeting with the Russian actress Alla Nazimova, who had long been an enthusiast of Strindberg's plays but had had little opportunity to appear in one in New York. Nazimova, too, had once found herself a supplicant before J. T. Grein, the arbiter of drama, in England. Her company, the St. Petersburg Players, had arrived in London from Russia in 1904, hoping to call attention to their Russian-language production of Chirikov's *The Chosen People,* a controversial Romeo and Juliet-style melodrama written in protest against the racist policies of the Czar. With Grein's backing, the company played for four weeks in London, and, as a result of its success, proceeded to New York. There, *The Chosen*

People found an audience among the growing Jewish population, and the critics were as enthusiastic as they had been in England. In 1906, when Lee Shubert, one of the influential men in New York theater, offered Nazimova a five-year contract and six months' pay for the time needed for her to learn English, she decided to stay in America.[8]

Nazimova had been an apprentice in Stanislavsky's Moscow Art Theater, where she had starred in plays by Ibsen, Dostoyevsky, and Chekhov. Her powers of persuasion were so considerable that she was able to convince Shubert that the vehicle for her New York debut should be Ibsen's *Hedda Gabler*, rather than a piece of Broadway fluff. The play was a success, and Nazimova developed into a major Broadway attraction, but in the following years she was given only mediocre pieces in which to perform. She longed to return to serious theater. When asked by a reporter in 1912 who her favorite playwright was, she answered, unhesitatingly, "Strindberg. He utters a great truth when he says 'Men and women hate each other always in the depths of their hearts. . . .' That is so true."[9]

This was not exactly the message Frida had been propagating in her lectures, but in Nazimova she had found a kindred soul, someone equally desirous of bringing contemporary European drama to the attention of American audiences. When Frida began lecturing on Strindberg, serious theater in America faced two obstacles. The first was the theater monopolies, or syndicates, which owned playhouses across the country, managed the major actors and actresses, and organized out-of-town bookings for maximum box-office results. Plays were devices to them, not vehicles for ideas. Subjects, characters, and plots were elements to be manipulated to please an audience. The second obstacle was a culture steeped in standards of prudery officially upheld by the law. Paddy wagons waited outside theaters to haul away cast members who dared speak censored lines. Organizations such as Watch and Ward in Boston and the Society for the Suppression of Vice in New York wielded considerable power. As a result, plays by Ibsen, Hauptmann, Chekhov, and, assuredly, Strindberg were rarely, if ever, produced. Strindberg's naturalistic plays such as *Miss Julie, The Father,* and *Creditors* acknowledged aspects of the struggle between the sexes that American authorities could not countenance. At the same time, his later work, dealing with more mystical themes, was virtually unknown.

Nazimova encouraged Frida to move beyond the lectures and direct plays by Strindberg. This was possible under the auspices of the Stage Society, a type of *Freie Bühne* set up in 1912 as a showcase for noncommercial drama. Professional actors participating for free starred in productions that were performed on Sundays and Mondays, when the theaters were closed to the public. The expenses were paid by the three hundred subscribers, and money remaining after the production went to the Actors' Fund.

Initially, the Stage Society's scheme had been threatened by the laws prohibiting performances on Sunday, but by an elaborate series of pretenses it was possible to call the Sunday-evening event a dress rehearsal. No tickets were issued, no programs distributed, and Stage Society members and their guests entered by the stage door, while the lobby and foyer remained dark. Two "real" presentations followed on Monday. An organization so admirably flexible welcomed a play by Strindberg directed by his widow, and the press was equally intrigued.

In December 1915, *Town and Country* published an article on Frida's plan to produce one or two Strindberg works, perhaps more, under the auspices of the Stage Society. Since the participation of "Strindberg's widow" was part of the appeal, the piece was accompanied by a glamorous photograph of Frida taken by the leading celebrity photographer, Arnold Genthe. In January,

The New York Times announced an even more ambitious plan: Frida intended to present a series of Strindberg's plays, including unpublished pieces. She declared that she wished to introduce American audiences to the later and more optimistic Strindberg, and to present him as the pioneer of the intimate theater, the "pioneer in whose footsteps Antoine, Gordon Craig, Stanislavsky, and Reinhardt have followed."[10]

For her first production, scheduled for mid-February 1916, Frida chose *Easter*, a play written in 1902 with a cast of six characters and the single setting of a glass-enclosed veranda. In three acts, taking place on Holy Thursday, Good Friday, and Easter, a family shamed by a father imprisoned for debt moves through despair and contrition to the resurrection of hope. At the center of the drama is a holy fool, Eleanora, the daughter of the house, momentarily home on leave from a mental institution. It was a role in which Strindberg skillfully deployed his awareness of the delicate balance between religious vision and mental instability, spiritual strength and psychological frailty. The part was to go to Nazimova, and her name gave the production extra cachet.

Rehearsals were fraught with conflict, and the opening night was delayed two weeks. "No Lily-Like Calm About This 'Easter'" a *New York World* headline read. Nazimova, who had virtually directed herself in her Ibsen triumph, bridled under Frida's imperious style, and was replaced by the far less seasoned but more pliant actress Kathleen MacDonell. There were doubts about the set, designed especially for the production by Norman Wilkinson, and there were issues of billing; Frida insisted that the stage manager was not to appear on the program as her associate director.[11]

The performance itself was well received. Although one reviewer found the note of suffering in the play too dominant, he declared that "there can be nothing but praise for the Strindberg production." *The New York Herald* described it as "sumptuously mounted," and "acted by a cast of superior excellence." The curtain calls for Frida and the cast were numerous.[12]

Deficient in the diplomatic skills required for theater, Frida directed no more plays by Strindberg, but her dedication to promoting his work continued. Since the money from her lectures was not sufficient to support her, she sought a new outlet for Strindberg in the burgeoning American film industry, which had its East Coast headquarters in New York.

The marketing of feature films was in its infancy when Frida arrived in New York. Although longer films were already being made in Europe, single-reel shorts were still the standard fare in the primitive theaters known as nickelodeons that had sprung up all over America. Since entry was cheap and profits depended on audience turnover, owners and managers resisted long performances. Nevertheless, in 1914, two film companies, the Lasky Feature Play Company, headed by Jesse Lasky and Cecil B. DeMille, and Famous Players Film Company, organized by Adolph Zukor, began to make feature films from adaptations of theatrical properties. Instead of being shown in nickelodeons, these longer productions were to be screened in theaters as elegant as those built for the stage, with ticket prices to match. When the two companies merged to form the Famous Players Lasky Film Corporation in 1916, Lasky and Zukor became the leading figures in a business transformed within a few short years from a supplier of inexpensive working-class entertainment to one that had become a serious competitor to the theater. Frida's familiarity with European playwrights was attractive to these early filmmakers, and she was hired by Fox Film to develop properties, including work by Strindberg.

It was with this assignment in mind that Frida sought out the Danish actress Asta Nielsen, a silent-screen star in Europe, who was briefly stranded in America by the war in 1917. Nielsen had received several proposals to appear in American films, but she was sufficiently satisfied with her European career to resist them. Nevertheless, she was intrigued when she was invited to meet with a representative of Fox Film by the name of Frida Strindberg. She knew that this had to be Strindberg's second wife, and recognized Frida immediately by her resemblance to Harriet Bosse.

Frida asked Nielsen if she would consider playing Henriette, a figure loosely based on Strindberg's memories of Dagny Juel, in an American film version of his play *There Are Crimes and Crimes.* Without Nielsen in the major role, she explained, Fox would not consent to the production. On a more personal note, she revealed that Fox's interest in the play was the first real break in her attempt to promote Strindberg in America. In the beginning, she said, she had submitted articles to various newspapers, but more often than not she had been confronted by editors who had no idea who Strindberg was. Her discouragement, more than anything else, convinced Nielsen that the filming of a Strindberg play in a country where his name had so little resonance was doomed to failure. Nevertheless, she found it "not uninteresting" to have met Frida.

> *She was a highly intelligent woman, who, clearly, was not living in the best of circumstances. Her hair hung in strands around a faded, once pretty face. . . . In the extreme heat she wore a tight, dark-green velvet dress that had seen better days and adding to its superfluity, it was draped with a train, which by brushing the ground and the asphalt enveloped the entire lower part of her body with clouds of dust.*[13]

A few months later, unable to find passage home and in need of money, Nielsen wrote Frida that she would reconsider the proposal. Delighted with this possibility, Frida invited her to visit the Fox studios in Brooklyn. Confronted by the chaotic conditions under which several films in various stages were being produced at the same time, Nielsen was convinced her original decision had been the right one.

I was taken to a space under the roof of a high building, that was not more than a quarter the size of our large "Union" studios in Berlin and to my amazement, I saw three directors working simultaneously in three corners of the studio on different films. In the fourth corner a set was being hammered together. Ear-splitting noise filled the hall. . . . Women in Rococo costumes, mingled with gentlemen in tuxedos and white ties and cowboys in leather pants. Sweat ran from the faces of the directors, workers and cameramen.[14]

Frida, who had confessed to Nielsen that she blamed herself for having failed to understand Strindberg while they were married, took Nielsen's rejection in stride. "It was clear to me that she needed a little lift," Nielsen wrote, "but despite the disappointment, she understood fully that only under dignified conditions could one present Strindberg on the screen."[15]

Frida's idea was prescient. When Nielsen was able to return to Germany, her first major hit was a screen version of *There Are Crimes and Crimes,* made in 1919. According to Nielsen, the film was then sold to America, but never shown. "The subject was considered too serious for American taste," she remembered.[16]

Frida did eventually succeed in the industry, but not as the purveyor of Strindberg. She understood that the film industry's commitment to a playwright was dependent on a star. Instead, she became a screenwriter under the pseudonym "Marie Eve."[17] By 1917, even the theater could no longer supply the number of properties the flourishing industry demanded, and a new market sprang up for original scenarios, or "photoplays."

The golden years for amateur writers would last until the

mid-twenties, when screenwriting became a profession. Movie magazines published more ads for photoplay-writing schools than for acting classes. A periodical dedicated exclusively to this aspect of the industry—*The Photoplay Author*—offered advice on technique, featured successful "photoplaywrights," and included a column on the state of the photoplay market. Film companies advertised avidly for scripts, promising to read all submitted manuscripts if they were typed and accompanied by a synopsis.

Marie Eve was successful as a photoplay author. Two of her stories—*The Death Dance* and *The Golden Shower* were made into films in 1918 and 1919.[18] Drawing on her cabaret experience, Frida made stage performers of the standard innocent heroines demanded by the early filmmakers. Her plots revolved around the lust and envy they aroused by appearing on the stage. "I have chosen film as a way of earning a living," she wrote in a letter in 1920. "First of all because now is the time for it financially, secondly because grammar doesn't stand in my way there, thirdly because I like writing the murderous trash, without it touching me morally or intellectually."[19]

By the time the war ended, in November 1918, Frida knew her way around New York. Familiar with film companies, magazine editors, and publishers, she had learned to survive by writing photoplays and articles and had even acquired an agent. Now that Europe was accessible again, she could expand her possibilities by returning to the familiar role of cultural go-between. But the break with her family remained absolute. She made no effort to find out how they had survived.

Her latest passion was for Russian writers, and she was eager to translate German editions of their work into English. She wrote to the Russian poet Aleksandr Blok expressing her admiration and asking to translate his poetry with the assistance of the

Irish writer Padraic Colum. Before long a new candidate, another Russian, presented himself as the writer whose career she believed she had been destined to foster. This time he was neither husband nor lover, since the connection remained an epistolary one until many years later. But once again Frida was dealing with a writer whose ideas about sex had brought him notoriety.

In 1903, the twenty-five-year-old Mikael Artzybashev completed his novel *Sanin*, which he called an "apology for individualism." Sanin, its hero, lives without moral restraint and advocates sexual emancipation, rejection of all authority, and the absolute freedom of the individual to pursue his own desires. Old-fashioned concepts of honor making outcasts of children born out of wedlock or shameful figures of men who refuse to duel are shown to be foolish and unnecessary.

At first no Russian publishing house would touch the manuscript, but in 1907, after the upheaval of the 1905 revolution, the book was printed and became an international sensation. Translations appeared all over Europe and *Sanin* cults became a phenomenon of student life. So familiar was the title that when a member of the Russian government referred to "*Sanin*-morals," he did not have to provide an explanation. In 1915, *Sanin* appeared in America under the imprint of B. W. Huebsch and, surprisingly, evaded the eyes of the New York Society for the Suppression of Vice.

Having published Joyce's *Dubliners* in 1911, Huebsch was the first of a group of Jewish publishers to challenge the conservatism of a predominantly Christian industry by bringing European modernism to America. Alfred A. Knopf followed in 1915 with a list of contemporary works by European and Russian writers. In 1917 Albert Boni, Horace Liveright, and Boni's uncle Thomas Seltzer founded Boni & Liveright and launched the invaluable Modern Library series.

Seltzer was the *eminence grise* of all three publishers. Born in Russia in 1875, he came to the United States when he was eleven and worked in a sweatshop until he could afford an education. When he graduated from the University of Pennsylvania at twenty-two, he was fluent in Russian, Yiddish, German, French, and Italian and began a career as a translator and editor. Many of the writers he promoted had figured in Frida's life. He translated Sudermann for Huebsch, Przybyszewski and Artzybashev for Knopf, and for the first two titles of the Modern Library chose Wilde's *Picture of Dorian Gray* and Strindberg's *Married.*[20]

The adventurous spirit of these fledgling publishers carried a price. Many contemporary European authors dealt with sex in a far more frank and provocative way than American writers. Before the First World War, according to one publishing historian, "there was virtually no eroticism in books published in the United States . . . little literary sign at all that the sexes were physically attracted to one another."[21] For that reason these new publishers were constantly being harassed by John Sumner, head of the New York Society for the Suppression of Vice. In 1915, Knopf knuckled under by destroying the plates of Przybyszewski's *Homo Sapiens,* his novel describing the sexual competition for Dagny at the *Schwarze Ferkel.* In the 1920s, however, when Seltzer and Liveright, at considerable cost to themselves, took their battle against the Society into the courtroom and won, they brought the American literary scene abreast of the European avant-garde.

In 1916, Seltzer had written an introduction to Artzybashev's play *War,* a tragic drama of men and women caught up in mindless patriotism. He introduced Artzybashev, along with Leonid Andreyev and Maxim Gorky, as one of the three great living Russian writers to have achieved world fame. Americans, he pointed out, were reading *Sanin* by the thousands, despite their puritanical tendencies. Although Seltzer criticized Artzybashev's contempt for any form of sexual morality in *Sanin*, saying that he did not take ethical factors sufficiently into account, he praised Artzybashev's ability to create characters that were powerfully alive.[22]

After *Sanin*, Artzybashev had continued to write pessimistic novels and plays in which sex played a central role. He also began to edit his own newspaper, *Svoboda*, which was suppressed at the start of the war. With his anarchist leanings, Artzybashev was not sympathetic to the war, or to the later Bolshevik coup, but he did not leave Russia until 1923, when the harassment became unbearable. Since his mother was Polish and a granddaughter of the great patriot Kosciuszko, he was able to emigrate to Poland. There, poverty-stricken, ill with tuberculosis, and under constant threat of extradition, he nevertheless continued to criticize the Russian regime in the émigré newspaper *Za Svobodu!*[23]

Translations of Artzybashev's books often appeared in pirated editions in the West, though no payments were made to author, translator, or publisher because Russia was not party to the international copyright agreement. To circumvent this, Artzybashev's German publisher, Georg Müller Verlag, translated his books from manuscript and copyrighted the translations before the books appeared in Russia. In the early twenties, desperate for money, the author laid claim to royalties owed him, and Müller, in turn, asked Frida to represent him in the English-speaking countries. Her job was to go after those publishers who had unwittingly assumed his work to be free and clear of obligation. No task could have appealed to Frida more than to give succor to a sickly yet defiant writer in exile, and soon enough she was referring to Artzybashev as "my Russian."

Frida's dedication to the task went far beyond the pursuit of those who had published illegal editions. She offered Artzybashev's work to American and British publishers, sought out translators, and dealt with lawyers and literary agents in England, France, and Germany. In the process, she funneled money directly to Artzybashev whenever possible. She herself translated two of his books from the German for Boni & Liveright in 1922: a novel, *The Savage*, and a collection of three plays, *Jealousy*, *Enemies*, and *The Law of the Savage*. Artzybashev provided a new preface for the latter, in which he offered an idealistic vision of sexual relations in the future, a blueprint for the same sexual utopia Hans Jaeger had dreamed of nearly forty years before.

Man will seek spiritual intercourse independent of sex; physical nearness independent of spiritual life. When spiritual attraction arises between man and woman, they naturally will bestow upon each other physical caresses, but this caress will not be obligatory and dominating in their relations. Then only will jealousy, betrayal. and deceit disappear. Man and woman will freely unite and freely separate, will interrupt and renew physical relations without unhappiness.[24]

Since her arrival in New York in 1914, Frida had drawn on all her resources—writing skills, literary connections, even the fascination of her own history—to make a place for herself in a foreign cultural landscape. She was approaching fifty, and the days of the "*grande amoureuse*" seemed to have passed. She was conscious of a new serenity, and sometime in 1918 she wrote a droll and very frank letter to John about the changes in her attitude toward life as well as her appearance.

My dear once friend,

In these days of forced spiritism you won't be surprised to see one of the dead come back (another question is whether you will be very unpleasantly affected by this untimely return). Let me reassure you therefore at once that the evil is not as bad as it may seem, for I'm really quite, quite dead. . . . I'll never again commit suicide because you are blind to my charms—I never never again shall resent any happiness you find. . . .

I had not a fair chance years ago. . . . I was a pretty sadly tracked human being and mildly hysterical in consequence.

I'm not a femme du monde any longer, neither in clothes nor in thoughts, but I have become a man whom you would like . . . as a friend. . . .

She concluded with a harsh assessment of America.

You'd like America where its brutality is unvarnished, where the people are not washed and smell the vulgar brute, for there at least it is genuine. But its efforts at culture, art, distinction or cleanliness are *odious. . . . I think Swedenborg meant them when he dreamt of the dirt-hell—but with no romance or fin-de-siècle perfume about it.*[25]

Her nomadic pattern of living continued. Her letters were mailed from the offices of her friends or her lawyer and in none of them did she refer to a permanent home. In June 1921, when she was interviewed from just such an office at 8 West 40th Street by *The New York Times Magazine*, she revealed how much she still relied on the past for her identity. She was not the subject of the article—it concerned a doctor she had known in Vienna—but it gave her free rein to express herself.

She pointed to the public library across the street. "I love it dearly," she said, "and when in New York I always manage to live close to it somehow. In a way it is my home. My friends are there and my family. My husband is there, complete now in 58 volumes of which one-fourth part deals with science. . . .

My father Friedrich Uhl, novelist, critic, connoisseur, and editor is also there. . . ."[26]

By the early twenties Frida was enough of a name in New York's artistic circles to be listed as one of the organizers of the United Artists Russian Relief Fund alongside well-known screen stars, actors, musicians, and writers. At the same time, she widened the scope of her dedication to the distant Artzybashev by soliciting assistance from everyone she knew, even writing pleading letters to Sudermann and John. After Artzybashev fled Russia in 1923 and lay ill in Warsaw, she redoubled her efforts. Many years later in a column in an Austrian newspaper, the humorist Roda Roda, who had known Frida in New York, recalled the extent to which she was willing to help her protégé in Poland.

One morning Frida appeared at the Hotel Astor, where the German writer Herbert Eulenberg was packing for his departure to Hamburg on the ocean liner *Nord*. In her arms she held an entire new wardrobe, complete with underwear, that she had convinced a wealthy New York art patron to buy for "her Russian." Eulenberg, she hoped, would be able to transport her prize in his luggage. But it was eleven o'clock on a Sunday, the boat was to leave at three, and there was no room in a single trunk for her acquisition. Frida ran down to Broadway, found a shop selling fabric and thread, and frantically began to sew a bag herself. But the homemade receptacle was far from finished as three o'clock arrived. Frida, tears of frustration in her eyes, was forced to relinquish "the trousseau," and it was as many separate pieces that it was deposited in the ship's hold. According to Roda Roda, a few months later Artzybashev confirmed from Warsaw the puzzling delivery of an American farm implement.[27]

Frida might have remained in America had she not received a letter from Kerstin in 1920—their first communication in seven years. Her daughter had discovered her whereabouts through a mutual acquaintance who had run across Frida in a New York bookstore. Kerstin, now twenty-six, was living in Munich. She had married the young publisher Ernst Sulzbach, and was the mother of a one-year-old boy. Her husband came from a prominent Frankfurt banking family and his father, Emil Sulzbach, was one of the city's most important music patrons. For Frida, the renewed contact with her daughter and the discovery that she was a grandmother appeared to be a miraculous reprieve, an opportunity to make amends, a chance to reflect and explain. Here, at last, was an intimate with whom she could explore the tangle of her experiences. Her first letters were effusive and forthright.

I can lie here all the night looking at the moon . . . and am with you. I know enough about you now to dream and then a happiness and peace comes into my heart that I have never known. . . . But that my mother stole you, extorted you from me from the time you were small, that is the only thing I cannot forget till I am on my deathbed. And even if I repeat to myself, that in exchange she protected you from harm and need, I still cannot forgive it. Once a life is broken in spirit, nothing makes it whole again after. It doesn't matter where one ends up, once one is off the track.[28]

She explored her insights into the abiding flaw that had determined the course of her life.

From the time I was young, I loved the most, where I was dealt with the worst and never looked for those who would be good for me, rather I clung like a slave, often without real love, to those who were bad to me. I believe all the misery in my life can be directly attributed to this since the really fine blossoming of personality does not come from tears, but from happiness. . . .[29]

Strindberg, inevitably, was exempted from this company. With him, Frida insisted, she had always felt happy in her heart, even if he had often made it impossible for her to express it.

When, soon after hearing from Kerstin, Frida made overtures to Max Friedrich, and did not hear from him immediately, she admitted to Kerstin that she had much to answer for. "If anyone is at fault for what he lacks, only I am," she wrote. "He is the sacrifice, for which I deserve the *bastonnade* (or, in fact, the life that became my share . . .)."

Even her memories of Wedekind had been tempered by time. "There was much good in him," she conceded to Kerstin, "but only someone with a store of simple tenderness as Tilly must have (I was too analytical and felt everything too deeply), a woman with faith and diplomacy (which I also lacked), could have the good part of him."

Kerstin, alas, was not the contented wife and mother Frida had greeted with such fervor in her first letters. She was unhappily married and, thus far, her attempts to find a profession—in teacher training and as an apprentice to a printer—had failed. At first, Frida urged her to continue searching for work, explaining that for her, being active had saved her from the evils of aging and stagnating. But when she began to sense that her advice was doing little to assuage Kerstin's misery, Frida decided upon a gesture that was the closest she could come to a demonstration of faith in her recently-restored child. Notifying her lawyer in Germany, she arranged to put her prize possession—the basket of letters from Strindberg—in Kerstin's safekeeping.[30] What Frida did not know was that by 1923 Kerstin's marriage was virtually over, and the sudden arrival of her valuable literary property offered a tempting way out of the financial difficulties of the young couple's separation. Without informing Frida, they decided to sell the letters to Bonniers, Strindberg's publisher.

When Frida heard about the transaction, her response was quick and sure: the letters were to be returned to the lawyer at once, even those addressed to Kerstin, since they all belonged exclusively to Frida herself.

Every page and note is my property and every page and note remains my property. That is not sweet of me. But it is quite intelligent. . . . So deliver it as quickly as possible, every bit and then wash your hands in innocence. I am sorry that you have such a hard-hearted mother—but you can't change that anymore—I am the way I am.

After the giving of the orders and the softening of the blow came the thoughts of the businesswoman. Frida asked Kerstin to find out what Bonnier had been willing to pay for the letters. "I would like to know if it was a good or a bad deal. In my view, it would be madness to sell the letters now. They will grow in value and the moment for them has not yet arrived."[31]

And yet the swiftness with which her child had seized the correspondence suggested that the moment would soon arrive. Frida's newly directed maternal instinct pointed the way. She proposed to Bonniers that they could buy the letters from her but only as part of a memoir of her marriage to Strindberg. The money would be used to help Kerstin, but Frida would be in control. Bonniers was eager, and in 1924, after a stay of ten years, Frida left New York for Europe. She was going to resume the maternal role she had rejected almost thirty years before. But with this decision, the hopeful phase of her renewed relationship with Kerstin ended.

· 10 ·

Family Reunion

UPON ARRIVING IN SWEDEN, Frida arranged for the sale of the Strindberg letters, the publication of her memoir, and, most important, Kerstin's share in these transactions. But the vehemence with which the fifty-two-year-old mother assumed her long-abandoned role was more than the thirty-year-old daughter could bear.

Kerstin was divorced, sickly, had little money, and might have been amenable to a helping hand. But Frida, never one to rely on tact, tried to use the Bonniers agreement to browbeat Kerstin into taking care of herself. The two women were soon at war, and letters of complaint rained down on Karl Otto Bonnier, the editor and head of the company, as well as on the lawyer for the Strindberg estate. Kerstin was so overwhelmed by her mother's manipulations that she refused to let her know where she was living; communication was maintained through representatives in Stockholm. Even Bonnier suggested the two take a break from each other.

Frida conceded to this necessity "... I cannot complain if a child I left to my mother to protect it from need, became hostile," she wrote Bonnier. "The intention was good but I understood too late, that anything else would have been better than that."[1]

These sad developments did not dissuade Frida from writing her book. For the next few years, dividing her time between Berlin and Vienna, staying with friends or in hotels, it was her major obsession. When, in 1925, she discovered that Wedekind's biographer, Arthur Kutscher, was in the process of publishing a second volume, she asked him to return her letters and make no reference to them. Wedekind had wanted no part in her life, she explained, and, therefore, there was no reason for her life to be mixed with his. She requested a "clean break in love and death" not only for her own sake, but also because public revelations of her time with Wedekind would affect the book she was writing, a book that was to benefit her daughter.

On a visit to Stockholm in the spring of 1926, Frida was interviewed by *Dagens Nyheter,* Sweden's leading newspaper. She presented its readers with the idealized picture of Strindberg she had created for herself: a father with great tenderness for children, a writer who suffered physically from having to conduct his marriage in a foreign tongue, a thinker who explained his ideas to her with "infinite patience and generosity." She was hard on herself. "When one is young," she told the interviewer, "one is brazen—I thought it to be the most natural thing to criticize the most celebrated writers in Austria and discuss *Faust* with extreme superiority." Strindberg, she insisted, had been far above her but it was precisely his preeminence that had affected the rest of her life. "Through him my existence was brought up to the higher plane and once you have felt the rapture of flying, you can't live without it, it becomes absolutely necessary."[2]

In all the excitement of her return to Europe, Frida did not forget "her Russian." By the mid-1920s Mikael Artzybashev was severely ill in Warsaw. Frida remained in touch with him, made sure he received the money due him, and, finally, in the last weeks before his death on March 23, 1927, went to nurse him in Poland. Although this was the only time she and Artzybashev had been face-to-face, she wrote Bonnier that after Strindberg, he had been her only other soul mate.[3] In the following years she sought help for his widow whenever possible.

Frida's vagabond existence ended with Maria Uhl's death in Mondsee in 1929. Her mother was eighty-five years old and had been withdrawn and out of touch for several years. Villa Uhl was bequeathed to Frida and Mitzi's son, Caesar Weyr, but Frida was able to acquire her nephew's share with the money she had received from Bonniers. Settling in the house of her childhood, she fired off letter after letter to the publisher as she struggled to complete her book and keep track of Kerstin. Her suggestions, questions, complaints, and complicated financial transactions may have tried Bonnier's patience, but he remained polite and encouraging and only asked Frida mildly if she couldn't keep her letters a little shorter. His forbearance was rewarded when he received the long-awaited manuscript in early 1932. Of all the responses that were to follow, none pleased Frida more than the first burst of praise from her editor after her years of chaotic dedication.

All in all, in my opinion, you have completed a literary task of importance. You have written a book that is not only of great interest because it deals with Strindberg, but because it gives a lively picture of the development of a young woman who could not extricate herself from Strindberg's power to enchant and charm. And, above all, for me and my wife, who knew the Strindberg of the 1890's better than most, how real, how like himself down to the smallest detail he appears here, with his ugly faults and his considerable winning and delightful appeal.[4]

If Bonnier thought peace would descend once Frida had turned in her manuscript, he was mistaken. He erred in choosing a young woman to do the translation from German to Swedish and thus awakened Frida's fierce possessive instinct regarding the language in which Strindberg had courted her. Wouldn't a man do a better job, she immediately asked Bonnier. He reassured her that there could not be a better choice than the thirty-two-year-old Karen Boye, one of Sweden's most talented young poets and the translator of Thomas Mann's *The Magic Mountain*. Unfortunately, he added that Boye was a great admirer of Strindberg's and knew most of his books thoroughly. Frida took the statement as a challenge and agreed to Boye's translation only if she was allowed supervision.

Complaints soon followed. Boye's translation was too free, it improved on the original, it was too ladylike, had the air of a student. Boye had no grasp of Strindberg's personality and used too contemporary a tone. Frida even asked if Boye understood the honor she had been given, but the imperturbable Bonnier held fast. Even when the book was published and praised, Frida remained convinced that she was the ultimate authority on Strindberg's language in the letters. In a final riposte to Bonnier on the matter, she could not resist specifying the source of her self-assurance. "I, myself, really believe, that for us women, the brain does not reside in the head. Please don't tell Frau Boye that. She doesn't understand it yet. When she once understands it, she will write very good books, or maybe she will no longer write any."[5]

Strindberg's Second Wife appeared in Sweden in 1934. The German version, titled *Love, Suffering and Time*, followed in 1936 and a revised and shortened edition, *Marriage with Genius*, was published by Jonathan Cape in London a year later. In 1939 a Danish translation, *Strindberg's Second Marriage*, was issued in Copenhagen.

Writing the memoir of her years with Strindberg gave Frida the rare opportunity to make up for what she now believed had been the shortsightedness of youth. As she had written Kerstin from New York, she felt she had begun to understand Strindberg only after suffering had made her more human, had given her some insight into herself. "He needed a lot [to put up with me]," she admitted.[6] The book was a successful blend of two stories. Frida's forgiving account of the courtship and marriage, and the unmediated intensity and passion of the original experience captured in the letters interwoven throughout the text. The two parts were so skillfully blended that, had the reader not known the outcome, the rocky course of the romance between the obstinate child-bride and the ardent but troubled genius would not have seemed doomed to failure until the very end.

Frida's narrative style was marked by playful humor and self-irony. Her capacity to be amused by her youthful self and her complicated husband provided the human dimension that was the book's greatest asset. Recalling an incident from their courtship, she describes how she had arrived late for an appointment with Strindberg, and he had admitted to his fear that she would not show up out of revenge. When Frida, nonplussed, asks why he would ascribe such a motive to her, he replies that she is a woman and he had, after all, attacked and insulted women.

> *Wonderful! How my self-esteem rose to be taken for an avenger of my sex. Dear heaven, if he only knew that I was no such tragedian, but only a dumb schoolgirl. . . . If he knew that. But he was never to know it. With the smile of the sphinx I sauntered to his side.*[7]

Another discussion pertaining to her sex ensued just before Kerstin was born. Strindberg had a theory that the pain of child-bearing was a myth created to cover up the reality that women experienced feelings of sexual pleasure during childbirth. He insisted that the myth still held for two reasons: the boundary between lust and pain was not easy to distinguish and women were liars.

Since no man had borne a child—till now—there were no unbiased witnesses regarding the feelings this act released. He expected that I, the woman to whom he was married, would finally assist in bringing the real truth to light. Naturally I agreed magnanimously: Who wouldn't want to unite the useful with the pleasant?[8]

The book was also enriched by Frida's ability to evoke the cycle of seasons that marked their brief union and reflected the shifting inner life of a young woman moving from naïve delight to reluctant disillusionment. Snow is crisp underfoot during the Berlin courtship, flowers begin to bloom in the months of their engagement, foul odors penetrate the close marital quarters in London, and isolating fogs close in on the *Häusel* on the Danube.

A critical success everywhere, the book received glowing reviews from writers including Knut Hamsun and the Danish author Karen Michaelis. In a charming letter, Thomas Mann, who protested that he was too busy to review the book as requested, wrote Frida that the greatest compliment he could give her was that the book had preoccupied him far more than he wanted it to.

Your book is of spellbinding interest; I read it daily, it distracts me irresistibly from that which I was so resolutely determined to concentrate on, and so my gratitude for the extraordinary gift and my thanks for it has something irritated about it, from which you should, nonetheless—why should I not say it openly—take more pride than in some less ambivalent response to your work.[9]

Those direct and positive responses in the published reviews, however, were sometimes preceded by ambivalence, as one German critic conceded.

Frida Strindberg, who wanted to set up a monument to the genius of August Strindberg in this book, has set up a monument to herself at the same time, proving herself equal to the subject of her great husband. When an extraordinary talent occupies itself with the extraordinary existence of an extraordinary spirit, a book emerges that we introduce, deliberately, as extraordinary. Saying this, the reviewer admits that he took up this book with a certain prejudice beforehand. For what does a book that was presumably intended as a justification by a woman have to do with the phenomenon of Strindberg? But when, filled with emotion, he put the book down, he was convinced that what lay before him was one of the best commentaries on Strindberg.[10]

Frida bathed in the success of her mission. She was no longer the woman behind the scene—whether as lover, translator, agent, screenwriter, publicist, or patron—of the writers and artists she admired. She was out front as Strindberg's representative. The same long letters that had overwhelmed Bonnier now went out to others who might help her promote Strindberg. To Jonathan Cape she broached the idea of publishing a complete English edition of Strindberg's work, to the civic authorities in Mondsee she outlined ideas for Strindberg tours and courses with headquarters at Villa Uhl, and through Anne Watkins, her agent in New York, she tried to have her book published in America. Watkins was very sympathetic and called the book "a magnificent work." She sent copies to Eugene O'Neill, Clifton Fadiman, and Henry Seidel Canby, among others. In the end, however, she had to write Frida about the sad truth of American cultural life in 1936. All the publishers she had approached had come to the same conclusion: there was no market for a Strindberg biography in America. Even the Modern Library, she added, had dropped Strindberg from their list.[11]

Frida pressed on. In the spring of 1937, she wrote to O'Neill asking him to rally American writers to protest "the 'death' of Strindberg the writer, twenty-five years after his death as a man." A decade after Frida's valiant efforts, Eric Bentley, writing in his book *The Playwright as Thinker*, published in 1946, reported no change in what was left of Strindberg in America.

He lay in the cold storage of college Scandinavian departments or tucked away in the littlest of little theaters. Miss Julie *or* The Father *turns up here and there in an anthology and the name of Strindberg has perhaps no associations in the public mind, unless it be the dim recollection of another lunatic genius who perhaps never left off beating his wife.*[12]

ALTHOUGH SHE MAINTAINED an international correspondence, Frida was living alone in a provincial town far from the great metropolises she was used to. Aging and isolated, no longer in touch with the cultural currents that had nourished her, she became increasingly eccentric. The feelings once inspired by her lovers were now bestowed on her dog, Ali. Letters were written in his name, and the baffled Bonnier received a lengthy manuscript describing his adventures. Her conviction of the importance of her role as Strindberg's savior also took on a note of self-delusion. In 1937 she wrote to Bonnier, "I am the woman who protected Sweden's Strindberg, when Sweden let him go. I am the woman who attempted to call him back anew and who is on the way to success."[13] Her constant focus on this goal blinded her to the danger of the growing influence of Nazi Germany. Politically, Frida could be astoundingly cavalier and misguided, as in a 1933 letter recommending her "old friend" Hanns Heinz Ewers to Bonnier, who was Jewish.

> *I am enclosing a letter I just received from Hanns Heinz Ewers. He is a personal friend of Adolf Hitler and Goebbels. He wants to sell my Strindberg memoir to the Cotta Verlag.... Would you want to work somehow with a German publisher, close enough to the regime to have the people behind it?*
>
> *And by the way, I am sending you an outstanding book—the "Horst Wessel" by Dr. Ewers. There is a psychological bent for good works among the young and an unbelievable love for the fatherland that has flamed up at the moment.*[14]

Bonnier's answer was terse. Under no circumstances, he told Frida, would he consider dealing with Germany whether independently or with a German publisher. As for *Horst Wessel*, he would not even think about it.[15]

For Frida, culture would always take precedence over politics, but by the mid-thirties such an attitude was not possible to sustain. The course she devised for herself was pragmatic opportunism. Writing to a supporter of her plans to organize Strindberg tours and courses in Mondsee in 1935, she reassured him that as a Swedish citizen, she avoided local politics. Appealing to his Austrian patriotism, however, she added that she would not tolerate anything against Austria, but neither would she become aggressive toward Germany. She tried to maintain a light touch by making a joke about the number of Jewish converts in Vienna, but also informed him that she had taken precautions to disassociate the project from any Jewish connections.

> *Today one can be Catholic without being Jewish. Even Viennese. (Admittedly one has to be careful in choosing which district to live in.)*

Not to be against. Absolutely not. But not to add spice, where it may be traced. It is a matter of tact and diplomacy, with an awareness of what is coming. . . .

And Frida knew what was coming, as her closing comments advocating caution in dealing with Bonnier revealed.

He is incredibly helpful, kind and good. But one cannot be completely Jewish—that doesn't work. Nowhere in the world. Nowhere, anywhere, for sure. No Swedish order will help against that.[16]

"Tact and diplomacy" would not be sufficient protection for her children, however. Fortunately, Kerstin, aware of the dangers facing her and her half-Jewish son under Hitler's racial laws, asked Bonnier if he could help them become Swedish citizens. As the head of Sweden's largest publishing house and the owner of several newspapers, he had the government's ear. Citizenship for "Strindberg's daughter and his grandson" was granted in 1933. By 1936 Kerstin was living in Stockholm.

After Germany's *Anschluss* of Austria in the spring of 1938 and the demolition of the Salzburg synagogue during *Kristallnacht* in November of that same year, Frida realized that her Swedish citizenship might not protect her from Germany's laws. Her Jewish grandmother was a real threat, and in desperation she and her nephew, Caesar Weyr, wrote to Poland to reassure themselves that on the wedding certificate of Uhl's parents, both bride and groom were registered as Catholic.

Max Friedrich, who had never given up the name Strindberg, faced different but equally serious problems in the years of the Third Reich. Frida's blindness to his case verged on the tragic.

In the early 1920s Max Friedrich had lived in Vienna and was a member of the circle of young intellectuals that gathered around the pioneering educator Eugenia Schwarzwald. What made Schwarzwald's salon different from other social sets in Vienna was its international character. She and her husband welcomed foreigners—journalists and students—even if they were in Vienna for a brief stay. Visitors, including Dorothy Thompson, Sinclair Lewis, Count Helmut von Moltke, Karen Michaelis, mingled happily with the young Austrian intelligentsia, many members of which had passed through Schwarzwald's unorthodox school and shared her liberal social leanings.

It was in this atmosphere that Max Friedrich met his first wife, the Austrian writer and journalist Marie Lazar, whom he married in 1923. A year later their daughter, Judith Maria Genia, was born. Although Max Friedrich and Marie Lazar were separated in 1927, and their friends in the Schwarzwald circle also went their different ways, the bonds of friendship that had been fostered in Vienna proved strong enough to maintain crucial international connections when Hitler and war appeared to have isolated them from each other.

In the late twenties, Max Friedrich began a career as a newspaper editor in Germany. By 1935 he had given up the complications of such a position under the Nazi regime to become a roving journalist and photographer. (Marie Lazar, who was Jewish, left Austria for Denmark with her daughter in 1933.) Max Friedrich's problems began in the summer of 1936 when he was sent on assignment to Spain by the Ullstein publishing group and photographed the clandestine delivery of bombers and pilots by Hitler in support of Franco.

Taking a break in Gibraltar in the midst of this assignment, Max Friedrich spent some time with Sir Percival Phillips, a friend working for the *Daily Telegraph*. Back in Seville, he was intent on being the first German journalist to interview Franco. The contact he hoped to cultivate for this was a German named Bernard, who was in charge of the delivery of weapons for the Spanish leader.

As soon as Max Friedrich entered his office, Bernard confronted him with a copy of the *Daily Telegraph* in which a story had appeared with the names of German pilots and the numbers of German airplanes. When asked if he was the source of the story, Max Friedrich vigorously denied it, but admitted that he had taken photographs at the airfield. He was then shown a photograph of himself and Phillips at a Gibraltar café. Phillips had written the revealing story.

Max Friedrich repeated his denials and reiterated that he was in Spain on assignment for Ullstein and his only purpose was to get an interview with Franco. Bernard agreed to telegraph the German publisher for confirmation, but kept Max Friedrich locked in a room until he received an answer. When he returned to release him, Bernard apologized for his suspicions, invited Max Friedrich to lunch with his German associates, and promised to arrange for the Franco interview.[17]

While they were having coffee in the lobby of the Hotel Kristina, Max Friedrich was suddenly approached by Arthur Koestler, a former colleague who had left Germany shortly after the Nazi takeover in 1933. In his book *Spanish Testament*, published in 1937, Koestler described this encounter and branded Max Friedrich a Nazi informer.

Koestler had come to Spain to hunt down for the British press precisely the kind of evidence that Bernard had accused Max Friedrich of passing to Phillips—the secret shipment of planes from Germany. In describing the group he observed at the Hotel Kristina, Koestler claimed that Max Friedrich rose and strolled by to see him more closely. "The man had recognized me just as I had recognized him," he wrote. "It was Herr Strindberg . . . he was a Nazi journalist and was correspondent in Spain for the Ullstein group." Koestler wrote that his former colleague had been a passionate democrat before Hitler, but insisted he had become a Nazi shortly thereafter. "I had nothing to do with him from then on," Koestler wrote, "but he was perfectly aware of my views and political convictions. He knew me to be an incorrigible left-wing liberal and that was quite enough to incriminate me."[18]

Feeling trapped, Koestler greeted Max Friedrich directly and introduced himself to Bernard, saying, "My name is Koestler. I'm from the *News Chronicle*." Only a few hours after being suspected of giving information to British newspapers, Max Friedrich was embraced by one of their journalists. He did not respond to Koestler, but after being asked, "Why won't you say hello to me?" several times, he recalled saying stiffly, "You see, Koestler, that we are engaged in an important discussion." But by then Bernard was looking at them both, certain of his suspicions. Koestler was ordered to leave the hotel, and Max Friedrich was thoroughly interrogated before Bernard was convinced that he and Koestler were not co-conspirators.

As soon as he could leave the Kristina, Max Friedrich found someone to notify Koestler that he was in trouble and should leave Seville as soon as possible. And, in fact, Koestler concluded his narrative of this episode in *Spanish Testament* by saying that, once back in his hotel, a colleague arrived and advised him to leave for Gibraltar immediately. "He was obviously acting as the mouthpiece of a higher authority," Koestler concluded, "but he refused to say whom. Eight hours later, I was in Gibraltar, twenty-four hours later I learned from private sources that a warrant for my arrest had been issued in Seville." This was followed by the fateful sentence. "So Strindberg junior had his say after all."[19]

Max Friedrich got his interview with Franco, but he was fed only canned phrases. Disgusted with political intrigues, he gave up journalism and began to work exclusively as a photographer in

Berlin. When *Spanish Testament* appeared in 1937 publicly branding him a Nazi, it was an accusation he could not publicly refute, since he was living and working in Germany. Instead, he took private measures and in 1938 applied for Swedish citizenship with the intention of moving to Sweden. The same ruling that had allowed him the name Strindberg—his birth within nine months of Frida and Strindberg's annulment—now enabled him to be legally considered the son of a Swede, and in 1940 he received his Swedish passport. By this measure, Marie Lazar, from whom he was not yet divorced, and their daughter, Judith, also became Swedish citizens. It allowed them to escape to the haven of Sweden's neutrality when the Germans invaded Denmark in 1940.

When he informed Frida of his plan to emigrate to Sweden, Max Friedrich forced her to face an issue she had been avoiding for years. After Max Friedrich was born, in August 1897, Frida did not write to Strindberg again until 1902. He never answered her few desperate letters that followed. Whatever information she received about him came from her mother. It was Maria Uhl, always intent on keeping scandal at bay, who told her that Strindberg had given permission for Max Friedrich to bear his name. Knowing Strindberg's acute sensitivity to matters of paternity—the entire plot of *The Father* revolved around this obsession—it is hard to believe that Frida accepted her mother's story. At that time, though, Max Friedrich was a child, Strindberg was far away, and Frida's own life was taking her elsewhere. It was a temporary way out of a dilemma.

After returning from America in the 1920s, however, and sensing possible complications now that her son was a published journalist, Frida urged him to change his name. But Max Friedrich, who for many years had had neither mother nor father to shore up his identity, was reluctant to give up the name under which he had already achieved a certain renown.

Frida had not pressed him further, but confronted with his decision to move to Sweden, she began to search for a document that would certify what her mother had vouched for. When it became clear that no such paper existed in her own archives or in Sweden, Frida understood that she had been party to a lie. Aware of what such a deception would have meant to Strindberg, not to mention the opening of the old scandal now that she considered herself Strindberg's representative, she was determined to prevent Max Friedrich from moving to Sweden if he did not change his name.

Her son could not agree. Taking another name at this juncture would appear to be a confirmation of Koestler's accusation. Reluctant to tell Frida about the incident in Spain, he offered a compromise. He would go to Sweden as Strindberg*h*—the additional letter at the end distinguishing him from the Swedish Strindbergs. This inventive proposal was sent to the Strindberg family lawyer and, although he approved in principle, the lawyer insisted that Kerstin have a say as well. She refused the compromise.

Kerstin had her own reasons for objecting to her half-brother's arrival. Now living permanently in Sweden, speaking and writing fluent Swedish, she had been accepted into the Strindberg family and had a close relationship with her father's eldest daughter, Karin, as well as with Harriet Bosse. Max Friedrich's presence would be a constant reminder of the scandals that had destroyed her childhood. Kerstin was also active in anti-fascist causes. She had heard of Koestler's accusation, knew that her brother had continued to work for German newspapers, and assumed he had made the necessary political compromises. She went the estate lawyer one better and took legal action against Max Friedrich to change his name immediately. She also rallied the Strindberg family to her cause and wrote to Frida that she could see how "Fritzl's story" distressed her. She assured her that for "those affected here, in other words, we sisters and the other heirs, you are an absolute hero and nobleman."[20]

Under these circumstances, Max Friedrich felt trapped and finally asked his mother to break the impasse. Perhaps to flatter her, he wrote, "I recently heard from the Georg Müller Verlag how brilliantly and with how much energy you went after the rights of Artzybashev. I cannot understand why, for once, this brilliance and energy can't be dedicated to the well-being of your children?" He closed on a poignant note. "In other families, it is thought to be an obligation, in these times, to stay closer together than usual. Only in ours, instead of this natural support for each other, there is hate, and instead of brotherly love, the perverse inclination to destroy the others and thereby ourselves."[21]

Frida refused her son's plea. Her life was no longer dedicated to the living. In her mind, she had done Strindberg a grievous wrong and all her energies now went into making up for it by spreading his name and protecting his reputation. Somehow she believed that the success of the book had erased her mistakes. Unfortunately for Max Friedrich, he was living proof that this was impossible. Frida became adamant. She refused to acknowledge his goodwill in agreeing to a change that would distinguish his branch of the family from the one that, according to her, had become "holy" in Sweden. She accused her son of clinging to the name to further himself. Even Marie Lazar, who had never written a book or an article under her married name, was now accused by Frida of masquerading as Strindberg's daughter-in-law. The irony was that the actions of both Max Friedrich and Marie Lazar in the antifascist cause gave them a heroic stature worthy of any name.

Living in Berlin and feeling relatively secure as a national of a neutral country, Max Friedrich had been able to demonstrate his real sympathies by providing a hideaway for a young Jewish man.

At that time, the number of Jews in Berlin able to escape the deadly transports to the East was rapidly diminishing. The most effective means of avoiding detection was to stay in the private homes of courageous Christians for brief periods of time. The young man to whom Max Friedrich gave shelter was a twenty-four-year-old named Herbert Strauss, who had, for the moment, been appointed an auxiliary rabbi to serve the remnant of the Jewish community. Max Friedrich was one of many who enabled Herbert Strauss to survive at that time, but he performed an additional service that galvanized Strauss and his girlfriend to risk an escape from Germany altogether. Clearly in contact with valuable sources, he gave the young couple the first news of the mass killings of the Jews in the extermination camps set up by the Germans in Poland. The two managed to make it to Switzerland, married there, and eventually emigrated to America, where Strauss, still alive today, became a widely published historian in New York.[22]

The German lawyer who pleaded Max Friedrich's case for the change of name to Strindbergh in Stockholm was Count von Moltke, the friend of both Max Friedrich and Marie Lazar from the Schwarzwald salon. Right from the start of the war, Von Moltke had actively resisted Hitler from the privileged position he held in the department of military intelligence. Until January of 1944, when his work was uncovered and he was imprisoned, and eventually hanged, he not only helped many Jews and others threatened by the Nazi regime to escape, but also worked with a group of like-minded friends to plan for the reformation of Germany after the defeat of Hitler. Both Max Friedrich and Marie Lazar were important contacts for Von Moltke. Max Friedrich's possession of a Swedish passport and the freedom to travel he gained thereby made him a useful informant and conduit. Marie

Lazar was Von Moltke's go-between in Stockholm. While on a diplomatic mission to Sweden in 1943, Von Moltke managed to get two crucial letters out to England with her assistance.[23]

Frida, isolated by the war and brooding about her own past, seemed incapable of grasping the drastic and desperate situations most people found themselves in under Nazi rule. She kept aloof from her neighbors and developed the reputation of being a stingy and suspicious loner. Neglecting the villa, allowing the garden to grow wild, she began to write and rewrite her will. In some versions, she focused on Max Friedrich, threatening his disinheritance if he created a scandal; in others it was Ali's fate after her death that seemed to concern her most. Should the dog be transported by passenger train to friends in Berlin or was a mercy shooting preferable when he was unsuspectingly being led on one of his favorite walks. The moment came sooner than anyone expected. After a fall in a shop on June 15, 1943, Frida entered the hospital in Salzburg for a dislocated shoulder. She seemed to be doing well until the bronchitis she had been suffering at the time she was admitted worsened, developed into pneumonia, and resulted in her death on June 28.

Kerstin, despite the years of battling with her mother, was devastated by the suddenness of Frida's death, as she wrote to a friend.

The old Mère has died and I am as miserable as a stone. As if our mother-daughter relationship was untroubled, harmonious, fulfilling, as if the last living person had been taken from me, that is how I sit here, feeling as terribly helpless and abandoned as never in my life. . . . I don't know who was with her or how she died, I simply believed she was immortal. That was an absolute conviction in my mind, she simply could not be killed. She always rose from the dead, was always there again when one least expected it. Vehement, wild, and uncontrolled, unharmonious and, nevertheless, complete in her way, smart as a woman seldom is and for herself so unmitigatingly . . . dumb, dumb and noble.[24]

After traveling through a continent at war to cope with Frida's estate in Mondsee, Kerstin discovered the chaos of her mother's papers. The precious documents of the family's past lay under threats from creditors, argumentative letters from publishers, complaints from the gardener, and dunning notes from the butcher for deliveries of special orders of dog food. "Only with a donkey's patience, page by page, drop by drop, can I work through this wildly foaming storm-scattered sea," she wrote her cousin Caesar. "Sometimes I think I am standing before a great lake and have to dive after precious stones sinking into slime and moving into oblivion. This family was UNIQUE, extraordinary and valuable." Among those "precious stones" was a packet of letters written by Friedrich Uhl—evidence of a lifelong affair with another Maria.[25]

AND SO AS Frida's life ended, revelations emerged that touched on its beginning—the link between her unorthodox childhood and the hidden life of Friedrich Uhl. For her father, as for most bourgeois nineteenth-century gentlemen, surface appearance had been crucial. Yet Uhl had been more drastic than most in his readiness to sacrifice all three women in his family to that cause. Luckily his ingenious solution to the dilemma of Frida—the temporary bestowal of a profession, rather than an arranged marriage—enabled her to escape her mother's and sister's fate. For a brief moment, Uhl had offered this daughter the vision of what it meant to be a man: she was granted ambition, she was given a purpose, she was permitted to taste the world. Since she was young, sensual, and amusing, as well as intelligent, the tribulations of love soon intervened, but she had gained something few women of her class were ever given—the awareness that she could fend for herself. It made her stubborn and it made her confident and it made her life a difficult one.

When Uhl generously acknowledged Ibsen's importance, he was passing the baton to the next generation. His contemporaries were concerned with concealing reality; Ibsen and his followers made a point of exposing it. And yet even Ibsen, who acknowledged that the consequences of social hypocrisy weighed heaviest on women, offered no vision enabling them to escape their fate. Nor could the men in Frida's life do so, despite living freely in bohemian enclaves, launching radical cultural enterprises, and writing freely about sex. Nothing could have been more indicative of the strange bifurcation between the sexes in Frida's lifetime than Karl Kraus's discussion on the nature of women in *Die Fackel.* In this debate, to which the two men who had fathered Frida's children were invited to contribute, no member of the gender under examination was given a say.

It was Frida who paid the price for her marriage to Strindberg and her liaison with Wedekind. After Strindberg, she had to make her way as a divorcée, after Wedekind as a divorced unwed mother. She was no longer respectable, no longer marriageable, and, for several years, her father kept his distance from her. Her place according to the social codes of the 1890s was with her children, and, financially, that meant relegation to the isolated hamlet of Dornach under her mother's thumb. To save herself, she refused to accept what was considered appropriate for her sex and opted for the male role instead. She kept the same distance from her children as men did, choosing to contribute to their upkeep rather than their upbringing. She kept no home, cultivated no domestic arts, remained free to move and travel. She became an inspired entrepreneur, confident enough to speculate, risk, and take initiatives. And she did not hesitate to take the lead when it came to pursuing or holding a lover.

Unfortunately, she was not adequately prepared for the life she sought, nor was she encouraged. A man with her talents would have been given training, an apprenticeship, the advice of a mentor and, finally, opportunity. Although her father recognized her writing skills, he saw her career as a stopgap measure keeping her out of his way until she was safely married. Strindberg, who initially praised her work, never felt comfortable with her forays into the public world of theater and publishing. And when the marriage came apart, he chose to use her aspirations as fuel for his ugly accusations. By the time she returned to Vienna, her experience in London, Munich, and Berlin had given her the makings of an editor, a publisher, an impresario, but such positions were not available to women. She learned to exercise her talents behind the scenes as an unacknowledged cultural go-between, but instead of the businesslike strategies of her male colleagues, she often acted on impulse and gave way to emotion. When she founded her own enterprise at last, it was her lack of practical experience, her ignorance of financing and administration, that did in the wildly ambitious Cave of the Golden Calf. Nonetheless, it did not keep her from what was perhaps a greater gamble: relying on her experience and talents to keep her afloat in the entirely unknown culture of the United States.

Although she had been with Strindberg for less than two years, he remained the most consistent factor in her life. He had been unjust and cruel to her. His alliance with her mother and daughter and his subsequent abandonment of them had disastrous consequences for Frida. Nevertheless, by an extraordinary act of self-preservation, she overcame bitterness and resentment to create an idealized image of her former husband. It gave her comfort, a sense of dignity, and the satisfaction of paying homage to genius. Ultimately it inspired the finest flowering of her own creativity with the writing of her book. By then she could say from the vantage point of middle age, "I see Strindberg as an immense flame which radiated and consumed."

There can be no doubt that Frida Uhl Strindberg was as difficult as she was intelligent. Every relationship, every undertaking was embattled. Whether it was her combative nature, the frustrations of a love life among the sexual sharks, or the need for control brought on by a precarious existence, she exhausted her lovers, her colleagues, her children. And yet the obdurate energy that was at its source propelled her to leave her mark on the culture of several countries—Austria, England, America, and Sweden—at a time when women were still struggling to have a say in one.

Coda: Max Friedrich and Kerstin

HAVING ACHIEVED SOME kind of reconciliation with Kerstin after Frida's death, Max Friedrich, in 1943, moved to Sweden as planned. Using the pseudonym Frederik Uhlson, he began writing articles for Swedish newspapers. Under his byline, he was introduced as an authority on Hitler's Germany and the author of a forthcoming book.

In early 1945, *Under jorden i Berlin* (*Underground in Berlin*), Max Friedrich's fictionalized version of his experiences among Jews who had escaped deportation and were living in hiding, was published. The story, which took place between October 1942 and the summer of 1943, offered the outside world one of the first pictures of the German network that existed to assist the victims of the Nazis, as well as several other aspects of the Final Solution. Since the book was published before the end of the war, it was probably thought necessary to present the information in fictional form. But both the name of the hero—Herbert Stauss—and the fact that one of his main contacts is a Swedish photographer indicate that Max Friedrich wanted the book to come as close to the documentary truth as possible.

Under jorden i Berlin was widely and favorably reviewed, and less than a year later, the truth emerged that Frederik Uhlson was Max Friedrich Strindberg, the son of Strindberg's second wife. A month later, articles began to appear in Swedish newspapers recounting Koestler's fateful encounter with Max Friedrich in Seville. Koestler's story was followed by Max Friedrich's own version of the events in Spain, as well as supporting evidence from reporters who done research in Germany and found that Frida's son had a distinct anti-Nazi reputation. When Max Friedrich returned to Germany to pick up his journalistic career there, no shadow cast a pall over the name he had refused to give up. After his retirement, he lived in Italy, where he died in 1978.

During the war Kerstin found a companion in Austrian immigrant August Moser, and together they were politically active in the *Freies Österreich* (Free Austria) group, a communist-oriented immigrant organization fostering contacts with the resistance. But Kerstin missed her close friends in Austria and was devastated by the news of the suicides and deportations of those who were Jews. Frida's death in 1943 and the departure of Moser, who went back to Austria when the war ended, added to her depression. On her first postwar visit to the land of her birth in 1946, she found herself estranged and in a constant state of outrage as she confronted an atmosphere in which fascism seemed far from defeated.

Nevertheless, in those difficult postwar years, Kerstin devoted herself to documenting the family legacy. For Bonniers, she helped prepare Strindberg's German letters for the collected edition, and she continued to work on a sequel to Frida's memoir of Strindberg—a volume eventually published under the title *Breven till min dotter Kerstin* (*Letters to My Daughter Kerstin*). She spent years obsessively piecing together, organizing, and making notes on her mother's voluminous correspondence in an effort to create a coherent archive. In her commentaries on Frida's life, she revealed a gift of writing worthy of her paternal inheritance. Her ironic summing up of her mother's attributes, for instance, did her justice.

She was without a doubt, in a certain sense, brilliant, inventive, imaginative. She bubbled over with suggestions, she gave tips from the refined artistic instinct of which she really had an overabundance.

She was witty, she had a baroque wealth of humor and a feeling for the comic and the grotesque. When she found herself erotically inclined toward a literary gentleman, she put her spiritual riches to work.

Organizing her mother's papers involved Kerstin in a new debate with her past, however, and her notes in the archive reveal her seeking answers to the difficulties of her childhood and frustrations of her adult life. Once more she confronts the overprotective attitude of Maria Uhl, who feared nothing more than that Kerstin might turn out to be a second Frida. Yet again she reviews the ill-fated reunion with her mother, when Frida's chaotic way of life and well-meaning but heavy-handed attempts to save her almost drove them apart a second time. Continually these assessments are suffused with the deepest regret of all: the unfulfilled dream of reunion with the father who had written her such enchanting letters before she could even read or write.

In going through her father's archives, Kerstin came upon Strindberg's 1905 note to Harriet Bosse. Her response to the letter in which he claimed to have "no scruples" about breaking with a child he had not seen since she was two, surprised even herself, as she noted in her diary. She was neither totally crushed nor destroyed. Instead, the discovery seemed to offer comic relief.

Strangely enough, I only long for a real drink after all this and then right away want to look into why he wrote that ridiculous letter.... Back home I say to myself, "Cheers Papa—one has to laugh—that's the way we are—father, mother, sons, daughters."[1]

By 1950, however, the past was taking a more tragic hold. Devastated by the sale of the house in Mondsee, Kerstin confessed to a friend that she had begun to wander around in confusion in the room that housed Frida's papers. "I feel I am in over my head and beyond my strength.... Since the winter I have been ill spiritually, if I can put it that way, and feel broken, no longer myself." Kerstin Strindberg died on April 30, 1956, and was buried in her father's grave.

PERMISSIONS ACKNOWLEDGMENTS

THE AUTHOR AND PUBLISHER are grateful to the following for permission to quote materials in copyright: Albert Bonniers förlagsarkiv (letters from Frida Strindberg to Karl Otto Bonnier, ms. by Max Friedrich Strindberg); Deutsches Literatur Archiv, Marbach am Neckar (letters from Frida Strindberg to Herman Sudermann, Arthur Kutscher, Cotta Verlag); Archiv, Kulturverein, Strindberg-Museum, Saxen (letters from Frida Strindberg, ms. by Else Bernstein); Münchener Stadtbibliothek-Monacensia (letter from Frida Strindberg to Max Halbe); *Selected Letters of Ezra Pound*, copyright 1950, Ezra Pound, reprinted by permission of New Directions Publishing Corp. (letter from Ezra Pound to Eustace Mullins); John Quinn Memorial Collection, New York Public Library (letters between John Quinn and Augustus John, diary entries, John Quinn); Harry Ransom Humanities Research Center, The University of Texas at Austin (proposal to Lecture Bureau, letter from Frida Strindberg to Mr. Christy); Carola Regnier, Munich (letters of Max Friedrich Strindberg to Frank Wedekind); Dep. Sulzbach and Strindbergsarkiv, Kungliga Biblioteket, Stockholm (letters of August, Frida, Kerstin, and Max Friedrich Strindberg, and members of the Uhl family); the estate of Augustus John and the Bridgeman Art Library (letters from Frida Uhl to Augustus John, letters from Augustus John to John Quinn); Wiener Stadt und Landesbibliothek, Vienna (letters from Frida Strindberg to Richard Schaukal and Karl Kraus); Wyndham Lewis Collection, Carl Kroch Library, Cornell University (brochure, J. S. Pond Lyceum, letter from Ford Madox Ford to Wyndham Lewis). For illustrations, thanks are due to the following: Albert Bonniers förlagsarkiv, Stockholm (Frida with "Ali"); Archiv, Kulturverein,

Strindberg-Museum, Saxen (Maria and Friedrich Uhl as newlyweds, Frida Strindberg, age eighteen); Munch-Museet, Oslo (*Zum Schwarzen Ferkel* by Edvard Munch); The Museum of the City of New York (portrait of Frida by Arnold Genthe); Norsk Folkemuseum, Oslo (portrait of August Strindberg by Christian Krohg); private collection (*The Way Down to the Sea* by Augustus John); Carola Regnier, Munich (Frank Wedekind); Dep. Sulzbach, Kungliga Biblioteket, Stockholm (Frida with Kerstin and Max Friedrich, ca. 1904, Kerstin Strindberg in her early twenties); Kristof Sulzbach, Stockholm (Frida Uhl, age 12); Wyndham Lewis Collection, Carl Kroch Library, Cornell University (Poster for "Cave of the Calf.")

NOTES

ABBREVIATIONS

AKS Archive, Kulturverein, Strindberg-Museum, Saxen, Austria.

DS Dep. Sulzbach 146, Kungliga Biblioteket, Stockholm.

LLZ Frida Uhl Strindberg, *Lieb, Leid und Zeit* (Hamburg-Leipzig: H. Goverts Verlag, 1935).

SB *August Strindbergs brev,* ed. by Torsten Eklund and Björn Meidal (Stockholm: Strindbergssällskapet, 1948–1999).

SL *Strindberg's Letters,* ed., comp. and trans. by Michael Robinson (Chicago: The University of Chicago Press, 1992).

1. THE EDITOR'S DAUGHTER

1. DS, Box 4.
2. For Strindberg's life, see Olof Lagerkrantz, *August Strindberg,* trans. Anselm Hollo (New York: Farrar, Straus & Giroux, 1979); Michael Meyer, *Strindberg* (Oxford and New York: Oxford University Press, 1987).
3. Friedrich Buchmayr, "Kurz Biographien," in *Die andere Welt—August Strindberg in Oberösterreich,* exhbn. cat. (Linz: Galerie im Stifter Haus, 1994), 80; Heinz Gerstinger, *Österreich, "Holdes Märchen und böser Traum": August Strindbergs Ehe mit Frida Uhl* (Vienna: Herold Verlag, 1987), 12 ff.
4. Friedrich Uhl, *Aus meinem Leben* (Stuttgart and Berlin: Cotta Verlag, 1908), 161.
5. Ibid., 12.

6. DS, Box 13.
7. *Wiener Zeitung*, May 17, 1925.
8. Kurt Paupié, *Handbuch des Österreichischen Pressegeschichte, 1848–1959* (Vienna and Stuttgart: Wilhelm Braumüller Verlag, 1960); Franz Stamprech, *Die älteste Tageszeitung der Welt* (Vienna: Österreichisches Staatsdruckerei, 1977), 316–58.
9. *Wiener Zeitung*, 225th Anniversary Issue, August 8, 1928.
10. Ibid., January 31, 1889.
11. Stamprech, *Die älteste Tageszeitung der Welt*, 318–20.
12. DS, Box 13.
13. LLZ, 14.
14. September 29, 1889, Strindbergsarkiv, Kungliga Biblioteket, Stockholm.
15. October 13, 1889, December, 12, 1889, June 1890, Strindbergsarkiv, Kungliga Biblioteket, Stockholm.
16. LLZ, 135.
17. Hermann Sudermann, *Heimat* (Stuttgart: Philip Reclam jun., 1980), 42. *Heimat* was to be one of the most popular plays of the 1890s and Magda a favorite role for such stars as Eleanora Duse and Sarah Bernhardt.
18. Ibid., 91.
19. DS, Box 1.
20. DS, Box 1.
21. DS, Box 1.
22. AKS.
23. AKS.
24. LLZ, 15.
25. DS, Box 9.
26. DS, Box 4.
27. Walter Berendsohn, "Frida Uhls Journalistik," *Dagens Nyheter*, April 5, 1950, 6.
28. December 31, 1892, Sudermann Archiv, Handschriften Abteilung des Schiller Nationalmuseums / Deutsche Literturarchivs, Marbach.
29. September 13, 1892, SL, I, 268.

30. Ola Hansson, "Vom künstlerische Schaffen," *Die Zukunft*, 3, 1893, 321; Carla Anna Lathe, "The Group *Zum Schwarzen Ferkel:* A Study in Early Modernism" (Ph.D. diss., University of East Anglia, 1972), 11, 13.
31. Adolf Paul, *Strindberg Minnen och Brev* (Stockholm: Ahlèn + Akerlunds Förlag, 1915), 20.
32. Carl Schleich in *Strindberg im Zeugnis der Zeitgenossen*, trans. by H. George Kemlein (Bremen: C. Schneeman Verlag, 1963), 94.
33. George Klim, *Stanislaw Przybyszewski* (Vienna: Igel Verlag, 1992), 41.
34. Gerstinger, *Österreich*, 36.

2. THE MISOGYNIST AND THE MAIDEN

1. August Strindberg, *Das Kloster*, in *August Strindberg*, *Werke in zeitlicher Folge 1898–1900*, Frankfurter Ausgabe, VIII-I (Frankfurt: Insel Verlag, 1992), 191–96.
2. Ibid., 210.
3. Ibid., 212–13.
4. February 8, 1893, SL, II, 454.
5. February 12, 1893, SB, IX, #2466.
6. DS, Box 4.
7. Strindberg, *Das Kloster*, 215.
8. Ibid., 216, 220.
9. The letter has disappeared but is quoted by Strindberg in *Das Kloster*, 220.
10. Meyer, *Strindberg*, 410.
11. March 4, 1893, *Wenn* nein, *nein! August Strindberg und Frida Uhl, Briefwechsel 1893–1902*, ed., comp., trans. Friedrich Buchmayr (Weltra: Bibliothek der Provinz, 1993), 26, 27.
12. March 6, 1893, SB, IX, #2486.
13. March 10, 1893, SB, IX, #2491.
14. March 12, 1893, SB, IX, #2495.
15. March 15, 1893, SB, IX, #2497.
16. Berendsohn, "Frida Uhls Journalistik."

17. Mary Kay Norseng, *Dagny: Dagny Juel Przybyszewska, the Woman and the Myth* (Seattle and London: University of Washington Press, 1991), 37–45.
18. Ragna Stang, *Munch, the Man and His Art*, trans. Geoffrey Culverwell (New York: Abbeville Press, 1978), 52; Patricia G. Berman, "Edvard Munch's Self-Portrait with Cigarette: Smoking and the Bohemian Persona," *Art Bulletin*, December 1993, 634–36.
19. Hans Jaeger, *Kristiania Bohème*, trans. Niels Hoyer (Hamburg: Adolf Harms Verlag, 1921), 130.
20. Norseng, *Dagny*, 45.
21. Dagny's union with Przybyszewski, which resulted in two children—Zenon and Iwa—was happy at first, but when they moved to Poland in 1898, it began to unravel. In letters and novels, he began to write about her as someone with a questionable past. Tragedy struck in 1901 when Dagny, with her little son, traveled to Tiflis with an unstable young man who had supported Przybyszewski's artistic ventures in Warsaw. When they reached their destination, he shot and killed Dagny and himself. See Norseng, *Dagny*, passim.
22. *August Strindberg, Werke in zeitlicher Folge*, VIII-I, 1140.
23. Strindberg, *Das Kloster*, 225.
24. DS, Box 4.
25. March 12, 1893, *Wenn* nein, *nein!*, 35.
26. DS, Box 4.
27. March 16, 1893, SB, IX, #2502.
28. March, 1893, *Wenn* nein, *nein!*, 42.
29. March 16, 1893, SL, II, 455.
30. March 21, 1893, *Wenn nein, nein!*, 48.
31. March 22, 1893, SB, IX, #2507; LLZ, 129.
32. LLZ, 129.
33. LLZ, 134.
34. LLZ, 136.
35. Stellan Ahlström, "Strindbergs Deutsche Freunde," in *Strindberg und die Deutschsprachigen Länder: Internationale Beiträge zum Tübingen Strindberg Symposium* (Basel: Helbing & Tichlenhahn, 1977), 49, 50.

36. DS, Box 4.
37. March 30, 1893, telegram, SB, IX, #2514, note 1.
38. March 30, 1893, *Wenn* nein, *nein!*, 54.
39. March 31, 1893, SB, IX, #2514.
40. DS, Box 4.
41. April 17, 1893, SB, IX, #2523.
42. April 16, 1893, *Wenn* nein, *nein!*, 60.
43. LLZ, 175.
44. LLZ, 188, 194.
45. The painting is in the collection of Strindbergsmuseet, Stockholm.

3. A WORKING WIFE

1. LLZ, 211–13.
2. LLZ, 218.
3. August 5, 1887, SL, I, 233.
4. March 20, 1888, SL, I, 270.
5. LLZ, 238, 239.
6. LLZ, 222.
7. To Birger Mörner, May 9, 1893, SL, II, 456.
8. To Birger Mörner, June 8, 1893, SL, II, 457.
9. LLZ, 11.
10. Meyer, *Strindberg*, 144.
11. LLZ, 243.
12. Strindberg, *Das Kloster*, 283.
13. June 26, 1893, SB, IX, #2565.
14. June 20, 1893, *Wenn* nein, *nein!*, 63.
15. July 6, 1893, ibid., 72.
16. DS, Box 4.
17. LLZ, 278.
18. DS, Box 4.
19. To Irma von Perger, February 24, 1894, in Richard Perger, "Neues zum Umkreis Uhl-Weyr-Strindberg," *Jahrbuch des Adalbert Stifter Instituts*, 2, 1995, 1.

20. August 3, 1893, SB, IX, #2614.
21. Strindberg, *Das Kloster*, 261.
22. August 7, 1893, SB, IX, #2621.
23. Strindberg, *Das Kloster*, 272–73.
24. August Strindberg, *Getting Married*, intro., ed., trans. Mary Sandbach (New York: The Viking Press, 1972), 71.
25. Meyer, *Strindberg*, 172–73.
26. Ibid., 164.
27. October 15, 1893, *Wenn* nein, *nein!*, 124–25.
28. LLZ, 356.
29. LLZ, 328.

4. A COUNTRY WIFE

1. Strindberg, *Das Kloster*, 282.
2. Meyer, *Strindberg*, 284.
3. Meyer, *Strindberg*, 189.
4. LLZ, 353–56.
5. June 19, 1894, SL, II, 473.
6. July 14, 1894, SL, II, 480.
7. DS, Box 4.
8. September 2, 1894, SL, II, 509.
9. August 26, 1894, *Wenn* nein, *nein!*, 137.
10. September 2, 1894, SL, II, 509.
11. September 11, 1894, SB, X, #2943.
12. DS, Box 4.
13. Julius Meier-Graefe, *Geschichten neben der Kunst* (Berlin: S. Fischer, 1933), 115.
14. Helga Abret, *Albert Langen: Ein europaischer Verleger* (Munich: Langen-Müller, 1993), 38.
15. DS, Box 4.
16. DS, Box 4.
17. Alexandra Thaulow, *Mens Fritz Thaulow malte* (Oslo: Gyldendal Norsk Forlag, 1929), 76.

5. BETRAYALS

1. August Strindberg, *Inferno and From an Occult Diary*, intro. and trans. Mary Sandbach (London and New York: Penguin Books, 1979), 101.
2. November 3, 1894, SB, X, #2987.
3. Ibid.
4. November 4, 1894, SL, II, 515.
5. November 6, 1894, SB, X, #2992.
6. November 8, 1894, SL, II, 518.
7. Strindberg, *Inferno*, 102.
8. November 9, 1894, December 8, 1894, SB, X, #3000, #3022.
9. LLZ, 513.
10. December 3, 1894, SL, II, 520.
11. LLZ, 588.
12. April 1895. *Wenn* nein, *nein!*, 161.
13. May 2, 1896, ibid., 167.
14. DS, Box 2.
15. June 1896, SB, XI, #3291.
16. Max Halbe, *Jahrhundertwende, Geschichte meines Lebens, 1893–1914* (Danzig: Verlag A. W. Kafemann,1935), 32.
17. Lou Andreas Salomé, *Lebensrückblick*, ed. Ernst Pfeiffer (Zurich and Wiesbaden: Max Niehaus Verlag, 1951), 125–26.
18. Frank Wedekind, *Diary of an Erotic Life*, ed. Gerhard Hay, trans. W. E. Yuill (Oxford: Basil Blackwell, 1990), 117–233.
19. Halbe, *Jahrhundertwende*, 29; Elisabeth Kleeman, *Zwischen symbolischer Rebellion und politischer Revolution* (Frankfurt am Main: Peter Lang, 1985), 87–130.
20. Ulrike Procop, "Elemente der Moderne: Bilder der Weiblichen bei Strindberg und Wedekind," in *Frank Wedekind, Texte, Interviews, Studien* (Darmstadt: Verlag der Georg Büchner Buchhandlung, 1989), 204.
21. Rolf Kieser, *Benjamin Franklin Wedekind, Biographie einer Jugend* (Zurich: Arche, 1980), passim.
22. June 25, 1896, SB, XI, #3307.
23. August 23, 1896, SL, II, 590.

24. September 11, 1896, SB, XI, #3372.
25. DS, Box 13.
26. December 4, 1896, SB, XI, #3442.
27. December 26, 1896, SB, XI, #3467.
28. December 27, 1896, SB, XI, #3468.
29. January 1, 1897, SB, XI, #3473.
30. January 14, 1897, SB, XI, #3481.
31. February 1, 1897, SB, XI, #3509.
32. February 27, 1897, SB, XI, #3533.
33. March 10, 1897, SB, XI, #3544.
34. April 4, 1897, SB, XI, #3577.
35. July 26, 1897, SB, XI, #3608.
36. Peter Jelavich, *Munich and Theatrical Modernism: Politics, Playwriting and Performance, 1890–1914* (Cambridge, MA, and London: Harvard University Press, 1985), 123–25.
37. January 20, 1897, Frank Wedekind, *Gesammelte Briefe,* ed. Fritz Strich (Munich: Georg Müller Verlag, 1924), 276.
38. April 1897, *Gesammelte Briefe,* 122.
39. Frank Wedekind, *Der Kammersänger, Gesammelte Werke,* III (Munich: Georg Müller Verlag, 1924), 203–40.
40. September 9, 1897, Nachlass Niederau.
41. Franziska Gräfin zu Reventlow, *Briefe 1890–1917,* ed. Else Reventlow (Frankfurt am Main: Fischer Taschenbuch Verlag, 1977), 23.
42. Franziska Gräfin zu Reventlow, *"Der gräfliche Milchgeschäft,"* Neue Rundschau, 8, 1897, 979–84.
43. Reventlow, *Briefe,* 384.
44. April 19, 1898, *Wedekind, Gesammelte Briefe,* 301.
45. July 27, 1898, ibid., 305.
46. *Max Halbe Nachlass,* Stadtbibliothek, Munich.
47. *Simplicissimus, A Satirical Magazine, Munich 1896-1944,* exhbn. catalogue (Munich: Haus der Kunst, 1978), 41.
48. Strindberg, *Inferno,* 248.
49. *To Damascus (Part 1)* in *Strindberg Plays: Three,* trans. Michael Meyer (London: Methuen Drama, 1991), 194.

50. August Strindberg, *Till Damascus III, Samlade,* Verk, Nationaluppla-gen, v. 39, ed. Gunnar Ollén, Stockholm: 1991, 316.
51. Meyer, *Strindberg,* 410.

6. CADS AND CABARETS

1. DS, Box 4.
2. Maria Weyr to Rima von Perger, February 24, 1894; Richard Perger, "Neues zum Umkreis Uhl-Weyr-Strindberg," 119.
3. Ingeborg von Rosen, *Konrad Pineus, Minnen och dagboksantekningar* (Stockholm: Norstedts & Söner, 1946), 99.
4. Harold B. Segel, *Turn-of-the-Cenury Cabaret* (New York: Columbia University Press, 1987), 1–83.
5. Ibid., 70–71.
6. Volker Kühn, *Die zehnte Muse, 111 Jahre Kabaret* (Cologne: VGS Verlagsgesellschaft, 1993), 14.
7. November 4, 1894, SL, II, 516.
8. Otto Julius Bierbaum, *Stilpe, Ein Roman aus der Froschenperspektiv* (Berlin: Schuster und Loeffler, 1897), 165–66.
9. Otto Julius Bierbaum, *Deutsche Chansons (Brettl Lieder),* (Berlin and Leipzig: Schuster and Loeffler, 1900), viii.
10. Ibid., 41.
11. Ernst von Wolzogen, "Frau Strindberg," *Die Propyläen,* 19 (1921–22), 75, 76.
12. Ibid.
13. Wilfred Kugel, *Der Unverantwortliche: Das Leben des Hanns Heinz Ewers* (Düsseldorf: Grupello Verlag, 1992), 34–75.
14. Von Wolzogen, "Frau Strindberg," 76.
15. Peter Jelavich, *Berlin Cabaret* (Cambridge, MA and London: Harvard University Press, 1993), 50–51, 86–92.
16. Jelavich, *Munich and Theatrical Modernism,* 139–85; Segel, *Turn-of-the Century Cabaret,* 159.
17. Christmas, 1902, *Wenn* nein, *nein!,* 184–88.

7. LOST BACCHANTE

1. DS, Box 4.
2. Ludwig Hevesi, Feuilleton, *Fremden-Blatt,* January 23, 1906, 15.
3. Letter to Irma von Perger, undated, "Neues zum Umkreis Uhl-Weyr-Strindberg," 123.
4. Arthur Schnitzler, *Tagebuch, 1903–1908* (Vienna: Verlag der Österreichischen Akademie der Wissenschaften, 1991), 25.
5. Paul Schick, *Karl Kraus* (Reinbek bei Hamburg: Rowohlt Taschenbuch Verlag, 1965), 34.
6. Arthur Schnitzler, *Tagebuch, 1893–1902,* 224.
7. April 10, 1905, *Schaukal Nachlass. Handschrift Abteilung,* Wiener Stadt und Landesbibliothek.
8. Schick, *Karl Kraus,* 39.
9. November 27, 1904, Kraus Archive, *Handschrift Abteilung,* Wiener Stadt und Landesbibliothek, #138805.
10. Undated, ibid., #138808.
11. 1904, ibid., #138799.
12. 1905, ibid., #138875.
13. Hartmut Vinçon, *Frank Wedekind* (Stuttgart: J. B. Metzler, 1987), 66.
14. Hilde Spiel, *Glanz und Untergang, Wien 1866 bis 1938* (Munich: Deutsche Taschenbuch Verlag, 1994), 60.
15. Hugo von Hoffmannsthal, *Gesammelte Werke in zehn Einzelbänden,* X (Frankfurt am Main: S. Fischer, 1979–80), 457.
16. Arthur Schnitzler, *Das Wort* (Frankfurt am Main: Fischer Taschenbuch Verlag), 1999, 141.
17. Otto Weininger, *Geschlecht und Charakter, Eine Prinzipielle Untersuchung* (Vienna and Leipzig: Wilhelm Braumüller, 1903).
18. Stefan Zweig, "Vorbeigehen an einem unauffälligen Menschen—Otto Weininger," in Joshua Sobel, *Weiningers Nacht* (Vienna: Paulus Manker, 1988), 85–87.
19. July 1, 1903, SL, II, 700.
20. Erich Unglaub, "Strindberg, Weininger, und Karl Kraus: Ein Überprufung," *Recherches Germaniques,* 18, 1988, 124, 125. See also Nike

Wagner, *Geist und Geschlecht: Karl Kraus und die Erotik der Wiener Moderne* (Frankfurt am Main: Suhrkamp Verlag, 1982), passim.

21. Erich Unglaub, "Strindberg, Weininger und Karl Kraus," 124.
22. August Strindberg, "Idolatrie, Gynolatrie," *Die Fackel*, October 17, 1903.
23. Thelma Hanson, "Karl Kraus och Strindberg," *Acta Regiae Societatis Scientiarum et Litterarum Gothoburgensis Humaniora* 36, 1996, 27.
24. Frank Wedekind, "Konfession," *Die Fackel*, December 31, 1904.
25. Franz Servaes, *Grüsse aus Wien* (Berlin, Vienna, Leipzig: Paul Zolnay Verlag, 1948), 175–76.
26. Undated newspaper account, AKS.
27. DS, Box 11.
28. DS, Box 13.
29. DS, Box 2.
30. Strindbergsarkiv, Kungliga Biblioteket, Stockholm.
31. August 18, 1903, *Gesammelte Briefe*, II, 101.
32. DS, Box 11.
33. March 2, 1907, SB, Vol. XV, #5503.
34. DS, Box 2.
35. DS, Box 11.
36. DS, Box 13.
37. DS, Box 2.
38. 1907, AKS.
39. 1907, *Wedekind Nachlass, Handschriftabteilung*, Stadtbibliothek, Munich.
40. AKS.
41. *Neues Wiener Journal*, January 26, 1908.
42. Letter to the press from Raul Markbreiter, January 1908, *Kraus Archiv, Handschriftabteilung*, Wiener Stadt und Landesbibliothek, #N. 164. 450.
43. January 1908, ibid., #138828.
44. January 1908, ibid., #138824.
45. January 1908, ibid., #138823.

8. WORSHIPING THE GOLDEN CALF

1. Margery Ross, *Robert Ross, Friend of Friends* (London: Jonathan Cape, 1952), 152–54.
2. Tom Pockock, *Chelsea Reach: The Brutal Friendship of Whistler and Walter Greaves* (London: Hodder and Stoughton, 1970), 155–65.
3. Ibid.
4. Ibid., 168.
5. May 17, 1912, John Quinn Memorial Collection, Manuscript Division, New York Public Library.
6. Michael Holroyd, *Augustus John* (New York: Farrar, Straus & Giroux, 1996), 261.
7. Ibid., 359.
8. October 27, 1910, John Quinn Memorial Collection—May 19, 1910.
9. May 19, 1911, ibid.
10. August 16, 1911, ibid.
11. September 3, 1911, diary, John Quinn Memorial Collection.
12. September 6, 1911, ibid.
13. To Kerstin Strindberg, 1923, DS, Box 4.
14. November 28, 1911, John Quinn Memorial Collection.
15. *The Sunday Times,* March 19, 1911, 6.
16. May 9, 1912, John Quinn Memorial Collection.
17. Included in John's letter to Quinn, June 19, 1912, ibid.
18. June 26, 1912, July 8, 1912, July 23, 1912, ibid.
19. Ashley Gibson, *Postscript to Adventure* (London and Toronto: J. M. Dent & Sons, 1930), 105.
20. Wyndham Lewis, *Rude Assignment*, ed. Toby Foshay (Santa Barbara: Black Swallow Press, 1984), 134.
21. Richard Cork, *Art Beyond the Gallery in Early 20th Century England* (New Haven and London: Yale University Press, 1985), 91.
22. Bokken Lasson, *Livet og Lykken* (Oslo: Gyldendal Norsk Forlag, 1940), 148.
23. *The Sunday Times,* June 30, 1912, 6.
24. Augustus John, *Chiaroscuro* (New York: Pellegrini and Cudahy, 1952), 233.

25. Manuscript Division, The National Library of Wales, Aberstwyth, NLW M522785D, Fol., 140.
26. John, *Chiaroscuro,* 233.
27. 1914, Wyndham Lewis Collection, Rare and Manuscript Collections, Carl A. Kroch Library, Cornell University, Ithaca, New York.
28. To Eustace Mullins, April 6, 1959, in Eustace Mullins, *The Difficult Individual Ezra Pound* (New York: Fleet Publishing Corporation, 1961), 98, 99.
29. "Les heures du cabaret," program, October 1913, Wyndham Lewis Collection.
30. To Mrs. Percy Harris, November 1913, ibid.
31. William C. Wees, *Vorticism and the English Avant-Garde* (Toronto and Buffalo: University of Toronto Press, 1972), 51.
32. Holroyd, *Augustus John,* 418.
33. Meyer, *Strindberg,* 560, 566.
34. DS, Box 8.
35. September 5, 1909, SL, II, 808.
36. DS, Box 8.
37. Ibid.
38. Tilly Wedekind, *Lulu, Die Rolle meines Lebens* (Munich, Bern, Vienna: Rutten und Loening Verlag, 1969), 82, 130.
39. Ibid.
40. *Wedekind Nachlass,* Stadtbibliothek, Munich.

9. IN EXILE

1. The National Library of Wales, Aberstwyth, NLW M522785D, fol. 140.
2. John, *Chiaroscuro,* 233.
3. Proposal sent to The Lecture Agency, Ltd., Manuscript Division, Harry Ransom Humanities Research Center, The University of Texas at Austin.
4. Rare and Manuscript Collections, Carl A. Kroch Library, Cornell University.

5. To Mr. Christy, Harry Ransom Humanities Research Center.
6. Associated Press, n.d., Library of the Performing Arts, Lincoln Center, New York; *Chicago Herald,* June 15, 1915; Associated Press. n.d.; *New York Star,* April 5, 1916.
8. Gavin Lambert, *Nazimova* (New York: Alfred A. Knopf, 1995), 1–131.
9. Ibid., 88.
10. *The New York Times,* January 19, 1916.
11. February 17, 1916; *New York Telegraph,* February 26, 1916.
12. *New York Herald,* February 28, 1916.
13. Asta Nielsen, *Die Schweigende Muse* (Munich: Carl Hansen Verlag, 1977), 285.
14. Ibid., 288.
15. Ibid.
16. Renata Seydel and Allen Hagedorff, *Asta Nielsen, Ihr Leben in Fotodokumenten* (Munich: Universitas, 1981), 140.
17. Letter from Frida to her nephew Caesar Weyr, May 19, 1943, DS, Box 4.
18. *The Death Dance,* Select Pictures Corp., July 1918; *The Golden Shower,* Vitagraph Co. of America, November 1919; see *American Film Institute Catalog, Feature Films 1911–20* (Berkeley: University of California Press, 1988), 200, 341.
19. To Kerstin Strindberg, 1920, DS, Box 4.
20. G. Thomas Tanselle, "The Thomas Seltzer Imprint," *Papers of the Bibliographical Society of America,* 58, 1964, 380–448.
21. Tom Dardis, *Firebrand, The Life of Horace Liveright* (New York: Random House, 1995), 154.
22. Thomas Seltzer, "Michael Artzybashev," *The Drama,* 21, February 1916, 1–10.
23. Sally O'Dell and N. J. L. Luker, *Mikhail Artzybashev: A Comprehensive Bibliography* (Nottingham: Astra Press, 1983), 20–22. For their answers to my queries regarding Artzybashev and the émigré circle in Warsaw, I thank Anna Frajlich-Zajac, Jerzy Giedroyc, Czeslaw Milosz, Tomas Venclova, Marc Raeff, Piotr Sommer, Walter Laqueur, and Federika della Casa Marchi.

24. Mikhail Petrovich Artzybasheff, *Jealousy, Enemies, the Law of the Savage* (New York: Boni and Liveright, 1923).
25. John, *Chiaroscuro*, 234–36.
26. Sunday, June 26, 1921, 10.
27. Roda Roda, "Wie Eulenberg von New York Abschied nahm," *Der Wiener Tag*, February 6, 1938, 19.
28. 1920, DS, Box 7.
29. 1923, DS, Box 7.
30. 1923, DS, Box 7.
31. 1923, DS, Box 7.

10. FAMILY REUNION

1. September, 1931, Albert Bonniers förlagsarkiv.
2. *Dagens Nyheter*, May 31, 1926.
3. April, 1927, Albert Bonniers förlagsarkiv.
4. March 17, 1932, ibid.
5. April 10, 1933, ibid.
6. 1920, DS. Box 7.
7. LLZ, 67.
8. LLZ, 388.
9. October 10, 1936, DS, Box 13, II.
10. *Deutsch-Schwedische Blätter*, April, 1937.
11. December 13, 1936, DS, Box 3.
12. Eric Bentley, *The Playwright as Thinker* (San Diego, New York, London: Harcourt Brace Jovanovich, 1987), 196.
13. 1937, Albert Bonniers förlagsarkiv.
14. April 22, 1933, ibid.
15. April 26, 1933, ibid.
16. February 25, 1935, DS, Box 4.
17. Max Friedrich Strindberg, *Meine Begegnung mit Köstler*, unpublished manuscript, Albert Bonniers förlagsarkiv.
18. Arthur Koestler, *Spanish Testament* (London: Victor Gollancz, 1937), 37–40.

19. Ibid.
20. DS, Box 3.
21. April 9, 1943, DS, Box 3.
22. In a conversation with Dr. Strauss in his apartment near Columbia University, he remembered Max Friedrich as a quick and intelligent man, but rather touchy, timid, and easily offended. He was sympathetic to the Jews, but not physically courageous. "All the more to his credit," according to Strauss, "that he was willing to take the risk of hiding a Jew." He also recalled that Max Friedrich had urged him to tell the world after the war that "he had saved a rabbi from death in Poland."
23. Michael Balfour and Julian Frisby, *Helmuth von Moltke: A Leader Against Hitler* (London: Macmillan), 184.
24. DS, Box 8.
25. September 1943, AKS.

CODA: MAX FRIEDRICH AND KERSTIN

1. Strindbergsarkiv, Kungliga Biblioteket, Stockholm.

INDEX